The People of Ghana:
Ethnic Diversity and National Unity

Godfrey Mwakikagile

The People of Ghana: Ethnic Diversity and National Unity

First Edition

ISBN-13: 978-9987-16-050-1

New Africa Press
Dar es Salaam, Tanzania

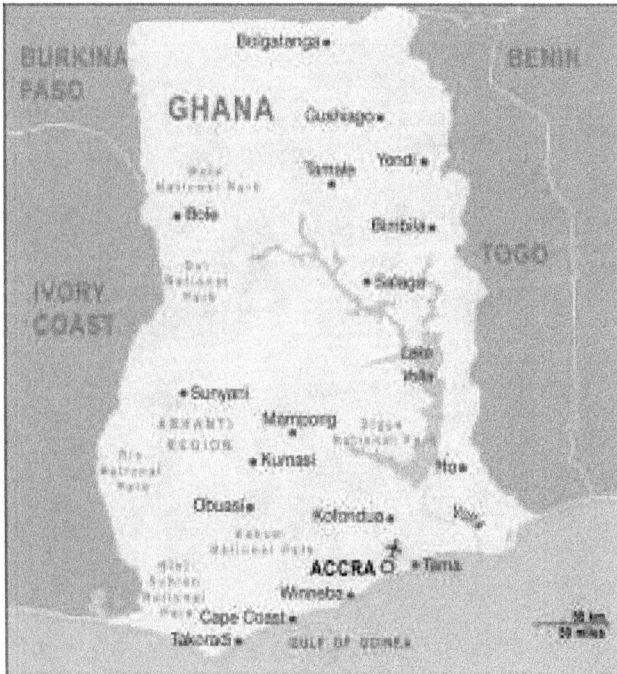

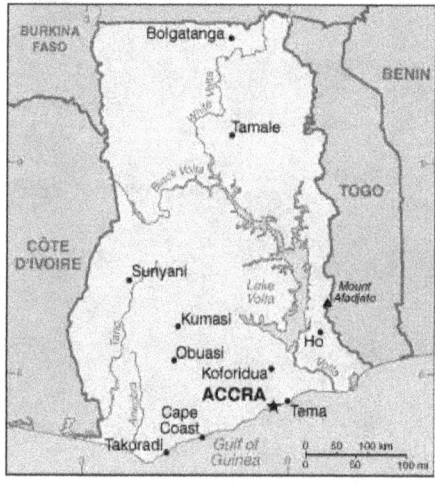

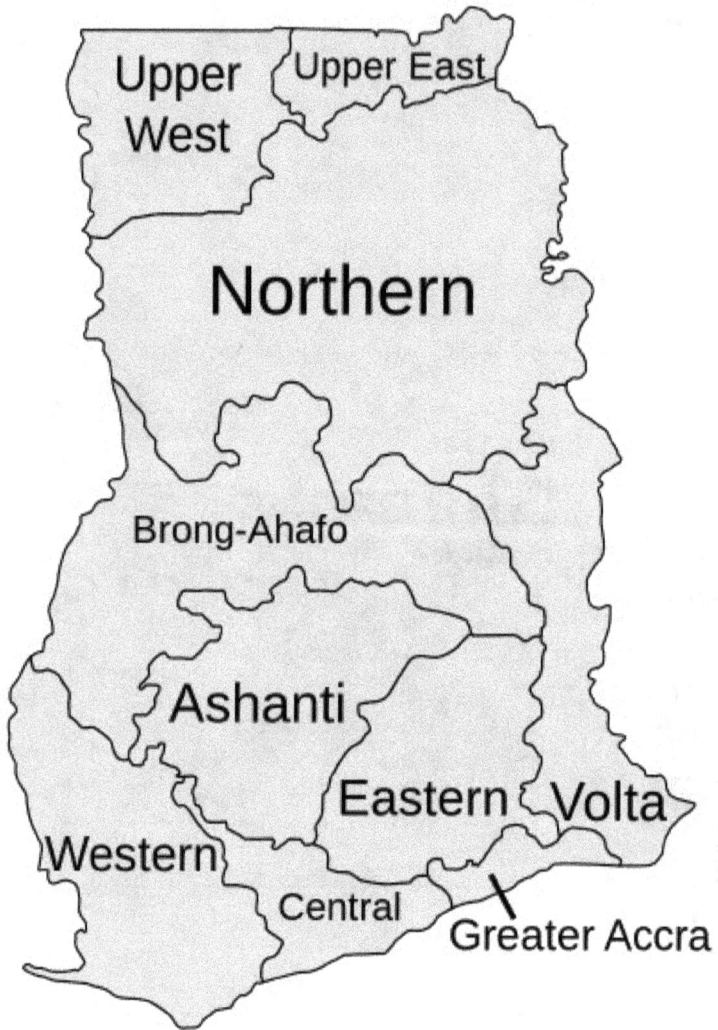

Upper West

Upper East

Northern

Brong-Ahafo

Ashanti

Eastern

Volta

Western

Central

Greater Accra

Introduction

THIS WORK is intended to provide basic facts about Ghana. It is an introductory text although it provides a comprehensive picture of the country and its people in many areas. It is also an in-depth study of some of the ethnic groups in Ghana and can be can be used as a complementary text together with other works for a probing analysis of the subjects covered here.

It may help some students learn important things about Ghana, one of the most fascinating countries on the continent with a unique place in history as the first black African country to emerge from colonial rule.

Some members of the general public who are going to Ghana, or who just want to learn a few things about the country, may find this work to be useful. I had them in mind when I wrote it. But I also had other people in my mind in order to introduce them to this African country in a simple, direct way without burdening them with a lot of details which students of Ghana or those who are interested in African studies probably need to know in their academic pursuits.

I deliberately kept this book "small," although brevity has its consequences, especially excluding a lot of details some people may find necessary in their attempt to learn a lot of things about Ghana; it is impossible to cover all the ethnic groups in detail in a book of this size. But that is the sacrifice I had to make to keep the book "short," simple and easy to read and understand.

I have done my best to provide basic facts about the regions and the people of Ghana which I believe are enough to satisfy the curiosity of many people who are not interested in an in-depth analysis of the history, politics and other aspects of this great African country.

The book has its shortcomings. And I take full responsibility for that.

I am also very grateful to the individuals and institutions whose works I have used to complement my analysis. Without them, I would not have been able to document parts of my work which I felt needed to be documented with full acknowledgement of the sources I have cited.

Special thanks to Professor Sidonia Alenuma-Nimoh, a native of Dagawie (land of the Dagaaba) in the northwestern part of Ghana, for her elaborate and incisive analysis of the Dagaare-speaking communities of West Africa which I have used to complement my study of the Dagaaba.

Also, thanks to Dr. Charlotte Kyerewaa Anokwa, an Akyem, whose autobiographical account has been very useful in providing me with some insights into the Akyem ethnic group which is an integral part of the broader picture of Ghana's demographic and ethnic landscape I have tried to present in my book.

I am also very grateful to Professor Cati Coe for her work on the Akuapem which has helped me to understand some cultural elements of this ethnic group; and to Professor Kwamina B. Dickson for explaining the identity of the Guan and their place in the history of Ghana as the country's first inhabitants.

My profound gratitude also goes to Anthony Y. Naaeke for his work on the Dagaaba I have used to broaden my understanding of one of the ethnic groups in northwestern Ghana; to Professor Ivor Wilks for his work on the Wala I have also cited in my study; also a lot of thanks to Solomon Salifu Tampuri, a Gonja, for his autobiographical work which has enabled me to understand the history and culture of his people; to Albin Akasanke for his nationalist perspective on Ghanaian identity that transcends ethnic loyalties he has presented in his autobiographical work.

I am also very grateful to Rita Muhammad, an African American, whose autobiographical work including her experience in Ghana provided another perspective on the country and on some ethnic groups in the areas where she visited and worked. Her work helped me broaden my understanding of the people in the area where she worked as a teacher for about two years.

I am also indebted to Professor Kwame Botwe-Asamaoah for his work which has provided me with some insights into the threats and violence Nkrumah and his government faced from tribalists and regionalists who wanted to divide the country along ethno-regional lines to the detriment of national unity; also, a lot of thanks to Nana Yaw Osei for his perceptive article on the imperative need for regional balance in political appointments for the sake of fairness, national unity and stability I have incorporated into my work.

Also special thanks to Professor E. Gyimah-Boadi and Richard Asante for their comprehensive analysis of ethnic structure, inequality and governance of the public sector in Ghana I have incorporated into my work and used as an analytical tool. The empirical evidence they have provided has played an equally important role in fortifying my central thesis.

And to the rest, whose material I have used in my analysis, thank you very much. I am equally grateful to them. Their works have served me very well in writing this book.

As an African, I feel it is my duty to write about Africa

as much as it should be the duty of other Africans to do the same thing. Unfortunately, non-Africans, in and outside Africa, write more about us than we do ourselves.

The number of books including textbooks written about Africa by non-Africans is staggering. That is in sharp contrast with the number of books written by Africans. More than 50 years after independence, we can not continue to blame our former colonial rulers for everything that goes wrong in Africa. That includes our failure to write books about our continent; we don't write enough.

And we don't always have to write about our own countries if we really believe we are one people as Africans. This reminds me of what Mwalimu Julius Nyerere once said about the oneness of Africa concerning the plight of African refugees which he felt was not being seriously addressed by the Africans themselves. He said it was a shame for Africans to be refugees in Africa.

It is indeed a shame for any people to be homeless and helpless in their own homeland. Africa is one. It is the homeland of Africans. Yet millions of Africans have been homeless through the years right there in Africa because fellow Africans don't care about them.

Nyerere backed up what he said with action. During his presidency, he gave citizenship to tens of thousands of refugees living in Tanzania. Even Shirley Graham Du Bois, the widow of Dr. W.E.B. Du Bois, who left Ghana after Kwame Nkrumah was overthrown and moved to Tanzania, acquired Tanzanian citizenship. She was very close to President Nyerere and wrote a biography about him. She died in China in 1977 as a citizen of Tanzania.

Nyerere also worked with Nkrumah, another staunch Pan-Africanist like Nyerere himself, even before he led Tanganyika to independence in 1961.

The constitution of the Tanganyika African National Union (TANU), the party that led the struggle for Tanganyika's independence, is almost identical to the constitution of the Convention People's Party (CPP) which won independence for Ghana under Nkrumah.

Nyerere was very much impressed by the CPP constitution and decided to use it in a spirit of Pan-African solidarity. And the CPP was, in terms of organisation and mobilisation, patterned after the Indian National Congress (INC, simply known as Congress in India)) led by Jawaharlal Nehru. Formed in 1885, it was the first nationalist movement to be launched in the British Empire in Asia and Africa and paved the way for other nationalist organisations in the British colonies.

Nkrumah himself was inspired by Mahatma Gandhi – Nehru's mentor – in his campaign for Ghana's independence and adopted the principles of nonviolent civil disobedience practised by Gandhi in India. He called it "Positive Action" and demanded "Independence Now."

Nkrumah and Nyerere were also some of the most relentless supporters of the African liberation movements and uncompromising opponents of the racist apartheid regime of South Africa.

During the struggle for independence in Tanganyika, Nyerere led a liberation movement, TANU, which included members of all races.

When the country won independence from Britain on 9 December 1961, he formed a multiracial cabinet. Its members included Sir Ernest Vasey as minister of finance; Derek Bryceson, minister of health, and Amir H. Jamal, minister of industry. Vasey and Bryceson were of British origin; Jamal, Indian.

It was a lean cabinet comprising only 12 members including Nyerere himself as prime minister. He was 39 years old and the youngest leader in the world during that time. He became president the following year when Tanganyika became a republic on 9 December 1962.

Amir H. Jamal was the most intellectual cabinet member in the first independence cabinet besides Nyerere and the longest-serving minister of finance in the country's history. He held other high-profile ministerial posts and was one of the most respected and most knowledgeable cabinet members. He also chaired the 35th annual meetings of the International Monetary Fund (IMF) and the World Bank Group and was a close friend of Nyerere.

A technocrat of high intellectual calibre, he was independent-minded and the best adviser Nyerere had. He had sharp political instincts but as a public servant never did anything for political expediency. His integrity was unimpeachable. I knew him when I was a news reporter.

Jamal's appointment and inclusion of other non-blacks in the cabinet in a country that was overwhelmingly black demonstrated Mwalimu Nyerere's commitment to racial equality not only in Tanganyika – later Tanzania – but throughout the world.

Also, Nyerere and Nkrumah were members of a group of leaders in the Organisation of African Unity (OAU) known as the Group of Six, according to Ahmed Ben Bella in an interview in Geneva, Switzerland, in 1995. The six leaders worked together on a number of issues including the Congo crisis and African liberation. They were also ideological compatriots.

Besides Nkrumah, Nyerere and Ben Bella, the other members of the group were Gamal Abdel Nasser, Ahmed Sékou Touré, and Modibo Keita. As Jorge Castañeda states in his book, *Compañero: The Life and Death of Che Guevara*:

"According to Ben Bella, these leaders had a group of their own within the OAU; they regularly consulted and conspired among themselves. Ahmed Ben Bella, interview with the author, Geneva, November 4, 1995....

Ben Bella considered Modibo Keita the senior and most respected member of the Group of Six....

Tshombe was despised by the leaders of the OAU, especially its most radical ones – the so-called Group of Six, consisting of Nasser, Ben Bella, Kwame Nkrumah of

Ghana, Sékou Touré of Guinea, Julius Nyerere of Tanzania, and Modibo Keita of Mali – who still blamed Tshombe for Lumumba's death." – (Jorge Castañeda, *Compañero: The Life and Death of Che Guevara*, New York: Alfred A. Knopf, 1997, pp. 277 and 280).

During his presidency, Nyerere also said African countries should open their borders to allow other Africans to settle in those countries.

Analogous to what he said about the plight of African refugees in Africa – which is their home and therefore they should feel at home – is my sentiment which I believe is shared by many of my fellow Africans concerning our collective responsibility to write about our continent.

It is a shame that some of us may not want to write about other African countries because they are not our countries and therefore not our responsibility to write about them in spite of our claim that we are one people as Africans and Africa is one. If we are indeed one people, and Africa is one, then all African countries belong to all of us as Africans.

Write what you want to write about any African country because every African country is your country.

That is why Kwame Nkrumah proclaimed in his speech when the Gold Coast won independence from Britain on 6 March 1957 and became the new nation of Ghana:

"The independence of Ghana is meaningless, unless it is linked up with the total liberation of Africa."

He stated on another occasion:

"Africa is one continent, one people, and one nation. The notion that in order to have a nation it is necessary for there to be a common language, a common territory and common culture has failed to stand the test of time or the scrutiny of scientific definition of objective reality."

13

He also said:

"I am not African because I was born in Africa but because Africa was born in me."

Welcome to Ghana.

Welcome to Africa.

The country and its regions

GHANA is one of the most well-known African countries. It also has the distinction of being the first country in sub-Saharan Africa to win independence.

Formerly known as the Gold Coast, Ghana won independence from Britain on 6 March 1957 under the leadership of Kwame Nkrumah, one of the most influential leaders in the history of post-colonial Africa.

During his presidency, Ghana became a leader in African affairs because of his own qualities as a dynamic personality and an uncompromising champion of African independence and unity.

The independence of Ghana, the first black African country to emerge from colonial rule, marked the dawn of a new era of freedom for the continent and the country's flag, designed by Theodosia Salome Okoh who died in April 2015 at the age of 92, symbolised that era and the spirit of independence at a time when almost the whole continent south of the Sahara was still under colonial rule. As she stated in an interview explaining the meaning of the flag – the design and the colours she chose:

"I decided on the three colours of red, gold and green because of the geography of Ghana.

Ghana lies in the tropics and blessed with rich

vegetation.

The color gold was influenced by the mineral rich nature of our lands and red commemorates those who died or worked for the country's independence.

Then the five pointed lone star which is the symbol of African emancipation and unity in the struggle against colonialism."

Ghana is bordered by Burkina Faso (formerly Upper Volta) in the north, Togo in the east, the Atlantic Ocean in the south, and by the Ivory Coast in the west. It has an area of 92,000 square miles.

It is one of the most prosperous countries in Africa.

The country has a population of 27 million. The majority of the people are Christian. Muslims constitute about 18 per cent of the population.

The first commercial contact with Europe involved trade in gold that was available in the region that came to be known as the Gold Coast. It was named by the Portuguese who where the first to establish commercial contact with the people in the region in the 1400s. They called it *Costa do Ouro* which means Gold Coast.

Other Europeans who were involved in the trade in gold with the indigenous people by the 1600s were the Dutch, the Swedes, the Danes, the Norwegians and the Germans. They built forts and castles along the coast from which they conducted trade with the indigenous people of the region. It was some of the same forts which were later used to carry on the Trans-Atlantic slave trade.

In the 1870s, the British gained a foothold and secured some parts they named the British Gold Coast. They expanded the area they controlled by conquering the indigenous people and eventually became the dominant power in the region. They established a colony which later became independent Ghana.

The country has a rich history including the tragedy of the slave trade. A very large number of African Americans and other people of African descent in the diaspora have roots in Ghana. As Dr. Nkrumah stated in his speech to celebrate Ghana's independence:

"There exists a firm bond of sympathy between us and the Negro peoples of the Americas. The ancestors of so many of them come from this country. Even today in the West Indies, it is possible to hear words and phrases which come from various languages of the Gold Coast." – (Kwame Nkrumah, quoted by Ali A. Mazrui, *Towards a Pax Africana: A Study of Ideology and Ambition*, London: Weidenfeld and Nicolson, 1967, pp. 60 – 61).

They are descended from the the Akan, the Ewe and other ethnic groups in Ghana and from other parts of the continent – Congo, Angola, and so on – including East Africa, especially Tanzania and Mozambique; although most of the slaves taken to the Americas came from West Africa.

There are five major ethnic groups – meta-ethnic categories of related groups – in Ghana. But the number of cultural and linguistic entities is higher than that. Rivalries among them is not unusual as is the case in most parts of Africa although the country has an excellent record as one of the most stable and peaceful on the continent:

"In 1960 roughly, 100 linguistic and cultural groups were recorded in Ghana.

Although later censuses placed less emphasis on the ethnic and cultural composition of the population, differences of course existed and had not disappeared by the mid-1990s.

The major ethnic groups in Ghana include the Akan, Ewe, Mole-Dagbane, Guan, and Ga-Adangbe.

The subdivisions of each group share a common cultural heritage, history, language, and origin. These shared attributes were among the variables that contributed to state formation in the precolonial period.

Competition to acquire land for cultivation, to control trade routes, or to form alliances for protection also promoted group solidarity and state formation.

The creation of the union that became the Asante confederacy in the late seventeenth century is a good example of such processes at work in Ghana's past.

Ethnic rivalries of the precolonial era, variance in the impact of colonialism upon different regions of the country, and the uneven distribution of social and economic amenities in post-independence Ghana have all contributed to present-day ethnic tensions. For example, in February 1994, more than 1,000 persons were killed and 150,000 others displaced in the northeastern part of Ghana infighting between Konkomba on one side and Nanumba, Dagomba, and Gonja on the other.

The clashes resulted from longstanding grievances over land ownership and the prerogatives of chiefs. A military task force restored order, but a state of emergency in the region remained in force until mid-August.

Although this violence was certainly evidence of ethnic tension in the country, most observers agreed that the case in point was exceptional. As one prolific writer on modern Ghana, Naomi Chazan, has aptly observed, undifferentiated recourse to ethnic categories has obscured the essential fluidity that lies at the core of shared ties in the country.

Evidence of this fluidity lies in the heterogeneous nature of all administrative regions, in rural-urban migration that results in inter-ethnic mixing, in the shared concerns of professionals and trade unionists that cut across ethnic lines, and in the multi-ethnic composition of secondary school and university classes.

Ethnicity, nonetheless, continues to be one of the most potent factors affecting political behavior in Ghana. For this reason, ethnically based political parties are unconstitutional under the present Fourth Republic.

Despite the cultural differences among Ghana's various peoples, linguists have placed Ghanaian languages in one or the other of only two major linguistic subfamilies of the Niger-Congo language family, one of the large language groups in Africa.

These are the Kwa and Gur groups, found to the south and north of the Volta River, respectively.

The Kwa group, which comprises about 75 percent of the country's population, includes the Akan, Ga-Adangbe, and Ewe.

The Akan are further divided into the Asante, Fante, Akwapim, Akyem, Akwamu, Ahanta, Bono, Nzema, Kwahu, and Safwi.

The Ga-Adangbe people and language group include the Ga, Adangbe, Ada, and Krobo or Kloli.

Even the Ewe, who constitute a single linguistic group, are divided into the Nkonya, Tafi, Logba, Sontrokofi, Lolobi, and Likpe.

North of the Volta River are the three subdivisions of the Gur-speaking people. These are the Gurma, Grusi, and Mole-Dagbane. Like the Kwa subfamilies, further divisions exist within the principal Gur groups.

Any one group may be distinguished from others in the same linguistically defined category or subcategory, even when the members of the category are characterized by essentially the same social institutions.

Each has a historical tradition of group identity, if nothing else, and, usually, of political autonomy.

In some cases, however, what is considered a single unit for census and other purposes may have been divided into identifiable separate groups before and during much of the colonial period and, in some manner, may have continued to be separate after independence.

No part of Ghana, however, is ethnically homogeneous. Urban centers are the most ethnically mixed because of migration to towns and cities by those in search of

19

employment.

Rural areas, with the exception of cocoa-producing areas that have attracted migrant labor, tend to reflect more traditional population distributions.

One overriding feature of the country's ethnic population is that groups to the south who are closer to the Atlantic coast have long been influenced by the money economy, Western education, and Christianity, whereas Gur-speakers to the north, who have been less exposed to those influences, have came under Islamic influence. These influences were not pervasive in the respective regions, however, nor were they wholly restricted to them." – ("Ethnic Groups," GhanaWeb).

Modernisation has also contributed to more diversity in demographic composition across the country. The people of different ethnic groups are found in all of Ghana's ten regions but in varying degrees. Still, different ethnic groups have more people in their own native regions than they do in other parts of the country.

However, there is great social interaction and cohesion among different groups, a phenomenon that has "blurred" distinctions in terms of ethnic loyalties and cultural identities, forging a new identity – Ghanaian – on the anvil of diversity.

Many Ghanaians have transcended ethno-regional loyalties for the sake of national unity although regionalism is still a factor in presidential elections and appointments, among other areas. As Nana Yaw Osei stated in his article, "Ghana: Loyalty, Regional Balance and Political Appointments":

"The politicians in Ghana are expected to love those who were loyal to them while in opposition but must remember, they were not only born as Ghanaians but are equally elected to serve the interest of Ghana not their party *apparatchiks*.

20

I personally wrote an article to remind ex-president John Dramani Mahama (JDM) on the dangers of appointing a lot of northerners in his government.

I received a severe backlash from that publication. Professor Stephen Addai also advised JDM on that same issue. Professor Addai was vilified and bastardized. Individuals he could not only teach but give birth to, described him as irresponsible. JDM and his National Democratic Congress (NDC) lost the 2016 presidential and general elections partly because his government alienated the Akan majority, The Ga-Adangbes and the Ewes.

President Akufu-Addo had appointed many people from Eastern Region (ER). For example, Nana Asante Bediatuo, Madam Gloria Akufu, Mrs. Ursula Owusu-Ekuful (an impeccable attorney, MP) and Messrs Dan Botwe (MP), Yaw Osafo-Marfo, Samuel Atta Akyea (A good Lawyer, MP), Kwasi Amoako-Attah (MP for Atiwa), Boakye Kyeremanteng Agyarko (MP and partly from Kroboland) and Ken Ofori-Attah all from the Eastern Region. Madam, Otiko Afisa Djaba is also partly from Eastern Region.

This writer is from Brong Ahafo and Ashanti Regions by virtue of paternity and maternity respectively. Eastern Region is my third region because throughout my job history in Ghana, I worked in the region. Eastern people are wonderful. I have more friends in ER than any part of Ghana. Nevertheless, having more ministers from Eastern Region is not healthy for national integration.

It is also not healthy for the New Patriotic Party (NPP) as a political organization. President Akufu-Addo like his predecessor, JDM, probably appointed people he could trust. Some people have argued that a leader needs people he could trust....

Are these people loyal to Ghana or president Akufu-Addo? Loyalty of appointees alone cannot suffice as an antidote for bad governance. The framers of the 1992 constitution of Ghana envisaged the importance of regional balance and national development....

Political appointments must be based on population and not only geographical considerations. Appointments must be proportional to the population. It will be unfair to have two ministers from Upper West Region (which has a small population) and two from The Northern Region (which has a large population).

Another way of ensuring proper regional balance is the idea of a nation. A nation is a group of people with a common language, cultural heritage and ancestry. A nation is not necessarily defined by geographical boundaries. Ghana becomes a nation when we consider all Ghanaians irrespective of their geographical locations on earth. Our ancestors are part of Ghana as a nation. Other examples are, Asanti, Akyem, Anlo and Krobo nations.

These include Asantes, Anlos, Akyems and Krobos in dispersion. For example, notwithstanding the fact that Mrs. Ursula Owusu Ekuful is a member of parliament for Ablekuma West Constituency in the Greater Accra region, she is a native of Akyem. Definitely, she adds up to the number of Akyems in government per the nation concept. Although managing electoral success is somewhat difficult than being in opposition, the nation concept must be factored into political appointments to assure Ghanaians of regional/ethnic balance.

Ghana is a unitary state with socially preposterous system of centralization and bureaucratic bottleneck. The son of Mr. Kofi Akote of Akwapem Guan and Madam Naa Atwee of Ga lineage, Kwadwo Adi, living in the Bumprugu Yoyoo area must definitely know some big men in Accra, before his passport or birth certificate could be fast-tracked.

A Cocoa Farmer in the Western Region or Brong Ahafo Region must come all the way to Tema Port for the purpose of clearing his/her goods. Not until the impractical system of centralization in Ghana is abandoned, every region needs a big man in Accra. Certain sectors like security require individuals who are loyal to the president. Apart from that regional balance and competence must be prioritized in national appointments.

Patriotism and competence must be raised above loyalty to the president. Loyalty promotes sycophancy, mediocrity and incompetence in governance. It is a tool dictators use to safeguard and sustain their inordinate and uncompromising political and social ambitions. Must we be loyal to our leaders when they are wrong? Assuming The Gambian army had been loyal to Yahya Jammeh, it would have had a calamitous implication on innocent Gambians.

I think President Akufu-Addo's government has not totally taken off yet. It will be a sort of bigotry to start criticizing him. However, as Plato observed "For a man to conquer himself is the first and noblest of all victories." It is based on this assertion that I think there are many appointees from ER (the Eastern Region). ER is made up of The Akyem, The Akwamu, The Akuapem, The Kwahu, The Asante and The Krobo.

What is particularly lamentable is that the Akyems appeared to be dominating in the list of appointees from ER.

Looking for individuals loyal to a leader is not a bad idea in its entirety. Nonetheless, loyalty cannot guarantee an excellent job performance. When we go to hospital, we don't look for physicians who are loyal to us.

This means that competence and appropriate regional balance not only loyalty are needed to transform our beloved motherland. The famous saying, "no taxation without representation" in the history of the USA must goad our leaders to prioritize regional balance in political appointments." – (Nana Yaw Osei, "Ghana: Loyalty, Regional Balance and Political Appointments," GhanaWeb, 23 January 2017).

23

Yet, in spite of all that, Ghana still stands out as one of the few African countries which have maintained unity and stability through the years under democratically elected leaders in spite of ethnic diversity which has been a source of conflict in some countries because of ethnic rivalries partly caused by domination of some ethnic groups by others.

Even when the country was under military rule, it remained united without any threats of fragmentation along ethno-regional lines. For example, Jerry Rawlings, the longest-ruling military head of state provided strong leadership and earned the country respect in Pan-African circles because he was an ardent nationalist and Pan-Africanist.

The respect and admiration he earned Ghana was sometimes reminiscent of the Nkrumah era when the country was a shining black star in the constellation of nations. Unfortunately, the black star faded after Nkrumah was overthrown. But he still left behind a united nation, a rare accomplishment on a continent where ethnic rivalries have threatened to tear countries apart through the years since independence.

One of the main factors which have contributed to ethnic integration in Ghana is fervent nationalism, especially under the leadership of Dr. Kwame Nkrumah who established a unitary state transcending ethno-regional loyalties and rivalries. This included integrating schools by mixing students from different ethnic groups and regions.

Integration of the civil service also played a major role in building national unity and solidarity among the people of different ethnic groups and cultural backgrounds whose identities were regionally entrenched.

Without strong leadership, national disintegration and even violence could have shattered the dream of establishing a stable and united nation.

Violence perpetrated by tribal and regional chauvinists

had already erupted in some parts of the country including the capital in an attempt to undermine Nkrumah's government. Nkrumah himself was the target of several assassination attempts through the years.

The strongest opposition to Nkrumah came from the Ashanti who wanted autonomy – virtual independence – for their region. In 1954, they formed a political party, the National Liberation Movement (NLM), led by Bafour Osei Akoto (who was the founder of the party) and Dr. Kofi Abrefa Busia, a relentless opponent of Nkrumah, although the party also had support in other parts of the country including the Eastern Region, home of Dr. J.B. Danquah, who is acknowledged as one of the founding fathers – the Big Six – of modern Ghana.

The NLM was formed after Dr. Busia's party, the Ghana Congress Party (GCP) which he formed in May 1952, won only one seat – out of 104 – in the 1954 election. Busia was the one who won the seat. Nkrumah's Convention People's Party won 72 seats.

Ironically, Dr. Danquah, Nkrumah's most celebrated opponent besides Dr. Busia, failed to win the election in his home region in the 1954 electoral contest when he sought to represent Akyem Abuakwa Central in parliament also as a candidate of the Ghana Congress Party (GCP). It was a humiliating defeat for the "doyen of Gold Coast politics," on his own turf, by his nemesis, Nkrumah whose party won the seat.

Besides the NLM, other political parties opposed to Nkrumah's policy of centralisation of power under a unitary state controlled by the Convention People's Party (CPP) included the Northern People's Party (NPP), the Muslim Association Party (MAP), the Togoland Congress (TC) which was resolutely opposed to the integration of British Togoland with the Gold Coast, and the Anlo Youth Organisation, a tribal party of the Anlo ethnic group in the southeastern part of the country but which – unlike the Togoland Congress – campaigned for the unification of

British Togoland with the Gold Coast yet strongly opposed Nkrumah and his Convention People's Party (CPP).

The 1956 election saw the CPP consolidate power by retaining control of the legislature when it defeated its opponents and even won support in all the regions including the opposition strongholds of Ashanti and the Eastern Region, averting the threat of national disintegration.

After the Gold Coast won independence in 1957 and became Ghana, the ruling Convention People's Party passed a law outlawing tribal, regional and religious political parties and any other parties which promoted sectional interests militating against national unity. This led to the merger of the different opposition parties to form the United Party (UP) under the leadership of Dr. Busia.

Opposition to Nkrumah and his CPP government intensified, with some of his opponents resorting to violence in an attempt to assassinate him and overthrow the government. They did not care even if they plunged the country into chaos as long as they succeeded in getting rid of him and his government. As Professor Kwame Botwe-Asamoah states in his book, *Kwame Nkrumah's Politico-Cultural Thought and Policies: An African-Centered Paradigm for the Second Phase of the African Revolution*:

"Having compromised on the federal issues with the provision of regional councils, the CPP government found itself having to combat secessionist threats, rebellion and violence. A statement by the opposition leader, Dr. Busia, foreshadowed these developments. He had warned the British government that a CPP victory in the 1956 election would be disastrous for the nation, and that the NLM was prepared to seek any means possible, including terrorism and undemocratic means, to eliminate the evil CPP (Awoonor: 168).

In March 1953, Dr. Busia debased 'the CPP of being

26

made up of agitators and revolutionaries, aided by a frantic band of propagandists who used imperialists as scapegoats to inflict the demagogy of the uneducated upon the country' (Ibid: 156).

Against this anti-democratic stance, was it surprising to see the relentless, systematically terrorist methods applied by the Opposition that culminated in the coup of February 24, 1966, that overthrew Nkrumah's government?

Should not the government at that time have considered Busia's statement as a threat to national security, worthy of arrest by the law enforcement agency?

Ghana was to witness the outcomes of this avowed violent statement by Dr. Busia, often referred to as the champion of democracy in Africa." – (Kwame Botwe-Asamoah, *Kwame Nkrumah's Politico-Cultural Thought and Policies: An African-Centered Paradigm for the Second Phase of the African Revolution,* New York & London: Routledge, 2005, pp. 121 – 122).

Nkrumah's opponents contended that he had suppressed the opposition with draconian legislation and the country was already drifting towards dictatorship, if it wasn't already one; although they conceded Nkrumah's party won a majority of the seats in the first election in 1951 in which the leading opposition party during that time, the United Gold Coast Convention (UGCC) whose acknowledged leader was Dr. J. B. Danquah, also participated. The party performed miserably and its leaders acknowledged that even according to the Danquah Institute:

"Nkrumah and a number of CPP leaders were arrested in early 1950 as a result of their 'Positive Action' methods aimed at immediate self-government.

In the February 1951 election the CPP won a plurality of seats and, bowing to the inevitable, the colonial administration released Nkrumah to become Leader of Government Business.

The UGCC was disbanded after its poor showing in this election, leaving a clear field for the CPP to operate as the sole independence movement for some three or four years.

By 1954, however, a number of regional- or ethnic-based opposition parties had arisen to challenge the CPP on the issue of political centralization and on the question of the unitary structure of the independence constitution. Within the area that was to constitute the new state of Ghana, these parties included the National Liberation Movement (NLM, advocating autonomy for the Ashanti region), the Togoland Congress (which opposed the integration of British Togoland with the Gold Coast), the Muslim Association Party, and the Northern People's Party (NPP).

The challenge of these parties to CPP dominance and particularly on the issue of constitutional structure represented a potential threat to the smooth transition to independence that the British authorities and the Nkrumah government so greatly desired. What might be interpreted as an impending crisis in national integration was tentatively resolved by the election of 1956 in which the CPP retained its majority position in the legislature and demonstrated at least marginal support in all regions of the country. This cleared the path for independence, which was granted eight months later. Under a new name, Ghana, the nation joined the British Commonwealth as an independent entity on March 6, 1957.

Still threatened by sectional and ethnic cleavages, the new government embarked upon a policy of political consolidation and the suppression of opposition.

One of the first acts of the government following independence was the proscription of sectional, regional, religious, and tribal parties. As a result, the NLM, NPP, and other minority parties merged as the United Party under the leadership of K. A. Busia, J. B. Danquah, and other opposition figures.

Subsequent acts of political suppression by the Nkrumah government such as the Preventive Detention Act of 1958 considerably reduced the effectiveness of the opposition party.

Many United Party members were imprisoned; others, like Busia, went into exile. Danquah, Ghana's first nationalist, died while under detention, having been one of several prominent people arrested following an unsuccessful attempt on Nkrumah's life.

Following independence, the major organs of the press and the broadcast media (owned and operated by the government) were employed to promote the objectives of the CPP government. The independent press was strictly censored. Formal opposition in parliament dwindled as members were detained, left the country or crossed over to the majority side. By the end of our time period, 1962, the United Party held only a handful of seats." – (Danquah Institute Public and Research Center, Accra, Ghana).

Out of desperation, Nkrumah's opponents started to use unconstitutional means, including indiscriminate use of violence killing innocent people among them children, in an attempt to oust him – even when they conceded his party, CPP, had won elections in 1951 and in 1956, one year before independence. As Botwe-Asamoah states:

"The Opposition's declared vow to rid the country of the 'Veranda Boys' or the 'homeless tramps and jackals' took the form of several bomb explosions, (and) assassination attempts on the lives of Nkrumah and the CPP followers. Earlier, Dr. J.B. Danquah also issued similar threatening statements on various occasions.

During the electioneering campaign in 1956, the NLM supporters in central Akyem Abuakwa constituency (in the Eastern Region) quoted the Omanhene Nana Ofori Atta II as saying that there would be no peace in the country if the CPP should win the election. In fact, fears were constantly

29

put into the people (this author, then a child, also heard it) that the CPP strongholds in Akyem Abuakwa would be destroyed by the 'oprem' (cannons) in front of the Omanhene's palace.

In our village, the NLM supporters vowed publicly that all 'strangers settllers' would be chased out of Akyem leaving their cocoa farms behind, should the NLM emerge victorious; in addition, they vowed that the CPP supporters would be made to plant their plantains inside their houses.

We the children from Ettokrom, who had to walk from Ettokrom to attend primary school at Osiem at the time, would run to hide in the bush, anytime we heard the approaching NLM Peugeot caravans, especially their resounding horns.

Kofi Awoonor's analysis of the events at the time is worth citing here. After the CPP won the election, the NLM kept up some degree of agitation in which secession was invoked as the last result 'to what it considered to be a constitutional impasse.' He continues:

> The political unrest persisted in the opposition enclaves of parts of Asante, the Volta area, and Accra where the sectarian movements for secession, Ewe unificationist and Ga sectarian claims against 'strangers' received more ominous and threatening support (Ibid: 188).

This situation posed a very grave threat to the political stability in the newly independent country, a serious factor sadly ignored by critics of Nkrumah policies.

On the even of Ghana's independence, the Opposition enclave in the Volta region, the Ewe Unification Movement, actually went into the bush to prepare for an armed insurrection. Accordingly, 'groups were set up armed with homemade shotguns' and 'formed themselves into a ragged guerilla army prepared to go into battle for their cause' (Mahoney: 160).

In the face of this, 'the Queen's governor-general in the Gold Coast was obliged to send troops' to the region to put down the 'Ewe revolt against the new government' (Ibid: 160).

Later, the leaders of the movement, S.G. Antor and Kojo Ayeke were arrested and jailed for masterminding the rebellion.

The CPP government's attempt to contain the unrest that erupted in Kumase, was prompted by the deportation orders, debated in the parliament, against Alhaji Amadu Baba and Alhaji Osman Lalam. These two non-Ghanaian Moslems 'were accused of financing the NLM and its thugs' (Awoonor: 190).

Three months after the Ewe rebellion, Nai Wulomo (Ga Chief Priest) launched another anti-Nkrumah movement, the Ga-Shifimo Kpee (the Ga Standfast Association), in Accra, with an opening prayer. As Awoonor indicates, 'a sheep was slaughtered and oaths were sworn against all 'strangers,' including Nkrumah who was accused of encumbering a Ga Constituency seat.

From then on the organization's youth wing, 'Tokyo Joes,' thronged themselves at vantage points in Accra, the seat of the government, hooting and jeering at Nkrumah and the CPP leaders. Strangely enough, J.B. Danquah, who had lost his bid in the election in Akyem Abuakwa Central, and S.G. Antor were present for the inauguration of what Awoonor characterizes (as a) 'revanchist organization.'

In order to buttress the Ga-Shifimo Kpee, taxi drivers and truck drivers went on strike in July 1956. This led to armed conflicts between the CPP youth, led by Oko Kolomashe, a fisherman of Bukom, 'and the Tokyo Joes, who had the support of Ga leaders' (Austin:372).

It was in response to these undemocratic and terrorist methods against national security interest that compelled the CPP government to seek the necessary legal measures, and rightly so, to consolidate the unitary system of government for which the people voted." – (Ibid., pp. 122 – 123).

31

He goes on to state:

"Ninsin legitimizes the Nkrumah government's emergency measures as a choice to the realization of a strong national unity free from both ethnocentrism and the 'danger of fragmentation,' or national fragmentation and rivalry.

With the voters' mandate, the CPP government 'committed its energies to forging national unity and making the nation strong' (Ninsin: 232).

Nkrumah had urged that 'in the highest reaches of national life, there should be no reference to Fantis, Asantes, Ewes, Gas, Dagombas, Strangers' and so forth.'; in contrast, 'we should call ourselves Ghanaians – the brothers and sisters, members of the same community – the state of Ghana' (Nkrumah, 1961: 168).

Continuing, he implored Ghanaians to purge from their own minds the ethnic chauvinism and prejudice of one group against the other. Otherwise, 'We shall not be able to cultivate the wider spirit of brotherhood which our objective of Pan-Africanism calls for. We are all Africans and Peoples of African descent, and we shall not allow the imperialist plotters and intrigues to separate us from each other for their own advantage' (Ibid: 168).

Here, Nkrumah not only understood the Opposition's continual undemocratic conspiracies and terrorist methods as a threat to Ghana's internal security, but he also viewed them in the broader context of his Pan-African project." – (Ibid., pp. 123 – 124).

As shown above, Ghana has faced threats to its national integrity through the years, especially in the fifties and soon after independence including the bloody political and civil strife of 1954 – 1956 during the general elections period (elections were held in 1954 and in 1956) instigated by the opposition whose regionalist and tribalist agenda encouraged subversion and the use of violence and fuelled secessionist sentiments. But the country has emerged intact.

Fortunately, most of the threats were not serious enough to plunge the country into civil war and break it up as some secessionists wanted to do.

However, Ghana would not have faced such threats if the opposition conceded defeat and accepted the results without causing turmoil after the Convention People's Party won all elections in the 1950s. Nkrumah's popularity in the fifties was indisputable, although he started losing some of that in the early sixties as he drifted towards authoritarian rule. But he is still an embodiment of Ghana even today despite his shortcomings.

Ghana has ten administrative regions. They are Upper West, Upper East, Northern Region, Brong Ahafo, Ashanti, Western Region, Central Region, Eastern Region, Volta Region, and Greater Accra which is the smallest in terms of area but with the second largest population after Ashanti.

Each of the regions has its own identity and distinctive attributes. Yet they all share a common identity as integral parts of one united country.

The Ashanti Region is home to the Ashanti kingdom, one of the most renowned political entities on the continent before the advent of colonial rule like the Buganda kingdom in Uganda and others elsewhere.

Inhabited mostly by the Ashanti people, also known as the Asante, the region is a major producer of gold and cocoa, the country's main exports. In fact, it is the largest producer of cocoa in the whole country.

The Ashanti are the largest subgroup of the Akan people. They constitute about 15 per cent of Ghana's population. Their main language is Twi.

The Ashanti are also known for having formed one of the most successful political unions on the African continent before the advent of colonial rule, the Ashanti Empire. It existed from 1701 to 1957 when it was officially abolished after the establishment of Ghana as an independent state under a unitary government.

The main city of Ashanti Region is Kumasi, one of the largest in Ghana. It is the region's capital. It is also the cultural and commercial centre of the Ashanti Region. And about a third of the entire population of the Ashanti Region live in the Kumasi metropolitan area. Also, more than 50 per cent of the people in the region live in urban centres. That is because a very large number of people live in the Kumasi metropolitan area.

The Ashanti king, Otumfuo Asantehene, is the spiritual leader of the entire region.

The region also has the largest natural lake in the country. It is called Lake Bosomtwe.

The Ashanti Region is also known for its religious ceremonies. The main ones are Akwasidae and Adae Kese. They are religious festivals in remembrance of leaders and heroes who are the "dead living." The spirits of the departed are believed to be very much a part of the living, interacting and guiding them in their daily lives. Consultation with the spirits of the dead leaders and heroes takes place during the Adae festival.

Other traditional celebrations are the Kente, Mmoa Nni Nko, Nkyidwo, Papa, and Yaa Asantewaa festivals.

About 78 per cent of the people in Ashanti Region are Christian. That is higher than the national average of 69 per cent. Muslims constitute 13 per cent of the population in the region which is lower than the national average of 16 per cent.

Some of the major tourist attractions in the Ashanti Region are Kejetia Market in Kumasi. It is also known as the Kumasi Central Market. It is an open-air market and the largest in Africa.

People who go to the market, especially, visitors, are advised to stay close to each other because it is very easy to get lost and lose one another. There are so many people and so many cars and other vehicles in and around the market that it is not uncommon for many people to get lost.

The market also has had a number of tragedies, especially fires destroying shops, stalls and merchandise. One of the worst outbreaks was in 2001 when more than 150 stalls were destroyed.

The market's location in central Kumasi has also given the city a distinct character. It is the heart of Kumasi which is also known as the Garden City because of its wide variety of flowers and plants. Kumasi also is home to Kwame Nkrumah University of Science and Technology, one of the most renowned institutions of higher learning in Ghana and on the entire continent.

Another administrative region, **Brong Ahafo**, is in the central west. It is the second-largest in the country. It is mostly inhabited by the Akans Brong and Ahafo after whom it is named. It is known for cocoa and timber production and for its agribusiness. Brong Ahafo is one of three largest producers of cocoa in the country. Most of the cocoa is produced in Ahafo, an area that borders the western part of Ashanti Region.

The northern part of Brong Ahafo is a major producer of grain and tubers.

Coffee, rubber and tobacco are also produced in the region.

The region is also a major producer of cashew nuts. Some of the nuts are used to produce brandy and wine in the town Wenchi which is also known for the Apoo festival celebrated in April-May every year.

The region has a variety of cultural attractions and wildlife including two national parks, although it does not draw many tourists the way neighbouring Ashanti does. But it has earned a place in the history of Ghana for being the home of the country's second prime minister, Dr. Kofi Busia, who became the nation's leader in 1969 after

Nkrumah was overthrown and replaced by a military regime in 1966.

Although Brong Ahafo is mostly inhabited by the Akan, there is one area where a different ethnic group constitutes the vast majority of the population. The area is Sene where the main ethnic group is the Guan, especially the Gonja which is the largest subgroup in the Guan cluster.

The Ewe and the Gurma are the other ethnic groups whose members are found in large numbers in Sene and Atebubu. They are the second-largest in those areas.

Ewes, who are a southern group, are found in large numbers in Sene because of their involvement in fishing on the side of the Brong Ahafo Region facing Lake Volta.

The Mole-Dagbon are the second largest group in all the other administrative areas of the Brong Ahafo Region; although a distant second to the Akan. The Akan constitute about 63 per cent of the region's population, and the Mole-Dagbon about 15.5 per cent. The Grusi are the third-largest with only about 4 per cent of the region's total population.

The other ethnic groups in Brong Ahafo are the Mande-Busanga, and the Ga-Dangme.

About 71 per cent of the people in Brong Ahafo are Christian, and 16 per cent Muslim. More women than men in the region are Christian and even in the entire country. Also more men then women are Moslem; so are those who practise traditional religions.

Muslims are a majority in two districts, Kintampo and Atebubu. They are mostly members of the Mole-Dagbon ethnic group.

Sene District has the largest number of people who practise traditional religion. It is also in Sene where you find the largest number of people who profess no religion at all.

The Brong Amafro Region also attracts many people from the northern part of the country because of its good climate and the availability of arable land. Another factor that accounts for this migratory pattern is the region's proximity to the north, making it easier for northerners to move into the region.

Almost 50 per cent of the people in Brong Ahafo can not read and write. But they are better off than their counterparts in the northern part of the country where the illiteracy rate is more than 70 per cent. The national average of the literacy rate is about 55 per cent.

More than two-thirds of the people in Brong Ahafo are engaged in agriculture. And the largest market in the entire region is in Techiman.

The Central Region was once a part of the Western Region. It was created in 1970 for administrative purposes because of the large number of people in the Western Region. There was a need for the creation of another region.

It is the third-smallest region after Greater Accra and Upper East. It is also the second most densely populated although it has lost a large number of people through the years because they have migrated to other parts of the country and elsewhere. People from other parts of Ghana and beyond constitute 25 per cent of the region's population. Some districts have almost 40 per cent of the people who came from other parts of the country.

The people of what is now the Central Region were the first In Ghana to come into contact with Europeans who first went there for commercial purposes. The region's capital, Cape Coast, was also the first capital of the Gold Coast. The capital was moved to Accra in 1877.

The region is also known for its festivals. There are 32 of them. Some of the most well-known festivals are Aboakyer held in Winneba, Bakatue in Elmina, and Fetu in Cape Coast.

Most of the people who came from outside the Central Region migrated from Ashanti, Eastern, Greater Accra, Volta and Western regions.

Like most parts of Ghana, the region is mostly rural. But its urban population increased from 28 per cent in 1960 to about 38 per cent in 2000. The most urbanised districts are Cape Coast, Awutu-Efutu-Senya and Agona. About two-thirds of the people in those districts are urbanised.

The Central Region has a lot of natural resources in commercial quantities. They include gold, diamonds, petroleum, natural gas, bauxite, beryl, kaolin, clay, columbite, tantalite, quartz, mica, granite and others. It is also known for tourism. Fishing also is one of the major economic activities in the region.

The region's dense forest has mostly been cleared in order to grow cocoa and oil palm trees. Timber is also produced in large quantities in the forest areas.

The Central Region also has plenty of fertile land.

It is also home to the University of Cape Coast, a renowned academic institution, and the University of Education-Winneba.

Its tourist attractions include castles and forts, a reminder of an era when the slave trade was thriving in the region and other parts of the country. Cape Coast Castle and Elmina Castle – which is the oldest trading post on the Gulf of Guinea – are world heritage sites recognised by UNESCO.

The vast majority of the people, at least 82 per cent, are Akan. The Guan are the second largest, constituting 6 per cent of the region's population, followed by the Ewe who are about 5 per cent.

Among the Akan people in the Centrtal Region, the Fante are the main group. They live mostly along the coast and are known in Ghanaian history for having formed one of the most successful political structures in the history of pre-colonial Africa, the Fante Confederation which existed from 1868 to 1874; before then, they had the Fante Confederacy, an allliance of Fante states which existed since the 1500s.

There are small ethnic groups in the Central Region. They are Mole-Dagbon, Grusi, Gurma and Mande-Busanga. Together, they constitute about 4 per cent of the region's population and are of northern origin.

The Central Region was also home to one of Ghana's presidents, John Evans Atta Mills who led the country from January 2009 until his death in July 2012, although he was born in the Western Region.

The Eastern Region is the sixth-largest in terms of area and the third-largest in terms of population after Ashanti and Greater Accra.

It is home to the Akosombo Dam which plays a major role in the region's economy and that of the country as a whole.

It was one of the major projects launched by President Nkrumah, although it was conceived by the British colonial rulers twenty years before then. Nkrumah wanted it to provide power for the rapid industrialisation of Ghana.

Building of the dam resulted in the creation of Lake Volta, the largest man-made lake in the world in terms of area. Lake Volta also is the third largest man-made lake in the world in terms of volume; the largest, Lake Kariba, is also in Africa located between Zambia and Zimbabwe.

But the creation of Lake Volta, which covers a substantial part of the Eastern Region, also led to disaster. Many people were uprooted from their traditional homelands and displaced. About 80,000 people were relocated. At least 700 villages were taken over by the Volta River Authority which oversaw the construction of the Akosombo Dam.

The vast majority of the people in the Central Region are Akan.

The flooding caused by the construction of the dam, leading to the creation of Lake Volta, also had a major impact on the environment.

The artificial lake, which is 250 miles long, covers a

large area of more than 3,000 square miles. That is 3.6 per cent of the entire area of Ghana.

The dam, which also provides electricity to other West African countries including Togo and Benin, was originally conceived by a British-Australian geologist, Albert Ernest Kitson, in 1915 but was not comprehensively mapped out until 1949.

Construction began in 1961 and the dam was officially opened by President Nkrumah himself in 1965, less than a year before he was overthrown on 24 February 1966 in a military coup masterminded by the CIA.

Although many people were uprooted and relocated in order to build the dam, a lot of benefits have been derived from it through the years. They include increased fishing and tourism.

But the people have also suffered because of a decline in agricultural productivity along the lake and its tributaries. The land around Lake Volta is not as fertile as the land that was overtaken by the flooding to create the lake and where tens of thousands of people once lived and earned a good living from farming before they were displaced and relocated. And increased agricultural activity has virtually depleted the soil of its nutrients, making it unsuitable to grow crops.

Agriculture further downstream has also suffered. Flooding which brought soil nutrients from upstream as the river flowed naturally was stopped by the dam, resulting in poorer soil.

The use of fertiliser in commercial agriculture which has been fuelled by the dam has also led to pollution of the Volta River; so has sewage and flows from cattle stocks in the area. Compounding the problem is the rapid growth of aquatic weeds which impede navigation and transport on the lake.

The people who live in the area have been affected by all that. The aquatic weeds have contributed to a decline in health among the people because they provide a natural habitat for black flies which cause river blindness, snails which spread bilharzia, and mosquitoes which are responsible for malaria.

The diseases have increased dramatically through the years since the Akosombo Dam was built, especially in the areas where the people were resettled after being displaced by the construction of the dam. The closer the people are to Lake Volta, the higher the incidence of disease. The hardest-hit have been children and fishermen.

The traditional economy of the people, dependent on the river, has also suffered because of a dramatic decline in shrimp and clam populations which are also an important part of their diet; it has also suffered because of pollution of the Volta River.

The human cost of the Akosombo Dam and its product, Lake Volta, can not be underestimated. Tens of thousands of people were not only uprooted and forcibly relocated; they lost their vital source of income and livelihood which depended on farming in their traditional homelands and on fishing in the Volta River.

They also lost their homes and their traditional burial grounds. Their communal ties were disrupted and social fabric torn, leading to loss of social values which were fostered in their traditional communities that no longer existed after the people were removed from their ancestral lands.

It was an incalculable human cost. No resettlement programme could repay that; and no resettlement programme could rebuild those ties and communities.

Indigenous knowledge including traditional methods of farming and other means of earning a living, which are a product of a local or native environment, was lost; a result of the displacement of the people from their traditional homelands.

The people were not only relocated to less fertile land; poor living conditions in the resettlement villages also took their toll, with some people dying and others leaving.

41

One resettlement village lost more than 50 per cent of its population in 23 years since the people were relocated there.

Therefore, the Volta River project has had a profound impact on the lives of the people in the area, leading to economic uncertainties and insecurities accompanied by increased poverty, despite its positive impact in some areas especially at the national level as a development scheme. The problems have been compounded by population pressure in the Volta-basin area.

Poverty has also played a role in fuelling migration in the Volta Basin, compounded by harsh living conditions in the resettlement villages. This movement of the people, from place to place, has been a major factor in spreading HIV in the communities in the basin. The spread of sexually transmitted diseases is inextricably linked to the construction of the Akosombo Dam. Thousands of men were involved in building the dam and attracted many prostitutes. Commercial sex has been thriving in the Volta Basin since then.

Besides the Akosombo Dam, other dams of the Volta River Hydro Development Project have also played a major role in creating conditions which have enabled bilharzia to spread in the area.

Another major dam in the Eastern Region is Kpong.

The region also has gold and diamonds. It also has large deposits of bauxite which have yet to be mined in commercial quantities.

The Eastern Region also produces in commercial quantities a variety of agricultural products – cocoa, rubber, maize, pineapples, cassava, palm oil, cashew nuts, mangoes, yams, rice, ginger, sweet pepper and others.

It also has important historical sites. The remains of the slave market at Abonse are one of the major attractions; so are the botanical gardens at Aburi as well as other attractions including cruises on Lake Volta and a chain of highlands, waterfalls and valleys.

The Eastern Region also stands out in the history of Ghana in one respect. The home of Tetteh Quarshie, the "father" of the cocoa industry in Ghana, is in the region. In 1870, he went to Fernando Po (renamed Bioko and a part of Equatorial Guinea) and returned to the Gold Coast in 1876 with some cocoa beans. The first cocoa seed was planted at Mampong in the region. It led to the establishment of the first cocoa farm in the country. His home is a major attraction to many visitors.

The region is also known for its traditional festivals including Akantukese, Bobum or Dipo, Klovo Sikplemi, Ngmayem, Odwira, and Ohum.

They are occasions for celebration, prayer, spiritual cleansing, and dedication, among other things.

The majority of the people in the Eastern Region are Akan. They constitute 52 per cent of the population. The second-largest ethnic group are the Ga-Gangme. They make up 19 per cent of the region's population. The third-largest are the Ewe, 16 percent, followed by the Guan constituting 7 per cent of the population.

The main language is Twi.

The Eastern Region also has the distinction of having produced two presidents of Ghana. One was Fred Akuffo who was the military head of state from July 1978 until June 1979 when he was overthrown and executed three weeks after being ousted in a military coup led by Jerry Rawlings who became the new military head of state. The other head of state from the Eastern Region was Nana Akufo-Addo, a civilian, who went into office in January 2017.

The region also produced Dr. J.B. Danquah, an elder statesman who was regarded as the "doyen of Gold Coast politics." He played a major role as the leader of Ghana's first political party, the United Gold Coast Convention (UGCC), which was formed in 1947 to campaign for independence.

In his speech in Accra on Ghana's 50th independence

43

anniversary on 6 March 2007, President John Kufuor paid tribute to the leaders who started and led the campaign for the liberation of their country from colonial rule. Steeped in the Danquah-Busia tradition, he claimed it was Dr. Danquah who gave Ghana its name. As he stated:

"This is a celebration not only for Ghana but also for the whole of Africa. For, March 6, 1957 changed the outlook of our continent and its status and role in the world forever....

I must pay homage to the first President of Ghana, Dr. Kwame Nkrumah, and his colleagues of the United Gold Coast Convention (UGCC) who in 1947 launched the last phase of the process towards independence. These colleagues were: J.B. Danquah, (who gave us the name GHANA), Paa Grant, the financier of the group, Obetsebi-Lamptey, Edward Akufo-Addo, William Ofori-Atta and Ako Adjei all of blessed memory.

Let me also pay homage to the first government of our nationals under Dr. Kwame Nkrumah. I must mention some of its stalwarts: K.A. Gbedemah, Kojo Botsio, Kofi Baako, Krobo Edusei, Imoru Egala and others of blessed memory. Of that pioneering group I acknowledge two men who are still alive and are here with us, K.S.P. Jantuah and Amuawuah.

I also must pay homage to the members of the then Opposition; to Prof. K.A. Busia, S.D. Dombo, S.G. Antor Victor Owusu, Joe Appiah, and others of blessed memory; and R.R. Amponsah and C.K. Tedam, who are alive and with us here.

They struggled to establish the culture of multi-party democracy in our country. But above all, let us give thanks and praise for the many Ghanaians throughout the years who have worked anonymously and often without reward to make our nation what it is today. For as our former Prime Minister, Dr. K.A. Busia, put it, and I quote him: 'It is by the devoted day-to-day service of many ordinary and unnoticed citizens that a nation achieves greatness'....

Fifty years ago, as the first African nation south of the Sahara to gain independence, Ghana under Kwame Nkrumah made the fight for independence of other African countries, its prime occupation. Nkrumah articulated this passion in these immortal words, which I quote: 'The independence of Ghana is meaningless, unless it is linked up with the total liberation of Africa.'" – John Agyekum Kufuor, "The Star of Africa," *The New Black Magazine*, Birmingham, England, March 2007).

It was actually Nkrumah who proposed that the Gold Coast should be renamed Ghana after it emerged from colonial rule in memory of an empire called Ghana that once existed in West Africa north of present-day Ghana. Dr. Danquah, who was the main leader of the UGCC, agreed with him.

Dr. Danquah will indeed be remembered in Ghanaian history for the role he played especially in helping found the first political party in the Gold Coast to campaign for independence; so will his colleagues in the UGCC. But he was eclipsed by Nkrumah who once served as the UGCC's secretary-general.

Nkrumah left the United Gold Coast Convention in 1949 to form his own party, the Convention People's Party (CPP), which finally led the Gold Coast to become the first black African country to emerge from colonial rule.

In his book *Interventions: A Life in War and Peace*, Kofi Annan explained why Nkrumah left the United Gold Coast Convention to form his own party. It is true he wanted "Independence Now" unlike the UGCC leaders who took a gradualist approach. But there was also another reason why he left.

They saw him as someone of lower social and economic status. He had just returned to the Gold Coast in 1947, jobless, and in spite of his high education did not fit in the social category of lawyers, doctors and others who had good income; some of them even came from the ruling class of traditional rulers, in sharp contrast with his background as the son of a goldsmith. As Annan stated:

"As in many other African colonies, it was soldiers returning from the Second World War, who had served in the British army, who began to question more fundamentally the iniquities of colonial practices.

They witnessed white British soldiers alongside whom they had fought and bled receive generous pensions, land, and other benefits in Africa – none of which were available to Africans. Together with leading members of Ghana's professional classes – lawyers, doctors and engineers – these veterans began a campaign for independence. As conservative members of society – by definition, those who had status and assets and privileges even under colonial rule – they were looking for a cautious, methodical change of regime. Their independence slogan was – tellingly – 'Step by Step.'

This was the group that formed the United Gold Coast Convention (UGCC) as their party, and decided to appoint as secretary a fiery, courageous activist, Kwame Nkrumah. A member of one of Ghana's smaller tribes, and the son of a village goldsmith who had gone on to educate himself in the United States and Britain, Nkrumah brought to the cause an impatience and a passion that could not, in the end, abide the gradualist tempo of Ghana's elite." – (Kofi Annan, *Interventions: A Life in War and Peace*, New York: Penguin Books, 2012, p. 18).

He went on state:

"Tired of their condescension toward him and their dismissive attitude to what they considered his rabble-rousing supporters, he broke away from the UGCC to found the Convention People's Party.
Nkrumah possessed more than just impatience,

however; he had a keen strategic mind and an ability to organize people that far surpassed that of his former colleagues. He soon became the indisputable driver of Ghana's independence." – (Ibid.)

The people of the Western Region and Ghana as a whole will always remember the role Nkrumah played not only in leading Ghana to independence, the first country in sub-Saharan Africa to emerge from colonial rule; he will also be remembered across the continent as a trailblazer and as one of the most prominent leaders of Africa's struggle for freedom.

Other regions of Ghana also stand out in different ways.

The Greater Accra Region is the economic and industrial hub of the country as well as its political centre. The nation's capital Accra is located in the region and is named after it.

The Greater Accra Region was a part of the Eastern Region until 1982.

It is also a major tourist centre because of the nation's capital which has a wide variety of attractions including government and academic institutions. Major attractions in Accra include the Osu Castle, the Kwame Nkrumah Mausoleum, Independence Square, and the Accra International Conference Centre.

The Greater Accra Region is also known for its traditional festivals by the members of different ethnic groups in the region, especially the Ga and the Adangbe.

The Ga festival is known as Homowo. The literal meaning of the term is "hooting at hunger" or "jeering at hunger." The festival is held in remembrance of a major famine which wreaked havoc among the Ga in the 1500s.

The famine was caused by drought. So, when rain returns, it is time for celebration.

Mainly a food festival, it is held in August every year and all Ga clans participate in it to remember the horrendous tragedy. It starts with the planting season in May before rains start. Maize is the main crop.

The dance the Ga perform to mark the festival is known as Kpanlogo. The celebration includes marches, playing drums, singing, and painting faces. Members of other ethnic groups can participate in the festival.

Other main festivals are Asafotufiam and Ngmayem.

All these festivals are very important occasions for strengthening communal bonds and even in resolving family disputes among the members of the Ga-Dangme ethnic groups.

The main ethnic group in the Greater Accra Region is the Akan. Its members constitute about 40 per cent of the region's population. The second-largest is Ga-Dangme, about 30 per cent, and the third-largest, Ewe, 18 per cent. But the Ga are the largest sub-ethnic group in the region, constituting about 19 per cent of the entire population.

Christians make up 83 per cent of the region's population, and Moslems, 10 per cent. Among Moslems, there are more men than women who are adherents of this faith.

Greater Accra has been the second most populous region since 1960 when the country became a republic after winning independence in 1957. One main reason for that is the magnetic power of Accra on the rest of the country, attracting large numbers of people in search of better opportunities in the capital city.

The Greater Accra Region is not well-endowed in terms of arable land. It does not have much fertile soil, a deficit that has a major impact on agriculture. It is basically a dry region.

It is also poor in minerals, with the exception of granite, salt and clay.

Of all the country's ten regions, **the Northern Region** is the largest. And its capital, Tamale, is the fourth-largest city in the country.

The region's land area is the same as the areas of

Eastern, Greater Accra, Volta and Western regions combined. It is also equal to the areas of Brong Ahafo, Ashanti and Greater Accra put together.

The region is drier than the southern parts of the country because it is close to the Sahel region and the Sahara desert.

The harmattan winds from December to February have a profound impact on the weather during those months, with temperatures ranging from 57°F at night to 104°F during daytime. But because the region is basically dry, humidity is very low, thus reducing the severity of high temperatures during the day.

The main ethnic groups in the Northern Region are the Mole-Dagbon who constitute 52 per cent of the population, the Gurma, almost 22 per cent, and the Akan and the Guan who together make up about 9 per cent of the region's population.

In the Mole-Dagbon group, the largest subgroups are the Dagomba and the Mamprusi. The Dagomba are about 33 per cent of the entire region's population.

Among the Gurma, the Konkomba are the largest subgroup, and among the Akan the Chokosi are. The Gonja are the largest among the Guan.

The languages spoken in the region are identified with particular districts. Dagbani, which is the language of the Dagomba, is the most widely spoken in the region; it is spoken in nine out of the region's thirteen districts. Gonja is spoken in three districts.

The majority of the people in the Northern Region are Muslim. They constitute 56 per cent of the region's population. Christians are about 19 per cent. A significant number of the people, about 21 per cent, are followers of traditional religions.

There are also important archaeological sites in the region such as Yikpa Bonso, Jentilkipe and Kpaesemkpe.

The region has been under strong Islamic influence for centuries, reflected not only in the adherence of the

Islamic faith among the majority of its people but also in the architecture and in the presence of ancient mosques. One is the Larabaga mosque built in the 1400s.

There are also remains of an ancient defence wall built at Nalerigu in East Mamprusi District in the 1600s which is a very important part of the region's history.

There are many graves in the region which are important historical sites. They include the mass grave of Dagomba warriors who were killed by the Germans at the battle of Adibo near Yendi, and the graves of kings including the grave of the most renowned king of the Gonja, Ndewura Jakpa, at Bipe in West Gong District.

Other graves include burial grounds of the Gonja who were massacred when they resisted and fought slave raiders. Their graves at Jentilkipe are important shrines.

The region was an important source of slaves. It was also a major battleground for those who fought against the invaders seeking to capture the indigenous people and sell them into slavery. There are many relics which are a reminder of that bygone era. One of those sites is Yendi. Another one is Salaga which still has homes of the slave traders and even wells which were a source of water that was used to bathe slaves before selling them for shipment across the Atlantic.

The people in the region also have important traditional festivals. The most well-known is the Damba, a product of Islam, which was originally an occasion to honour and celebrate the birthday of Prophet Muhammed. It no longer has such religious significance and is now an occasion for entertainment including playing music, dancing, riding horses and other festivities.

The region's economy is based on agriculture. But hunting and forestry are also important to the region's economy.

The Northern Region has a low density of population because of its harsh climate. The climate has also been a major factor in emigration. Many people have moved out of the region in search of better opportunities elsewhere.

The region is also home to the Dagbon kingdom founded by the Dagomba people in the 1400s A.D.

The Northern Region also produced one of Ghana's presidents, John Dramani Mahama, who served from July 2012 to January 2017. He assumed office after his predecessor, John Atta Mills, under whom he served as vice president, died on 24 July 2012.

The Northern Region also produced one of Ghana's vice presidents, Alhaji Aliu Mahama. He served as vice president for two terms under President John Kufuor from January 2001 to January 2009. He died in November 2012, about four months after President Mills did.

In the far northeastern part of the country is **the Upper East Region**. It is the second smallest in terms of area after Greater Accra.

It is located in the traditional kingdom of Dagbon which stretches across northern Ghana. Part of the kingdom straddles the Ghanaian-Togolese border. A small part of it also stretches into the Ivory Coast.

The region is also bordered by Burkina Faso, formerly Upper Volta, in the north.

Like the Upper West Region, the Upper East was a part of the Northern Territory which was a British protectorate during colonial rule. In 1960, the territory was divided into two regions, Northern and Upper. In 1983, the Upper Region was divided into Upper East and Upper West while the Northern Region remained intact.

The main ethnic groups in the region are Bimoba, Bissa, Buli, Frafra, Kantosi, Kasem, and Kusasi. They fall under four main categories: Mole-Dagbon, Grunsi, Mande-Busanga, and Gurma.

Interspersed among them are other people from different parts of Ghana and beyond although in much smaller numbers.

In spite of its positive impact in terms of integration, ethnic diversity has sometimes resulted in conflicts in the region, best exemplified by what happened in Bawku East District where fighting between the two dominant groups, the Mamprusi and the Kusasi, erupted in 2008:

"The country may have a reputation for peace but the news from Bawku is of hatred and violence.

There are fears that a long-standing chieftaincy dispute between two ethnic groups, the Kusasi and the Mamprusi, is spiralling out of control despite a heavy military presence and a dusk-to-dawn curfew which has been in place since the beginning of the year.

Over the weekend (21 – 22 June 2008), a man from the Mamprusi community was apparently looking for a missing animal when he was set upon and killed by a mob from the rival Kusasi ethnic group. According to residents of Bawku town, some Mamprusi disguised in military attire set out to retaliate.

Fearing they were soldiers, men ran away leaving mostly women and children in the hands of the mob.

They were butchered with machetes. At least 13 people were killed including women, children and a six-month-old baby.

Emmanuel Bombande from the West Africa Network For Peacebuilding (WANEP) has been working to reconcile the rival communities for several years.

He says it is an ominous sign that for the first time women and children have been targeted. The use of military uniforms is also a dangerous development.

'If other groups of people can now wear the military uniform to attack, then nobody knows anymore what is happening on the ground. And that is sending panic and people are leaving their homes. There is a complete deterioration in confidence – even in the military to be the protector of civilians.'

Security forces have made dozens of arrests but there is fear of a vicious cycle of revenge attacks.

There are a number of other chieftaincy disputes in

Ghana which have yet to be resolved....

Ghanaians are proud of what is a relatively peaceful country. But the news of violence in Bawku is for some people a sign that the peace should not be taken for granted....The example of what happened next door in Ivory Coast proves that a reputation for stability can all too easily be shattered." – ("Bid to End Deadly Ghana Clashes," BBC News, 25 June 2008).

Such conflicts may be ignited by minor incidents but the root causes go deeper, often to colonial and precolonial times. They are symptomatic of a bigger problem. As Felix Y. T. Longi states in "The Kusasi-Mamprusi Conflict in Bawku: A Legacy of British Colonial Policy in Northern Ghana," in *Ghana Studies*:

"Post-colonial Africa has witnessed a phenomenal increase conflicts of various magnitudes, mostly arising out of disagreements over a variety of issues including onwership of land, succession to chieftaincy titles, and resource allocation, among others....

Ghana is among the few countries in West Africa perceived to be oasis of peace in a sub-region otherwise characterized by civil wars, rebel activities and general instability. This image of Ghana, however, only masks a festering wound of communal violence, inter-ethnic conflicts and armed confrontations in the Northern part of Ghana.

The root causes of these conflicts, which have almost become persistent, are largely traceable to the introduction of secular political authority/chieftaincy in areas which, before colonialism, were described as stateless or acephalous. The security of the entire country has often been compromised by the scope of unrest, wanton loss of lives and property, waste of the nation's scarce resources and the dislocation of people." – (Felix Y. T. Longi, "The Kusasi-Mamprusi Conflict in Bawku: A Legacy of British

Colonial Policy in Northern Ghana," in *Ghana Studies*, Volume 17, 2014, p. 157).

He goes on to state:

"Generally, scholars are divided in their discussion of the roots causes of inter-ethnic conflicts that occur in Northern Ghana as a result of disputes over succession to a chieftaincy title or office. One school of thought traced the genesis of these conflicts to attempts by anthropologists and the colonial administration to categorize societies in that part of the country into acephalous/non-centralized and centralized groups, while the other school of thought identified other factors beyond the colonial enterprise. This paper examines the genesis of the Mamprusi-Kusasi conflict in Bawku within the context of the first school of thought....

The Kusasi – who claim to be the autochthones – and the Mamprusi – seen by Kusasi as warrior new-comers – have remained the dominant groups...in Bawku....

At the heart of the Kusasi-Mamprusi conflict is an agglomeration of issues about litigations over allodial rights and chieftaincy. Both the Kusasi and the Mamprusi claim allodial ownership of Bawku, claims which are shrouded in their narrative histories of origin and derived from claims of autochthony. The Alhassan Committee which investigated land ownership in Northern Ghana in 1978 identified first-comership as one of the bases to claim of land ownership.

In Bawku, answers to the question of the first settlers are inconclusive and highly controversial. For one to dissect the question of the first settlers of Bawku, it is imperative to discuss the migration-and-settlement histories of the Mamprusi and the Kusasi." – Ibid., pp. 157 – 159. See also pp. 157 – 176).

It is true that colonial rulers caused a lot of problems

when they imposed their own political structures on the indigenous people and even destroyed some traditional institutions; although they also used traditional rulers to facilitate imperial rule through indirect rule. Where such rulers did not exist, colonial administrators appointed chiefs and imposed them on the people. But it is also true that some conflicts predate colonial rule.

Many African "tribes" were already in conflict with their neighbours, fighting over land and other resources, long before Europeans came. Also, there is no question that in many cases, colonial rulers did take advantage of the situation and exacerbated conflicts in order to "divide and rule," although the people were not really united – except by their common identity as Africans – and demonstrated that by attacking and fighting each other. They were nothing to each other except as enemies. This may be dismissed as a Eurocentric view of Africa's precolonial past. But there is empirical evidence to support that in different parts of the continent. Inter-tribal conflicts were nothing new in precolonial times, although they were not as widespread as the colonialists sometimes claimed they were just to justify imperial rule.

Both schools of thought mentioned by Longi above are valid in their own contexts. The causes of some conflicts are rooted in the precolonial past. And there are those which are attributable to colonial policies. Then there are conflicts whose causes overlap, rooted in the precolonial era and in the colonial period, reinforcing each other and compounded by misguided policies of the colonial rulers and even of post-colonial governments.

In the case of Bawku, the conflict between the Kusasi and the Mamprusi was both precolonial and colonial in terms of origin:

"Conflict between the Mamprusi and Kusasi ethnic groups is long-standing over some decades and has resulted in sporadic and recurrent   outbreaks of serious violence resulting in destruction of property and death on many occasions. In an extended discussion of the politics of northern Ghana, Bawku in the Upper East Region of Ghana is cited as 'the most intense example of tribal rivalries in the last forty years' but whose origins belong in the pre-colonial period.

Hostility between the Kusasi and Mamprusi is probably as old as the state of Mamprugu itself, since the town of Pusiga, less than ten miles distant from Bawku, was one of the first stopping places for the band of invaders who established the Mamprusi Kingdom.

One colonial administrator in the 1930s traced the history of such hostilities, culminating in open warfare in 1895 after the Mamprusi Nayiri felt he had been insulted by the people of Kugri (Kelly 1974).

Since Ghana's independence in 1957 the Kusasi and Mamprusi have largely given their support to various regimes and opposition movements, who have generally obliged by enskinning and deskinning competing candidates for the Bawku chieftaincy as required by their supporters." – ("Bawku: Mamprusi-Kusasi Conflict," RRT Research Response, Refugee Review Tribunal, Australia, 9 October 2009, pp. 1 – 2).

Unscrupulous politicians have exploited the situation to promote their own interests and political agendas to the detriment of the communities they claim to represent. This has been the case especially during the post-colonial era:

"In the 2000 elections over 50 people were killed in disputes following the alleged NDC claim that an NPP government would reinstate the Mamprusi chieftaincy (Ayee 2001: 7). Most recently, in December 2001, violence broke out following a dispute between a Kusasi and a Mamprusi at a lotto kiosk in the Sabongari district of the town. Subsequent tit-for-tat attacks led to at least 29 deaths and 36 serious injuries on the day of 6 December alone.

...It would be wrong to identify a single cause for the violence and division in Bawku, as in other areas of the north.

In addition to the Mamprusi/Kusasi rivalry there was considerable resentment at the role of Hawa Yakubu who, as a Busanga, was resented by both tribal groups as something of an outsider in Bawku. Additionally, her refusal to allow a younger candidate to take her place as NPP candidate further stimulated local resentment against a wealthy candidate who was unwilling to allow others to share in the benefits of office (Kelly, Bob and Bening, R. B. 2007, 'Ideology, regionalism, self-interest and tradition: An investigation into contemporary politics in northern Ghana, *Africa*, Vol. 77. No. 2, pp. 200, 201).

A 2003 analysis published for the Netherlands Institute of International Relations also emphasised the complexity of issues involved in understanding conflict in the Upper East Region of Bawku:

> Indeed the Bawku conflict brought into play a complex matrix of structural and contingent factors that makes the disaggregating of the events particularly difficult.
>
> The area in which the conflict occurred is ethnically heterogeneousand has one of the lowest income (80% living in extreme poverty) and literacy (26.3% of adults functionally literate) rates in the country. It is a relatively densely populated area with over 100 residents per kilometer. There is relatively strong religious (66%) and ethnic (64%) attachment by the populace. Voter consciousness is high and party affiliation (NDC, NPP and PNC) strong with 2000 voter registration figures of 95 per cent.
>
> Additionally simmering disputes over the Bawku skin have persisted for years. A number of the protagonists have been brought before the courts, but to date no credible insights have been gained into the motivation for and execution of the attacks (Hughes, Tim 2003, 'Managing group grievances and internal conflict: Ghana' country report. Working Paper 11, Netherlands Institute of International Relations, June, pp. 57-58).

A frequently cited study by Christian Lund provides

further information concerning the history of conflict in recent decades, including overlapping issues of land ownership, ethnicity, chieftaincy and others, including the unresolved issue of the Bawku skin (signifying entitlement to the throne):

The skin is the symbol of chiefly authority in northern Ghana, equivalent to the stool in the south. It symbolizes the chieftaincy and the throne. When a chief is enskinned, he is seated on the skin of an ox sacrificed for the occasion. In normal parlance, chiefs who are forced to abdicate are de-stooled, not de-skinned.

According to Lund:

A wide range of political – including party-political – and economic competition over chieftaincy, land, markets, names of places and other issues are thus cut to fit the ethnic distinction as conflicts over rights and prerogatives are constantly rekindled.

These competitions are played out through a variety of political practices ranging from legal procedure, through party politics, administrative exclusion, home town association activity, cultural festivals, symbolically charged, well-choreographed receptions of dignitaries, to bloodshed....

The fact that the conflict is pattern entrenching does not mean that loyalties do not sometimes cut across the ethnic divide. But it means that such movements are easily denounced and considered invidious.

Obviously, internal rivalry among Kusasis and Mamprusis, inter-ethnic marriages and political alliances *contre nature*, all occurring as opportunities arise, do not easily conform to the entrenched pattern (Lund, Christian 2003, 'Bawku is still volatile: ethno-political conflict and state recognition in Northern Ghana,' *Journal of Modern African Studies*, Vol. 41, No. 4, p. 589).

In the article by Kelly and Bening referred to above, they point out that all the areas of Ghana are ethnically mixed, with the north being 'particularly heterogeneous, including as indigenes seven distinct language groups, each with numerous dialects.' Of these, the most significant is the Mole-Dagbane, which includes 'the languages spoken by the Dagomba, Mamprusi, Kusasi, Dagaaba and Builsa, who can be found in almost all areas of the north' (pp. 183-84).

Where outbreaks of conflict occur they have often arisen over relatively trivial incidents. The Guinea Fowl War (1994-95) began as the result of a fight between a Konkomba and a Nanumba man over a guinea fowl at a market near Bimbilla in January 1994:

The quarrel quickly degenerated into ethnic abuse, threats of oncoming war, and violence in which the Konkomba man severed a finger. The following day the son of the Konkomba man injured in the fight sought out the Nanumba man on his farm and shot him, after which large-scale Konkomba-Nanumba fighting broke out in Nanun, and quickly spread to Dagomba and Gonja-controlled areas.

Two days after the start of the war, the Konkomba minority in Tamale, numbering about 5,000 people at the time, were attacked by youths from the majority ethnic groups and forced to flee. The fighting centred around the Oti river region, mainly outside the district capitals that were protected by the army.

Almost all Dagomba, Nanumba, and Gonja settlements along the Bimbilla-Yendi road were burnt and February-March saw intense fighting in seven districts (Jönsson, Julia 2007, 'The overwhelming minority: traditional leadership and ethnic conflict in Ghana's Northern Region', CRISE Working Paper No. 30, Centre for Research on Inequality, Human Security and Ethnicity, University of Oxford, p. 19).

Ongoing incidents of violence since 2008 seem to indicate similarly localised and minor disputes can become the basis for inter-group conflict on a larger scale.

An Integrated Regional Information Networks (IRIN) report in June 2008 referred to a meeting between then President Kufuor with Bawku members of parliament and local leaders:

Kufuor said the local officials should be 'ashamed' of the events in Bawku where 17 people have been murdered in a new spat between the Mamprusi and Kusasi ethnic groups in the last week that locals say started in a dispute over the theft of a horse.

Bawku has a long history as a flashpoint town in Ghana. In 2001 at least 28 people were killed there when factions clashed in another battle apparently sparked by a relatively small crime, the destruction of a small shop.

....The international human rights group Amnesty International has expressed concern about the lack of political will to solve the crisis. The group said in a statement that the failure to resolve the conflict stems from a 'game of hurt no one in order to win all votes.'

President Kufuor has held two separate rounds of talks with leaders of the two rival ethnic factions this year ('Ghana: Conflict in north could threaten elections,' Integrated Regional Information Networks (IRIN), 27 June 2008).

The BBC reported that at least four people had died during fighting between members of the two groups in May of 2008 (BBC, 'Ghana: Four killed in Ghana tribal clash' 6 May 2008).

At the beginning of May 2009, *The Chronicle* reported that 28 people had been arrested for questioning following the shooting of two people in Bawku ('Ghana: Let's be sensitive with Bawku matters' 5 May 2009, *All Africa*, source: *The Chronicle*).

Further violence occurred a few weeks later, shortly after the visit of President John Mills to the area." – (Ibid., pp. 2 – 4).

Although such conflicts have erupted now and then through the years, they are not the norm in the Upper East Region or in the north as a whole despite the potential for ethnic violence in varying degrees in different parts of the country not just in the Upper East.

In terms of climate, the Upper East is a very dry region because of its proximity to the Sahel.

Its main products are crops which grow in hot and dry regions, especially millet, sorghum and rice. The region also has a lot of cattle.

It also has an ancient market at Bolga, a town that was an integral part of ancient trade routes from Mali and Nigeria, going all the way down to the coast. The trade route from Mali passed through Burkina Faso and down to Bolga. The one from northern Nigeria went through Bawku. They met at Bolga where they merged and stretched south.

The region is also a repository of historical narratives on the slave trade in the form of oral tradition and relics. There are slave camps and even a hollow baobab tree in which some of the people whom were captured were kept, waiting to be sold. The baobab tree is in Widnaba.

Slave camps and other relics associated with the traffic in human beings are in Paga Nania and elsewhere in the region. Nania was a major slave market for those who were captured in what is now Burkina Faso and other parts in the north.

The market was located in a rocky part which came to be known as Rocks of Fear. The local name for that was Pinkworo, emphasising the fear the rocks inspired among the victims of the slave trade as a place where they were going to be auctioned.

A rocky outcrop that was used as a vantage point for observation by the slave raiders stil exists there; so do water troughs in the rocks from which the captured victims drank water. Also on the site are grinding stones the captives used to grind millet and other cereals to eat. Indents in the rocks where they ground the cereals are clearly visible even today; a rueful reminder of the diabolical traffic in human beings which took place in the not-so-distant past.

Tongo Whistling Rocks are another major attraction in the Upper East Region. They are granite rocks. They "whistle" in November and December, producing an eerie sound when the harmattan winds blow through the region from the Saraha desert.

The region has very poor soil for cultivation. The soil comes from granite rocks which form the foundation of the region. Valleys have better soil but it is not easy to till and is waterlogged during floods. The soil is sandy and clay.

Erosion also is a major problem in the region.

The long dry season is harsh on the vegetation. The grass is scorched by the sun or is destroyed by bushfires.

The people themselves have made things worse by destroying the environment, exacerbating semi-arid conditions and making it virtually impossible to grow anything.

In spite of the arid conditions and high temperatures, heat is not as intense as it would have been had humidity been high. Low humidity in the region alleviates harsh conditions associated with high temperatures and makes life tolerable even if not comfortable.

The Upper East Region has many traditional festivals throughout the year marking a good planting season or celebrating harvest. The people also thank God for a bumper harvest and pray to Him for better days ahead.

The festivals are Fao, Feok, Gologo, Kakube, Kobina, Paragbiele, Samanpiid also known as Kusaasi, Willa, and Zumbenti.

The region also has a unique demographic composition in terms of worshippers unlike other parts of Ghana with the exception of the Upper West which in some fundamental respects is a twin to the Upper East.

The majority of the people in the Upper East are followers of traditional religions. They constitute about 46.5 per cent. Christians are about 28 per cent and Moslems, almost 23 per cent.

The largest number of people who practise traditional religions live in Builsa District. They constitute almost 64 per cent of the district's population. The lowest percentage of traditionalists, about 23 per cent, is in Bawku East. The dominant religion in Bawku East District is Islam. At least 51 per cent of the people in the district are followers of Islam.

Christianity is not a dominant religion in any district in the Upper East Region. But Catholics are the majority among Christians in the region.

The Upper East is the least urbanised region in Ghana followed by the Upper West Region.

The Upper West Region was the last to be formed. It

was created by the military head of state Jerry Rawlings in 1983. It is the seventh-largest region and is known for being the home of Dr. Hilla Limann who was president of Ghana from September 1979 until December 1981 when he was overthrown by Jerry Rawlings.

Dr. Limann was seen by his supporters as an embodiment of Nkrumaism and had strong support among Nkrumah's followers when he ran for president. Even after he was no longer president, he was actively involved in political activism as a Nkrumaist and worked with Nkrumah's followers and admirers. In contrast to that, Rawlings said although he admired Nkrumah, he was not a Nkrumaist.

Dr. Limann is still remembered in the Upper West as the region's most prominent son.

There are two major ethnic groups in the region: the Mole Dagbon who constitute about 76 per cent of the population, and the Grusi, about 18.5 per cent. The Wala, a subgroup of the Mole Dagbon, and the Sissala who are a part of the Grusi, are the largest subgroups. Each of the subgroups constitutes about 16 per cent of the region's population.

Like other indigenous people in Ghana and elsewhere in Africa, they have their own tribal homelands.

The Dagaba – also known as Dagaaba – live in the west, the Sisaala in the east, and the Wala mostly in Wa District which is also home to the town of Wa, the region's capital.

The Dagaba and the Sisaala are Christian and animist in very large numbers unlike the Wala, the majority of whom are Moslem. In fact, Wa, the regional capital, has the highest percentage of Muslims among all the cities in Ghana.

In terms of religious beliefs, Christians slightly outnumber Muslims in the Upper West Region. About 36 per cent of the region's population is Christian, and 32 per cent Moslem. Followers of traditional religions are not far behind. They are at least 29 per cent of the region's population.

Catholics are the majority among Christians.

Wa District has the largest population. Almost 40 per cent of the people in the region live in Wa.

Tha main languages spoken in the Upper West Region are Dagaare, Sissali, Wale, and Lobi.

Dagaare spoken by the Dagaaba and Waali spoken by the Wala (who are also known as Walba) are mutually intelligible languages. Dagaare also is the fourth-ranked indigenous language in Ghana in terms of the number of people who speak it, surpassed by Twi, Ewe, and Dagbane.

Houses in the Upper West are similar to those in the Upper East, made mostly of mud, but are shaped differently. In the Upper West, they are rectangular, while in the Upper East they are round.

Muslim traders from the the north, mainly Mali, have had a profound impact on the region's architecture which in many cases is patterned after mosques, especially the Larabanga mosque; they are the ones who built the mosque which continues to influence architecture in the region even today. However, the presence of Christianity in the Upper East and Northern Regions prevented this style from spreading there.

The Upper West has many traditional festivals – Bagre, Bongngo, Dumba, Kala, Kakube, Kobine, Paragbiele, Singma, Willa, and Zumbeti.

They are a reflection the people, the way they live, the values and cultures they cherish. They also usher in new seasons. The people even assess the performance of their traditional rulers to see if they are fit to continue playing that role.

The people of the region are well-known for their handicrafts and intricate skills of spinning and weaving among other things. Their products include traditional clothes, musical instruments including xylophone, carvings, pottery, and a variety of items produced by traditional blacksmiths.

The Upper West Region also has a rich history. Among its important historical sites are caves where the people sought refuge during slaves raids, and where captives were kept before their long one-way journey to the Atlantic coast for shipment to the Americas.

Another important historical monument is the Gwollu Slave Defence Wall that was built to protect local residents from slave raiders.

The region's poor climate has a profound impact on the people. The dry season is very long, from October to May, forcing many of them to leave and seek employment in other parts of the country, mostly in the south.

Crops grown in the Upper West include millet, maize, groundnuts and rice. Goats, sheep and pigs are the main domesticated animals in the region.

The local alcoholic drink called *pito* from millet is a very important part of life in the region. It is a cultural feature and distinguishes the region from other parts of Ghana, among other things.

The Volta Region has a special place in the history of Ghana because of how the new nation was formed. Formerly known as the Gold Coast, the area of what is Ghana today includes a region which was known as British Togoland and whose inhabitants voted to become an integral part of Ghana.

There was strong opposition among the Ewe in British Togoland to any kind of integration with Ghana. Instead, they formed the Togoland Congress (TCP) in 1951 to campaign for the unification of the Ewe people who lived in two separate colonial territories.

They wanted to unite with their brethren across the border in French Togoland to establish an independent Ewe state but lost the vote in a UN-supervised plebiscite in March 1956. The majority of the people – 58 per cent – in British Togoland voted to unite with Ghana. A significant minority, 42 per cent and overwhelmingly Ewe, voted against such unification.

They lost the vote because members of other ethnic groups live in the region. Non-Ewes voted to be a part of Ghana although some Ewes also did.

Located east of Lake Lake Volta, it is the only region that covers all climatic and vegetational belts from the coastal south to the northern part of the country.

The region's economy is based on agriculture, forestry and hunting. But one district, Keta, depends mostly on fishing.

The Ewe constitute about 69 per cent of the region's population. The second-largest group is the Guan, 9 per cent of the population; and the third-largest is the Akan, 8.5 per cent of the population. The fourth-largest is the Gurma. The Gurma live mostly in the northern part of the Volta Region and constitute 6.5 per cent of the region's population.

The Guan comprise 18 subgroups, and the Akan more than 19.

The Volta Region has other ethnic groups besides the Ewe, the Guan, the Akan, and the Gurma, although there may be a perception it is an Ewe region because the Ewe constitute the vast majority of the population, almost 70 per cent.

Like other parts of Ghana, the Volta Region has people from almost every ethnic group in the country. In fact, members of eight major ethnic groups live in the region. The other four major groups – besides the Ewe, the Guan, the Akan and the Gurma – are the Mole-Dagbon, the Grusi, the Mande, and the Ga-Dangme. They constitute more than 7 per cent of the region's population.

In terms of religion, the overwhelming majority of the Ewe, the Guan and the Akan are Christian. And the majority of the Hausa, Kyamba, Kotokoli, Kokomba, Nanumba and Gurma are Muslims; this is especially the case in the northern part of the region.

A little more than 67 per cent of the people in the Volta Region are Christians. Almost 22 per cent are traditionalists, adhering to traditional religious faith. And at least 5 per cent are Muslims.

More women than men follow traditional religious beliefs; about 22 per cent of the women and 21 per cent of the men do. And more men than women practise Islam.

There is a campaign among some people in the Volta Region to create another regional entity, Todzie Region. The entire southern part of Volta Region would form the new region, an area was once a part of the Gold Coast.

This seems to be a part of a trend in different parts of the continent where many people are demanding more freedom to manage their own affairs all the way down to the grassroots level instead of being told what to do by those in power at the centre in a distant national capital.

It is a form of decentralisation which could lead to the creation of more administrative units – regions or provinces and districts – in different countries if those in power concede to such demands.

It is a populist demand fuelled by the failure and the unwillingness of those in power, at the centre, to listen to the people and address their problems.

The Volta Region also serves as a bridge between Ghana and Togo in terms of fostering relations between the two countries. And its capital, Ho, has a very large market which draws people from Togo and all parts of the region.

The Western Region is located in the southwestern part of the country. Ghana's southernmost area, Cape Three Points in Ahanta West District, is located in the region. In June 2007, crude oil in commercial quantities was discovered at Cape Three Points, a small peninsula.

The region is also known for its abundant rainfall, the highest in Ghana, and for its green hills. Because of high rainfall, humidity is high in the region between 70 and 90 per cent.

It is also a very fertile region.

The Western Region also has 40 per cent of the forest reserves in the whole country.

It also has a large number of small and large-scale gold mines which are an important part of the region's economy together with oil production.

During colonial rule, what is now the Western Region was a part of the Western Province. The Western Province comprised what is now the Western Region and the Central Region. It was a very large province. Cape Coast was its capital. In July 1960, the Western Region was formed when the Central Province was created out of the former massive colonial province.

The Western Region is home to the twin cities of Sekondi and Takoradi, known as Sekondi-Takoradi, which is also the region's industrial and commercial centre. They became twins in 1946.

Sekondi is the capital of the Western Region. It is older and bigger than Takoradi and has great historical significance. The Dutch built Fort Orange there in 1642, and the English built Fort Sekondi, also known as Fort George, in 1682. Both were trading posts and right next to each other.

Sekondi also enjoyed economic prosperity after a railway was built in 1903 connecting the seaport to the interior where minerals and timber were produced.

Takoradi also is historically significant. The Dutch built another trading post there, Fort Witsen, in 1665. The city also has a deepwater seaport which was built in 1928. It is Ghana's first deepwater seaport.

Sekondi-Takoradi is also known for shipbuilding. Other major industries in the twin-city metropolitan district include cocoa processing, timber and plywood production, crude oil, and railway repair. The twin-city metropolis is on the main railway lines to Accra and Kumasi.

It is also known as the Oil City of Ghana because of the

large amounts of crude oil discovered in the Western Region. It has attracted many people from all parts of the world because of the oil discoveries with high potential for investment and job creation in the oil industry and related fields.

The region has five major ethnic groups: Wassa, Sefwi, Nzema, Ahanta, and Aowin who are also known as Brossa. Smaller ethnic groups include the Pepesa.

The Wassa constitute about 12 per cent of the region's population; the Sefwi almost 11 per cent; the Nzema 10.6 per cent; the Ahanta 6.3 per cent; and the Aowin 2.5 per cent.

Besides the languages of the five main ethnic groups, Fante is also spoken in the region. It is the second most widely spoken language especially in the southern part of the region. It is also the medium of instruction in many primary schools in the Western Region. Twi is widely spoken in two parts of the region, Sefwi and Bibiani, as much as Fante is.

Besides Fante, Nzema is the only other language that is used as a medium of instruction in primary school.

The Fante constitute the largest group of people who have migrated into the Western Region. They migrated mostly from the Central Region many years ago and have become an integral part of the population just like those who are native to the region. The Fante make up 18.2 per cent of the region's population, making them the largest ethnic group although non-indigenous.

Other Ghanaians who have migrated to the Western Region are the Ashanti (Asante), 7 per cent of the region's population; the Ewe, about 6 per cent of the population, Brongs, 3.4 per cent of the population; and the Kusasi, about 3 per cent of the region's population.

Most of the people in the Western Region are Christian. They constitute 81 per cent of the region's population. Muslims are 8.5 per cent of the population. And only 1.5 per cent of the people practise traditional religions.

Traditional festivals include Kundum by the Ahanta and the Nzema in honour of their ancestors. The Ahanta and the Nzema are neighbours.

The Kundum festival involves feasting, playing drums and dancing. It is also a celebration of harvest and an integral part of the culture of the Ahanta and the Nzema. It was originally a religious festival used to expel evil spirits.

The land of the Ahanta is also one of the most fertile parts of Ghana.

Other festivals in the Western Region are Eddie by the Wassa during harvest; and Alluolie or Eluo – a yam festival – by the Aowin and the Sefwi. As Dr. K. Y. Daaku, a Sefwi, stated about the festival and his people in his article, "The History of My People (Sefwi)":

"The Sefwi were composed of a number of states, but despite this they remained as one community. They celebrate a common annual yam festival which is called the Alluolie or Eluo....

All the three states of Sefwi share a common culture in spite of the fact that they all came from different places. They share a common dialect, Sefwi, have a common Yam Festival, Alluolie, and a common deity, Sobore.

Although the Sefwi dialect is grouped with other Akan languages, it is mostly unintelligible to the other Akan speakers. Linguistically the incoming Akans from the east and other regions have had their language very much overlaid with the Aowin-Bono dialect. Now Sefwi shares this common dialect, with the Aowin, Nzema and Anyi-Baule in the Ivory Coast.

In their common yam festival, the Alluolie, they celebrate the end of the farming year, and offer food and drinks to their ancestors – a practice which is not dissimilar from the Ohum and Odwira festivals of the Akans.

On the other hand, the second festival, the Alie, is not

70

celebrated by all the stools, but only by members of the Asona clan in the three states.

The importance of this festival lies perhaps in the fact that it serves as one of the only connecting links between the two Wenchis of Bono and Sefwi. Formerly celebrated only in Wenchi, but not taken up by the Omanhene of Anhwiaso and such places as Chirano, Subiri and Kesekrom, it has much in common with the celebration of the annual Apo festival of Wenchi in the Bono states.

In both the Alie and the Apo food which is cooked for the ancestors is placed at the outskirts of the town and merry-making women dance up and down the streets at times exposing their naked but well decorated bodies to the onlookers.

In the worship of the tutelar deity Sobore, the three states also have a common identity. The deity is supposed not only to protect the states from all calamities but it is also a fertility god. Admittedly each state had its own shrine and priests but in all essentials the method of worshipping is similar.

It appears that the Sobore predates the establishment of the modern Sefwi state. This may explain why only the local dialect and not Twi and only locally made wine from the raffia palm are used in worshipping Sobore. It is highly probable that the worship of this stream Sobore, was taken over from the Aowin." – (K. Y. Daaku, "The History of My People (Sefwi)," 22 June 2012).

The Western Region is also a major historical site. It has a number of forts along the coast built by the Portuguese, the Dutch, the British and the Germans. The first were built by the Portuguese in 1512. Others followed through the centuries and played a major role in the Trans-Atlantic slave trade.

The Western Region also produced Ghana's first president, Kwame Nkrumah. Another president of Ghana, JohnAtta Mills, was also born there although he is identified as one of the famous people from the Central Region.

But it was Nkrumah who earned the Western Region a special place in the history of Ghana because he was the country's first prime minister and president; also because of his stature as a continental leader.

He led Ghana to become the first country south of the Sahara to win independence. He was also the first and last leader to call for immediate continental unification under one government.

He also incurred the wrath of the Western powers, especially the United States, Britain, France and West Germany with his policies advocating African independence and unity. He was a relentless champion of African liberation. He was described as a threat to Western interests and as someone who had done more than anybody else to undermine American interests in Africa.

The military coup which led to his ouster was organised and masterminded by the CIA station chief in Accra, Howard T. Bane.

A former American ambassador to Ghana also said US officials including himself were infuriated by Nkrumah's book, *Neo-Colonialism: The Last State of Imperialism*, and was one of the reasons American leaders decided to overthrow him:

"One of the people who provided a written eyewitness account of what took place during the coup was Preston King, an African American living in Accra.

It was a very bloody coup, contrary to what the new military rulers and American officials claimed, that it was bloodless; a claim also made by Robert Smith who once served as the American ambassador to Ghana – he also once served in Nigeria – and was a veteran of African affairs at the US State Department. As he stated:

'They had had enough and Nkrumah was overthrown in

72

a coup. They did this in relatively bloodless fashion.

While Nkrumah was in the air flying to Red China, he was met on the ground in Peking by his Chinese host and it fell to them to inform him that he was no longer Head of State in the Republic of Ghana. So that was a fascinating time in a fascinating country....

Nkrumah dropped the straw that broke the camel's back, so to speak, in that he published a new book called *Neo-Colonialism (The Last State of Imperialism)*...which was simply outrageous. It accused the United States of every sin imaginable to man. We were blamed for everything in the world.

The book was so bad that I remember the then Assistant Secretary, G. Mennen Williams, called me up and gave me that book and said, 'Bob, I know this is bad. I don't know how bad. I want you to take it home tonight and read it. You're not going to get any sleep and I apologize for that, but on my desk, by eight o'clock tomorrow morning, I've got to have a written summary of this because I have called the Ghanaian ambassador in at ten o'clock tomorrow morning. We're going to protest this book.'

There had already been advance publicity so we knew it was bad, but we hadn't had our hands on a copy. And it was everything we feared it would be. It was awful.

And the next morning – of course, he had me in on this meeting as the note taker – a lovely, old man, Michael Ribiero, was the Ghanaian ambassador. Hated Nkrumah privately, but was a good soldier trying to put the best face on this, a career officer in their foreign service and very respected here and in Ghana.

Governor Williams, of course, was a relatively mild-mannered man. I had never heard Soapy Williams raise his voice until that conversation. Neither have I ever heard an ambassador get a tongue lashing like Ribiero got from Assistant Secretary Williams that morning. He, unfortunately, tried a couple times to interrupt the

73

governor when he was making a point. He had my notes in front of him. And at one point, when Ribiero interrupted him, said, 'Just a minute, Mr. Ambassador, don't interrupt me. I'm not through.' And he continued to go on.

He was raising his voice. He was shaking his finger in the ambassador's face. And it was a very painful, hour-long interview. To put it mildly, he protested vigorously the contents and publication of this book.

I think the publication of that book might also have contributed in a material way to his overthrow shortly thereafter.'"– (Godfrey Mwakikagile, *Western Involvement in Nkrumah's Downfall*, Dar es Salaam, Tanzania: New Africa Press, 2015, pp. 134 – 136).

The Western Region produced a son who will never be equalled in the history of Ghana. There will never be another Nkrumah.

The people

THE people of Ghana are divided into five major groups identified with or linked to specific regions.

In the northern part of Ghana are the Mole-Dagbani; in the east, the Ga-Adangbe; east of Lake Volta are the Ewe. And in the central and southern parts of the country are the Akan who constitute about 50 per cent of the country's population. The Guan live mostly on the Akuapem Mountains.

As a pluralistic society, Ghana is known for its ethnic, linguistic and cultural diversity. It is also characterised by a geographical divide which roughly corresponds to religious identity, the north being predominantly Muslim, and the south, Christian. As Robert Yaw Owusu states in his book, *Kwame Nkrumah's Liberation Thought: A Paradigm for Religious Advocacy in Contemporary Ghana*:

"In the 1960s, Ghana recorded about one hundred linguistic and cultural groups.

The major ethnoliguistic groups are Akan, Ewe, Mole-Dagbane, Guam, and Ga-Adangbe. These major groups have subdivisions and share a common cultural heritage, language, and origin. Of these ethnic groups Akan is the most predominant with 49.1 percent of the population followed by Mole-Dagbane with 16.5 percent, Ewe 12.7

percent, and Ga-Adangabe with 8 percent.

Linguistically, the Akan, Ewe, and Ga-Adangbe ethnic groups form what is generally classified as the Kwa language family group (75 percent).

The other general language family group in Ghana is the Gur-speaking people (25 percent). The latter group includes the broadly defined Gurma, Grusi, and Mole-Dagbane people groups in the north." – (Robert Yaw Owusu, *Kwame Nkrumah's Liberation Thought: A Paradigm for Religious Advocacy in Contemporary Ghana*, Trenton, New Jersey, USA: Africa World Press, Inc., 2006, p. 193).

He goes on to state:

"Despite this diversity and divisions, no part of Ghana is ethnically homogeneous. In religious outlook, however, most of the Gur-speaking people groups in the north have predominantly Islamic influence, whereas the majority of the Kwa-speaking groups in the south have been influenced predominantly by Christianity and Western culture. Underlining each of the two religious divides is the pervasive influence of the African primal or traditional religion....

From its pre-colonial era to the present Ghana has always exhibited religious diversity or pluralism. Pluralism implies the acceptance of diversity." – (Ibid., pp. 193, and 195).

Although each ethnic group has its own language, there are many languages which are mutually intelligible, reflecting a common origin of the people who speak those languages, and shared culture.

Eleven languages have virtual official status. Twi is the most well-known Ghanaian language, having assumed the status of "national language" – but only in some parts of Ghana where it is widely spoken, mostly by the Akan

76

people.

Even many foreigners, including African Americans, have heard of Twi. Some of them have even learned or want to learn the language.

But all the native languages have equal importance. They collectively give Ghana her unique identity as a nation. Every ethnic, cultural and linguistic group is an integral part of Ghana.

In acknowledgement of that, the government decided to translate the national anthem into the country's native languages and announced that when Ghanaians were celebrating their 60th independence anniversary in March 2017.

According to a report, "National Anthem, Pledge, Translated into Local Languages," in the *Daily Graphic*, Accra, 13 March 2017:

"Ghana's National Anthem and the National Pledge have been translated into 11 local languages to foster easy assimilation, patriotism and national cohesion. The 11 local languages are Ewe, Asante Twi, Akuapim Twi, Mfantse,Dagaare, Dagbani Dangme, Ga , Gonja, Nzema and Kasem.

The translation was made possible by the Ghana Bureau of Languages,the National Commission for Civic Education (NCCE) and a researcher, Mr John Amoah, who initiated the idea to have the two national assets translated into Ghanaian languages.

Translated works

Launching the translated works in Accra on Friday, Prof.Emeritus J.H. Kwabena Nketia said the spirit of nationalism, self-confidence and unity could be fostered if the country found innovative means to depend on herself instead of being over-dependent on what the colonial masters left the country.

The renowned musicologist and composer also underscored the need to find innovative ways of reinforcing the spirit of independence struggle which was self-reliance, among other characteristics, for sustainable development.

He said the present practice whereby the Anthem and Pledge had been relegated to the background by schools would not augur well for nation building.

He said the recital of the Anthem and Pledge should be made universal for every Ghanaian to understand the sacrifices made by our forebears in attaining independence for the country.

Office holders

Prof. Nketia stressed the importance for public office holders to recite them from the heart and reminded them that the positions they occupied was as a result of struggles and sacrifices.

He said a time would come when Ghanaians could accompany the recitals of the two national assets with traditional Ghanaians musical instruments as another innovative way of reinforcing the spirit of self-reliance.

The Chairperson of NCCE Ms Josephine Nkrumah, said the translation would help promote and sustain Ghana's democracy as well as instil patriotism and unity in Ghanaians.

She commended Mr Amoah for coming up with the idea to translate the Anthem and the Pledge into local languages which the NCCE and the Bureau of Languages supported wholeheartedly.

Partisan politics

She said now that the National Anthem and the National Pledge were in local languages, people and schoolchildren reciting them would pause and reflect on

78

their true meaning which would help foster unity and oneness.

Ms Nkrumah was also of the opinion that the local languages would help evoke a sense of national pride and national unity to prevent partisan politics from tearing the country apart.

Sense of pride

Mr Amoah appealed to Ghanaians to limit the use of English language in running the affairs of the country, since it was not the mother tongue.

He said most skills could be acquired by schoolchildren if they were allowed to think and acquire them through their mother tongues.

Mr Amoah also appealed to the government to publish parliamentary proceedings and the Hansard in local languages to increase the understanding of issues." – (Abdul Aziz and Theresah Esson, "National Anthem, Pledge, Translated into Local Languages," *Graphic*, Accra, Ghana, 13 March 2017).

And according to another report:

"Yesterday (13 March 2017) Ghana launched the translation of the national anthem into 11 other local languages. The launch was overseen by Ghana's National Commission for Civic Education (NCCE).

The national anthem was compiled and translated by a researcher identified as Mr. John B.K. Amoah. The translation was done in commemoration of the country's 60th independence anniversary.

The languages include Akwapim Twi, Ashanti Twi, Dagaare, Dagbani, Dangme, Ewe, Ga, Gonja, Kasem, Fante and Nzema. The NCCE has confirmed that the meaning of the anthem was not lost in these several other versions.

Mrs. Josephine Nkrumah, the chairperson of the NCCE said the translation will go a long way in fostering patriotism, nationalism as well as 'some civic understanding of what we are as Ghanaians.

'They engender patriotism, national unity and a sense of national pride.

'Today, on social media, we often find it humorous or comic when (a) clip goes viral on a Ghanaian fails (sic) an attempt at reciting or singing the national anthem, both young and old alike.

Often than not, this failed attempt further reveals a lack of understanding of the lyrics in the English language.

In essence, this implies that the sense of national pride and patriotism is lost on us, if we lack an understanding of what we recite or sing.'

She went on to say that the translation into several languages gives a sense of unity....

Mrs. Nkrumah agrees that the translation of the Ghana national anthem and the national pledge would make it easy for the different tribes to recite and most importantly understand what they say.

The national anthem and pledge of every nation is a significant piece of identity which only makes sense when the people havean understanding of what they are singing or saying....The national anthem was originally composed by Mr. Philip Gbeho in 1957 (grandfather of the late BBC presenter and reporter Komla Dumor).

Mr. Amoah, who made these translations available, has called for the naming of the Ghana flag as 'The Banner of Hope'....

J.H. Kwabena Nketia, emeritus professor and first African director of the Institute of African Studies, University of Ghana, formally launched the translated versions of the national anthem and the national pledge." - (Amara Onuh, "Patriotism: Ghana Translates National Anthem into 11 Local Languages," *AnswersAfrica*, 14 March 2017).

It was a wise decision. In a multiethnic society like Ghana where each ethnic group has its own language, it is virtually impossible to choose one "tribal" language and make it the national language or the language in which the national anthem is sung. Members of other "tribes" will undoubtedly see that as an imposition and a marginalisation of their identities and cultures.

Post-apartheid South Africa took the same approach. The country has 11 official languages. The national anthem is sung in five of the most widely spoken ones.

All that is in sharp contrast with what goes on in East Africa where Kiswahili (popularly known as Swahili) is the national language of four countries – Tanzania, Kenya, Uganda, and Rwanda which adopted it in February 2017 as her official language – and can not be claimed by a single tribe as its own.

It is also a vital tool of regional integration in East Africa where it is the dominant language; which would have been the case in West Africa as well if there was an African language that was non-tribal and was widely spoken throughout the region as Swahili is in East Africa. A Rwandan newspaper, *The New Times*, had the following report on the country's adoption of Swahili as an official language:

"Members of the Lower House yesterday passed the organic law establishing Swahili as an official language. Swahili joins Kinyarwanda, English and French as the country's fourth official language.

For now, the language will primarily be used for administrative purposes, appearing as one of the official languages in some official documents.

Appearing before the lawmakers to provide insight into why the law is necessary, the Minister for Sports and Culture, Julienne Uwacu, explained that the decision was motivated by both obligation and a variety of many other benefits.

'Rwanda joined the East African Community (EAC) in 2007 and in the statute that establishes this bloc, Swahili is universally used in the region and members are requested to make Swahili one of their official languages,' Uwacu said.

'Swahili as an official language is, on one hand, fulfilling what we are required to do as a member country but, on the other hand, it's a way to increase the benefits that Rwandans can reap from economic integration.'

Uwacu told the MPs that the East African Passport was meant to have started being used in January this year and requested that because of this urgency, the law is passed without it necessarily going through standing committees for further review.

However, the lawmakers expressed mixed feelings on the law.

MP Jean Baptiste Rucibigango said that though Swahili is not a language that is historically used in Rwanda, it is one of the most popular in East Africa and would definitely be of added value.

He wondered how it would be incorporated in schools as a foundation.

'It's one of the languages that we can compare to Spanish and English when it comes to how popular it has become in this region and I am in support of this law. The draft law says that the language shall be used in administration but I don't see anywhere where it says it will be taught in schools or used in research. How is this going to be done?' Rucibigango asked.

Presidential Order

In response, Uwacu said that a Presidential Order would detail when Swahili would be incorporated in school curriculum.

'We are going to introduce a curriculum and teaching

material and we will definitely take advantage of the relationship that we have with other partner states who already use the language,' the minister said.

MP Jean-Marie Vianney Gatabazi wondered whether the Government was ready for such a transition in terms of budget, calling it an 'expensive undertaking.'

'The moment this law is gazetted, there are so many things that need to change in terms of documentation, for instance,' he said.

MP Juvenal Nkusi agreed and also reminded fellow lawmakers that as a member of the EAC, Rwanda had ratified the bloc's treaty making the language which is already officially recognised by the members automatically applicable.

'Are we seriously going to adopt a law because of the East African passport? In the EAC treaty, is Swahili not recognised? Did we not ratify that treaty? Doesn't that automatically make it applicable in Rwanda? Would it stop the passport from being functional? Then there is also the cost. For a language that is already applicable here, why are we giving ourselves the burden of this cost?' he wondered.

To this, Uwacu said that the process would be gradual but reminded the MPs that in the recently revised budget, there is money that was set aside specifically for the EAC passport.

On adopting the language, she said that the process is gradual and reminded that there is a lot to benefit from learning Swahili, especially since East African countries had opened their borders to each other's citizens.

MP Theobald Mporanyi requested to know numbers indicating how many Rwandans speak Swahili, wondering if it was necessary to adopt another language." – (Nasra Bishumba, "MPs Approve Law Making Swahili Official Language," *The New Times*, Kigali, 9 February 2017).

The status of Kiswahili as a major African language has

also been acknowledged by some prominent West Africans including Ghanaian author Ayi Kwei Armah and Africa's first Nobel laureate, Wole Soyinka, who have called for the adoption of Swahili as the official language for the whole continent. Coincidentally, Ayi Kwei Armah once lived in Tanzania and taught at Chang'ombe College of Education in Dar es Salaam in the seventies.

The non-tribal nature of Kiswahili has enabled the language to play a major role in promoting unity and fostering harmony among the people of East Africa. No group has been marginalised linguistically. Therefore, members of different ethnic groups can not say the language has been imposed on them by one "tribe" as would have been the case had Twi, for example, been officially declared to be the official language of Ghana, with the Akan – who speak it as their native language – being the dominant group.

Although the Akan are the largest group in Ghana, smaller ones have equal status in the country as fellow citizens.

Akan speakers are predominant in the Ashanti, Brong Ahafo, Central, Eastern and Western regions.

Other languages recognised by the government as major mediums of communication, although regional in character, are Fante (also known as Fanti or Mfantse), Ewe, Ga, Dangme, Dagbani, Dagaare, Gonja, Nzema, and Kasem.

English is the official language of Ghana. As in most African countries, the language of the former colonial rulers is the official language. It is rare to find an indigenous African language that has the status of national or official language except in countries where the vast majority of the people belong to one ethnic group. Botswana is a good example. Tswana is the major indigenous language. It is spoken or understood throughout the country where about 80 per cent of the people are Tswana.

Another exception is Kiswahili in East Africa where it has the status of national language, although some people don't consider it to be a typical African language because of its "Arab" origin. It is essentially a Bantu – an African – language, although its vocabulary includes some Arabic words. But it is true that there would be no Kiswahili had Arabs not settled in large numbers in East Africa where they have lived for more than 1,000 years.

They have intermingled and intermarried with the indigenous people, especially along the coast, for centuries; it was mostly Arab men cohabiting with and sometimes marrying African women, not African men cohabiting with or marrying Arab women.

The interaction led to the development and evolution of a language that came to be known as Kiswahili as the people tried to communicate using a mixture of Arabic and African languages. But there is no question that Kiswahili is predominantly Bantu in origin.

That is in sharp contrast with what prevails in most African countries including Ghana where not one but a number of indigenous languages are dominant.

The best example in the case of Ghana is Twi spoken by the Akan who are also the largest group in the country and one of the largest in West Africa and on the entire continent. They are also some of the most influential people in Ghana.

Akan

THE Akan are the largest group in Ghana. They also constitute the majority of the people in neighbouring Ivory Coast. Altogether, there are at least 20 million of them in both countries.

The term "Akan" refers to a collection of different ethnic groups. They are collectively identified as "Akan" because they are related in one way or another and have basically a common culture and history.

They are essentially the same people collectively constituting a larger or a macro-ethnic group within which are different ethnic groups which have their own identities. Yet, they share a common identity. If the Akan were a nation, they would be "nations within a nation," each Akan group – Ashanti, Fante and so on – being a nation.

In Ghana, they are indigenous to the southern-central and southern parts of the country. They include the Ashanti who are some of the most well-known people in Africa. Another major Akan group is the Fante (also known as Fanti).

Other Akan groups are the Abbe, Abinghi, Abidji, Aboure, Abron, Adjukru, Ahafo, Ahanta, Akuapem, Akwamu, Akye, Akyem, Alladian, Anyo, Aowin, Assin, Attie, Avatime, Avikam, Baoule, Chokosi, Denkyira, Ehotile, Evalue, Kwahu, M'Bato, Nzema, Sefwi, Tchaman, Twifu, and Wassa.

The Akan language – whose main components are Twi and Fante – is used in primary school as a medium of instruction and is even studied at the university level in Ghana. It is also taught in universities in other countries including the United States where – as in Britain and in a number of other countries – the major African language that is taught has always been Swahili (Kiswhili); it has an advantage over other African languages because it does not belong to any particular tribe or ethnic group – it belongs to everybody, in fact to all Africans, because it is a product of many African languages in East Africa whose speakers migrated from West Africa, especially east-central Nigeria and Cameroon, about 3,000 years ago.

One of the official languages of the African Union, Swahili is the lingua franca of East Africa just as Twi in the "lingua franca" of Ghana.

The culture of the Akan people is matrilineal in terms of inheritance and succession. Their culture has had such a profound impact that it still survives in many communities of the African diaspora especially in Jamaica and other parts of the Caribbean, as well as South America and even in some parts of the United States, mainly in the south, where the descendants of slaves taken from the Akan region of Ghana and the Ivory Coast live.

The Akan culture was so strong in Jamaica that it suppressed and wiped out other African cultures. Other African slaves, new arrivals who were not of Akan origin, were forced to abandon their cultures and adopted the Akan culture when they were integrated into the slave communities on the island.

One of the most important elements of Akan culture is the traditional religion. It has a lot in common with other traditional religions of West Africa based on the existence of God as the supreme being and creator of the universe. But He does not interact with the people.

That is in sharp contrast with the teachings of Christianity based on the belief that God is active and intervenes in human affairs on daily basis. He is all-powerful, all-knowledgeable, and all-present – He is everywhere all the time.

Like many people of other Africans religions, the Akans also believe in the existence of spirits, of departed ancestors, who are active in human affairs and assist and guide the living in their daily lives especially when they are consulted and sought for assistance through rituals and ceremonies.

God has different names in Akan culture. He is the Almighty (Brekyirihunuade, Nyame, Nyankopon). He is also known as "the Great Designer" or "the Great Spider" (Anansi Kokuroku), and the Infinite Inventor (Odomankoma). The Akan also believe God has a wife, Asase Yaa, who is sometimes known as Mother Earth, and is second to God in terms of authority and power.

Akan culture is also one of the dominant aspects of daily life in neighbouring Ivory Coast where the Akans constitute the largest group of 8.5 million out of a total population of about 23 million. In Ghana, there are 11.5 million Akans out of a total population of more than 27 million.

Ashanti

The Ashanti, who are the largest among all the groups which collectively constitute the Akan meta-ethnic group, are also the largest single ethnic group in Ghana. They are also one of the largest in West Africa and on the entire continent.

The name Ashanti is a corruption or an anglicized version of Asante, the original name of the people.

They are known for their rich culture and history, including their fierce resistance against imperial conquest by the British. They fought one of the bloodiest wars in British colonial history.

They are also known as major producers of gold and golden items. The most important symbol of their "nation" is the Golden Stool, the throne of their king. It also has great spiritual significance as the home or residence of the spirit of the Ashanti nation.

One of the most important items of their identity which has also helped them earn international recognition is the kente cloth. It is sold worldwide and stands out among other items as an intricate pattern of fabric and artistry. It is also one of the symbols of Ghana's national identity, worn by national leaders and others including the first president, Dr. Kwame Nkrumah, and his cabinet members. Even Julius Nyerere wore the kente cloth in his first official portrait when he became prime of Tanganyika after he led the country to independence from Britain on 9 December 1961.

The Ashanti are also known for their highly elaborate and expensive funerals, a practice that demonstrates how much they value life that has been lost although they also believe, like members of most African "tribes," death is only a transitional phase – a passage to another world of spirits who include ancestors who help guide the living in their daily lives.

The funerals are expensive because many people attend them. They include not only immediate family members but members of the extended family even if they live far away and in other countries. They make every effort to attend funerals. The number of those who attend funerals is also large because people from neighbouring places also attend the funerals, making them even more expensive.

Funerals also provide occasions for the people to resolve some matters and carry on business in different areas. They take advantage of the large gatherings to discuss important matters involving families, land and other things.

The Ashanti are also known for their skillful artwork, making a variety of items including masks which are traditionally very important in different ceremonies. They also make sculptures, capturing the essence of their cultural identity as do other products.

As in most traditional societies in Africa, the Ashanti have an extended family system. The maternal side is predominant among the Ashanti. The mother's clan plays a vital role in the lives and destinies of family members.

Elders also play a very important role in the lives of the people, providing guidance.

Marriage is a vital institution in Ashanti culture and divorce is strongly discouraged. Polygamy is practised although many men no longer marry more than one wife; that is also the case in most communities across the continent even among the most traditional and conservatives ones, especially among young people because of the influence of modernisation which has had a profound impact on the traditional way of life.

But even with modernisation, traditional ways still shape the lives of many Africans; the Ashanti being no exception. In fact, even in towns and cities, many Africans follow their traditional ways, combined with modern practices which are essentially of European origin, producing a cultural hybrid that is neither typically African nor European. As an American saying goes despite its racist and derogatory connotations, "You can take a Negro out of the ghetto, but you can't take the ghetto out of the Negro."

The same applies to most Africans. You can take them out of the village but you cannot take the village out of them. In fact, village life is central to the integrity and wellbeing of most Africans, maintaining strong social bonds and respecting their cultures; an observation underscored here in the case of the Ashanti which is equally applicable to the members of other ethnic groups on the African continent:

"Although some Asante now live and work in urban centres, they remain primarily associated with village life. They are mainly farmers who produce plantain, bananas, cassava, yams, and cocoyams for local markets and cacao for export.

The basis of Asante social organization is matrilineage, a localized segment of a clan whose members claim descent from a common female ancestor. Members of the lineage assist one another in activities such building houses, farming, and clearing paths and in funeral rites.

Since the Asante believe that every individual is made up of two elements – blood from the mother and spirit from the father – paternal descent is also recognized and governs membership in exogamous *ntoro* divisions that are associated with certain religious and moral obligations." – (Asante in *Encylopaedia Britannica*, 2000).

According to Ashanti tradition and mythology, *ntoro* is the spirit of a person which determines and shapes his/her character.

The Ashanti live in a well-structured society whose hierarchy is determined by the elders. And although women play a very important part in this matrilineal society, they are also confined to certain roles because of their gender:

"The head of the lineage is chosen by its senior men and women; females are prohibited from holding this position because of menstrual taboos forbidding contact with sacred objects.

The lineage head is responsible for internal peace and relations with other lineages and, as custodian of lineage stools, which embody the spirits of ancestors, is the mediator between its living and dead members.

Every important lineage head also has a stool as a symbol of the office. The village chief is chosen from a particular lineage, which differs from village to village; his main task, with the advice of his council of elders, is to settle disputes within the community." – (Asante, *Encyclopaedia Britannica*).

The village has always been central to life in traditional societies across Africa. That is also the case with the Ashanti.

Critical to the wellbeing of the village, besides communal living and responsibilities, is the role of the elders who are the custodians of the customs and traditions of the Ashanti. They are also the final arbiters in disputes involving property, families and other matters.

They are also responsible for arranging and overseeing traditional ceremonies which are an integral part of Ashanti culture.

Without the elders, the villagers have no focal point to rally around. They provide the nucleus of village life, cultural and social, as well as political and spiritual.

One African American, Rita Muhammad, who wrote about her experience living in Ghana and showed reverence for the Ashanti during the two years she spent there, stated the following in her book, *At Home! Abroad*:

"As I buried my mother in December of 2005, I promised her and myself that I would pursue my desire to return to Africa. I heard of an organization that sent teachers to Africa for one year to teach. So, in February 2006, I applied; in May 2006 I was accepted, and was told I would be assigned to Ghana, West Africa, and in September 2006, I left the United States to live my first year in Africa.

I was thrilled to be returning to Ghana, since that is where I felt most at home. However, when I returned this time, things were different. In 1994, I was a tourist. Tourists don't quite see and feel the real country....However, this time, I wasn't in Ghana for 18 days. I was there for one full academic year, 10 months...from September 2006 until July 2007.

Since I had previously traveled to Ghana and fell in love with capital city of Accra, I was truly looking forward to going back. But this time it was not the city of Accra, a bustling and growing metropolis, to which I was assigned. Instead, it was Berekum; some 8 – 10 hours drive, towards the interior of the country, into the mountains, away from Accra....

Berekum is indeed a small, rural town. It is located northwest of Accra, in the Brong Ahafo Region and is one-and-a-half hours drive from the border of Cote d'Ivoire. Its well-known neighbor, in the Ashanti Region, Kumasi, is approximately 2 hours drive away.

As I rode in the van, I realized I was getting farther and farther away from what I knew as the developed metropolitan area. The farther we drove, the more unpaved highways, dirt roads, and thatched homes we passed. I was surprised to see the lack of color on the buildings. Everything seemed grey, dull yellow, brown or beige. The children were playing in the dirt fields; some with no shoes on their little feet.

I didn't know what to make of all this. I don't remember seeing this before. When you are toured, you are indeed shown the better area. All countries want to put their best face on for those visiting. So, my ride was as if I had never previously visited the country." – (Rita Muhammad, *At Home! Abroad*, CreateSpace, 2012).

She went on to state:

"I was awakened as the driver was turning into the campus of Berekum Teacher Training College, my home for the next two years!

As I opened my eyes all I could see was lush, green, tall trees. I felt as if I was being driven through a rain forest. The campus was absolutely beautiful....I was overjoyed. There was a peaceful, calm spirit on the campus. It really felt good....

All but a few of the teachers were men, who have studied extensively and who spoke English well. I couldn't help but notice their wives, who are primarily housewives, didn't speak any English at all. Many women over thirty years old, in this small village community, never attended school. Though education through middle school is mandatory, many do not see the importance of educating girls, though that concept is changing and more and more girls are also being educated....

So, here I am wondering how am I going to communicate with the women in my new community. Though my presence was welcomed by the women, it was also intimidating to some. So, I didn't want to be seen just socializing with men simply because they spoke English. After all, what would their wives think?

Well, that was just the beginning of my concerns. Unbeknownst to me, I would soon face challenges that would leave me crying myself to sleep each night, while vowing to leave the next morning.

Berekum is definitely different from the capital city of Accra, and initially presented several challenges. The first and foremost was the realization that not only did most of the women on campus not speak English, but most in the entire city of Berekum do not speak English. This was my biggest challenge in the beginning because I was looking forward to socializing with my sisters....Additionally, women in various societies carry the proper protocols of that society, and a lot can be learned about a culture by studying women.

So this was a real blow to me. Since English is the official language of Ghana, I just took it for granted that everyone spoke it....Being unable to speak Twi, and not being made aware that I should learn the indigenous language before I arrived, made my initial indoctrination into the area difficult.

However, that didn't stop me from trying. After the vice-principal walked me through campus, he then walked me through this small town, introducing me to store keepers, and showing me where to purchase my dry goods, fruits and vegetables.

As we walked from store to store, I remember thinking I had never seen such a small, rural town in my life. Being raised in California metropolitan cities was a far cry from Berekum. I was fascinated and wanted to drink in as much as I could....

The main road was paved, but most of small streets were not. The buildings looked as if they would fall down under the weight of a strong storm. The store keepers were all sweeping in front of their shops and I couldn't help but notice that though the town was old and little disheveled, it was also relatively clean. No trash and paper on the ground at all. Ghanaians are generally clean people. Always sweeping, wiping or cleaning something. The two years I was there I never once entered a dirty house. The home may need repairs and the walls may need paint, but there was rarely filth and dirt." – (Ibid.)

She then had an experience that shocked her and which many African Americans – some of them prefer to call themselves black Americans – who have visited Ghana have also experienced:

"As I walked through the town I noticed everyone stopping and staring. I mean really staring; like they had never seen a Black person before.

Wait a minute! I'm in Africa! They're Black too!! Why are they staring at me? I look like you! We are the same I was thinking to myself.

The children would smile and wave. The men would smile and say hello, while the women would just stare, a blank stare.

It was during these walks through the town, that I realized, once again, the only people who spoke English were the brothers, and most of them were under 30 years old.

I met a young brother who owned a video store and who had previously traveled overseas. His English was good. I asked why they stared at me so intently. While in the capital city of Accra, during our 7 days of orientation, I didn't get a lot of stares. I got some looks, but mostly people would say hello and ask where I was from. No big deal.

But Berekum was quite different. I was getting so much attention, as opposed to just blending in, so I asked my brother with the video store why I was stopping so much traffic. He said, 'my sister, you stand out so much, it's as if watching someone in bright colors walk through a black and white picture.' He explained that foreigners rarely come that far into the interior of the country, and if they do, they are white people.

He explained that they see me as an *abruni*. I remember hearing the children call me that. 'A what?' An *abruni*, which literally translated, means 'white people.'

Oh my God1! What! I am not even a little bit light-skinned at all. I am a dark-skinned Black woman. I don't remotely look mixed or anything, so why on earth would my people call me a white person? I was mortified.

He explained that is a general term used to identify all foreigners. I told him I was not a foreigner and I was clearly not a white person, so I won't accept being called *abruni*. I told him I am family who was kidnapped from the Motherland, and although estranged, I'm still family and will not accept being called *abruni*.

He smiled and said, then whenever yo hear them say *abruni*, stop and tell them who you are. Well, that's easier said than done since I don't speak their language and they don't speak mine. However, over the next two years, I would do just that, whenever feasible.

There were men, women and children who would say to me, *abruni*, *abruni*, and I would stop, pull up my sleeve, point to my brown skin and their skin and say, 'no *abruni*. Sister.' Every time I did that I would get either a big hug or a huge smile and they would all agree, and say, 'yeah, Seestah.' At that moment, my new motto became: 'It's all about education.'

We, Blacks in the Diaspora, must be there on the continent, engaged with our brothers and sisters, so they will know who we are." – (Ibid.)

"Obruni" is a term that rankles many African Americans; its use in reference to these descendants of African slaves being interpreted – and rightly so in some cases – as a rejection of these children of Africa by their brethren at home. As Cidney Holliday stated in her article, "American 'Obruni': Black Americans Considered Anglo in Ghana," published in a black newspaper which is described as "The Voice of The Black Community," *The Charlotte Post*, Charlotte, North Carolina, USA:

"At the start of my second week in Ghana I have been

96

many places and seen so many different things.

I think that one of the most challenging things for me to work with has been my level of incompetence with the languages spoken here. There are many beautiful dialects and languages spoken all across the world. During spring break I went to Taziè, France, with my school. There were many Portuguese, French, and German students there but English was the dominant language. There is a dominating expectance that people should know some English here in Ghana, but I felt somewhat dumb that I don't in return know any Fante.

Fante is the language spoken in the region of Ghana where our guest houses and internships are located. When I hear the language spoken it all seems so fast and confusing. However there are certain words I have come to know. For example Akwabaa means welcome. I saw this word for the first time when exiting the plane from London. It was painted alongside Ghanaian figures and beautiful landscapes in the airport in Accra.

Another word I have become very familiar with is 'Obruni.' This term translates directly to 'white person.' I have had some people tell me that the term doesn't solely mean white person as in white skin, but any 'Anglo-acting' person, including myself.

Children in the area will run up to our group, a multiracial group of young people, and yell 'Obruni! Obruni!' and run away quickly laughing and waving the entire way home. As an African-American I thought that they would see that my skin was like theirs, my heritage is shared in this land – I am not a 'white person.'

One evening a group of friends and I went out to a night spot. I was talking to a person of my own age; he also called me an Obruni. I told him, 'No I am not an Obruni, why would you say that?' He told me that I should not be offended; this word is for all foreign people. He told me the word 'Bibini' meant black woman, and black means all black people collectively.

He told me I wasn't quite a black person, like a

Ghanaian woman, but a 'Bibini-Obruni:' a black-white person.

On the streets walking to markets, with its organized chaos and multitude of scents of colors and textures, I have been called 'mulatto,' 'my African American sister' and some words which I did recognize as Fante, but didn't care to have translated for my own sake.

My fellow African American students from Davidson have talked about colorism and what it means to be black-skinned in a nation full of others who look similar to you, but still clearly differences in skin tones and aesthetic features. Now that I have been here a week I have wondered hard about what does it actually mean to be dark skinned, light skinned, or even African American.

We, as black Americans, categorize, assign, and praise and shame each other for principles I feel we cannot quite put our finger on when put in a place where we are technically part of the majority.

When I work with the school children, they are always amazed that we, the African American students, are like them in color but not in language. I had a 10-year-old student at the school I work with named Vanessa, come to me and ask, 'Madame, you speak Fante?'

When told her no, she said 'So you Obruni?' When I told her no again, she paused, thought hard, and then expressed that I was indeed an Obruni.

These thoughts even coming from people much younger (or older) than me resonate on a very deep and retrospective level for me. It's like everything I have been taught to know about myself, regarding race and skin color, has all been flipped.

It's an amazing experience to be here, but complicated nonetheless." – (Cidney Holliday, "American 'Obruni': Black Americans Considered Anglo in Ghana," *The Charlotte Post*, Charlotte, North Carolina, USA, 5 June 2014).

Some of these experiences and exchanges – and the dissonance in relations between Africans and African Americans as well as Afro-Caribbeans – have been captured and addressed in the works of other observers. As I state in one of my books, *Relations Between Africans and African Americans: Misconceptions, Myths and Realities*:

"What is sometimes so disturbing about some of these negative remarks by Africans when they talk about African Americans is that they come from different parts of the continent, delivering the *same* message of indifference towards American blacks. And because they are not orchestrated or coordinated, they give the impression that hostility or indifference towards black Americans is a pervasive phenomenon among Africans on the African continent and in the United States as well as in other parts of the world where Africans live. That is simply *not* true.

Yet, conflicting signals now and then coming from some Africans only reinforce the notion or the perception that Africans in general don't want to have anything to do or have nothing to do with black Americans. And it is not just because they are Americans that they don't want them; it is not because these African Americans were born and raised on American soil, although that may be one of the reasons, such as jealousy. These African descendants in the diaspora are even denied their African heritage by some Africans who call them 'white.' And as Kofi Glover, a Ghanaian professor of political science at the University of Southern Florida, bluntly states:

'Whether we like it or not, Africans and African Americans have two very different cultures.'

I am not saying that Glover is one of those Africans who say black Americans have nothing to do with their African cultural heritage or are not African at all; I'm simply saying that he is emphasizing what is an indisputable fact: there are fundamental cultural differences between Africans and African Americans.

The culture of black Americans is essentially European, *not* African. And they should admit that, however cruel and reprehensible the manner in which this Euro-American culture was acquired by them.

They have been immersed and submerged in the culture of their European masters and rulers for centuries, although there are still remnants of African culture across black America.

It is not their fault that they lost their African cultural identity – which many of them are trying to reclaim – but it is also true that when they lost it, they became Europeanized culturally, although they did not and could not become European for the simple reason that they were still an African people. And that causes some misunderstanding between the two sides, with some Africans going to the extreme and calling black Americans not African at all, as demonstrated by the following examples.

When some African Americans went to Kenya in the mid-1990s – I think they were business executives or some other kind of businessmen and may be even scholars – and said they were also Africans, their Kenyan counterparts, black Africans, said, no, they were not; they were 'white Africans' born in America, as reported by *The Economist*, obviously because they lost their African culture and identity after centuries of slavery and living in a predominantly white country of which they had become an integral part.

In Ghana also, a significant number of Ghanaians don't accept black Americans as Africans and even have a term, *obruni* in the Twi language, they use to describe them; the term also means 'foreigner.'

They call African Americans 'white.' The word *obruni* is used in that context, meaning white, and may be even in a derogatory sense – or to maintain distance – by some people in the case of black Americans; in spite of the fact, the indisputable fact, that many of these very same black Americans whom they call 'white' originated from the same place, Ghana, are members of their tribes – the Fanti, the Ewe, the Ashanti and others – and even of their own families.

They are their blood relatives, no matter how many centuries apart, separated since the slave trade. As Malcolm X said in one of his speeches, 'There is no tree without roots, and branches without a tree.' And as Ghanaian president, Dr. Kwame Nkrumah, stated: 'All peoples of African descent whether they live in North or South America, the Caribbean or in other parts of the world, are Africans and belong to the African nation.'

And it is consoling to our brothers and sisters from the diaspora when they find out that not all Africans feel this way and treat them as total strangers or outcasts. They learn this when they deal with different Africans in the United States itself; they also find out about all this when they go to Africa and meet many Africans who welcome them and embrace them.

There are some problems now and then, here and there, but the hospitality extended to African Americans by Africans makes many of them feel at home in Africa; be it in Ghana, Tanzania, Nigeria, South Africa, Kenya, Senegal, Gambia, Zimbabwe, Namibia, Swaziland, Togo, Benin, Uganda or any other black African country. As one African American, Imahkus, who moved to Ghana with her husband, states in an excerpt from her book, *Returning Home Ain't Easy But It Sure Is A Blessing*, published in *Escape From America Magazine*:

'Ahead of us loomed this enormous, foreboding structure. The sight caused me to tremble; I almost didn't want to go inside. The outer walls were chipped and a faded and moldy white exterior. The sea had eaten away some of the mortar. It was gray and dismal as we climbed the steep steps, following the sign leading to the reception area. When we entered the reception area of the Cape Coast Castle Dungeons a smallish man with a bright smiling face met us. His name was Mr. Owusu and he had been working there as a receptionist and sometimes Guide, for many years.

After introductions were made all around, Mr. Owusu, our guide began the tour around the Castle. Entering the inner part of the castle overlooking a large courtyard, our guide gave us the background history of the Cape Coast Castle Dungeons. This was one of the more than sixty castle dungeons, forts, and lodges that had been constructed by European Traders with the permission of local rulers (the Chieftaincy) and stretched for 300 miles along the West Coast of Afrika to store captured Afrikans, until a shipload of enslaved Afrikans could be assembled, for shipment to the West.

Unbelievable, twenty-seven of those houses of misery were located in Ghana. Various European oppressors had occupied the Cape Coast Castle Dungeons during the Trans-Atlantic European Slave Trade. It began with the Portuguese in the 1500's, followed by the Dutch, then the Swedes, the Danes and finally the English who occupied it in 1665. It remained under their control, serving as the seat of the British Administration in the Gold Coast (Cape Coast) until they re-located their racist regime to Christianborg Castle in Accra in 1877.

Our next stop was the Palaver (which means talking/discussing) Hall, the meeting place of slave merchants, which also served as the hall used in auctioning off our ancestors. The room was huge, the only light coming from the windows which lined both sides of the walls; one side facing the ocean, the other side overlooking the town; a bare room, echoing the voice of our Guide, a haunting echo, which reverberated off the walls, as the Guide explained how they bargained and sold us.

When slave auctions were not going on, Palaver Hall was used as a meeting place for the Governor, Chiefs and other visitors. We then moved on to the Governor's apartment and the church, which I felt like burning down! But nothing could prepare me for what we would experience next.

We descended the stairs into a large cobble-stoned courtyard and walked through large double wooden doors, which lead into a long, dark, damp tunnel.

The stench of musty bodies, fear and death hung in the air. There was no noise except the thunderous crashing of the waves against the outer walls and the roaring sound of the water. Deeper we walked, into large, dark rooms which had served as a warehouse for enslaved Afrikan people awaiting shipment to the America's and Caribbean.

This was the Men's Dungeon. As we stood in that large cavernous room the air was still, the little ventilation that was available came from small openings near the 20-foot high ceilings. Our ancestors had been kept underground, chained to the walls and each other, making escape impossible.

The mood of the group was hushed, as several people started crying. We were standing in hellholes of the most horrific conditions imaginable. There were no words to express the suffering that must have gone on in these dungeons.

I became caught up, thrown back in time. I was suddenly one of the many who were shackled, beaten and starved. But I was one of the fortunate souls to have survived the forced exodus from their homelands to be sold, branded and thrown into those hellholes, meant to hold (600) people but which held more than 1,000 enslaved Afrikans at one time. The men separated from the women, as they awaited shipment to the Americas. According to our Guide, the chalk marks on the walls of the Men's Dungeon indicated the level of the floor prior to the excavation of the floor, which had built up over years of slavery with feces, bones, filth, etc.

As the guide continued to describe the horrors of these pits of hell I began to shake violently; I needed to get out of there. I was being smothered. I turned and ran up the steep incline of the tunnel, to the castle courtyard, the winds from the sea whipping my face, bringing me back to the present. I couldn't believe what I had just experienced. How could anyone be so cruel and inhuman?

Following the guide we proceeded across the massive courtyard and down another passage way to the Women's Dungeon, a smaller version of the Men's Dungeon but not so deep underground, it had held over 300 women at any given time.

As we entered that dark, musty, damp room, the sound of the crashing waves was like muffled, rolling thunder. A dimly lit, uncovered light bulb hung from the ceiling on a thin, frayed wire. After standing silently for a time in this tomb, the Guide began to lead the group out. I was the last person left in the room when the Guide turned and said he was continuing the tour. 'Please,' I said, 'I'm not ready to leave, just turn off the light for me and I will join the group shortly.' As the group walked silently away, the tears would not stop flowing. I dropped to my knees, trembling and crying even harder.

With the light off, the only light in that dungeon came through one small window near the very high ceiling, reflecting down as though it were a muted spotlight. Darkness hung in every corner.

As I rocked back and forth on the dirt floor, I could hear weeping and wailing...anguished screams coming from the distance.

Suddenly the room was packed with women...some naked, some with babies, some sick and lying in the dirt, while others stood against the walls around the dungeon's walls, terror filled their faces.

'My God, what had we done to wind up here, crammed

together like animals?'

Pain and suffering racked their bodies, a look of hopelessness and despair on their faces...but with a strong will to survive. 'Oh God, what have we done to deserve this kind of treatment?'

Cold terror gripped my body. Tears blinded me and the screams wouldn't stop. As I sat there violently weeping I began to feel a sense of warmth, many hands were touching my body, caressing me, soothing me as a calmness began to come over me. I began to feel almost safe as voices whispered in my ears assuring me that everything was all right.

'Don't cry,' they said. 'You've come home. You've returned to your homeland, to re-open the Door of No Return.'

Gradually the voices and the women faded into the darkness; it was then that I realized that some of the screams I'd heard were my own. The eerie light beaming down from the window was growing dimmer as day began fading into night. As I got up from the dungeon floor I knew that I would never be the same again! 'After years of wandering and searching, I have finally found home. And one day, I wouldn't be leaving again.'

The book that you hold in your hands, *Returning Home Ain't Easy But It Sure Is A Blessing*, speaks to the visions of our ancestors and demonstrates the efforts both positive and negative, the humor, the tears and the frustrations of a Diaspora Afrikan family diligently working and struggling within the blessings of being back in our ancestral homeland. It faces the startling realities plagued by those of us who are trying to return home.

Realities of the fact that many of our continental Afrikan born brothers and sisters have very little knowledge of the Afrikan people born and raised in the Diaspora that resulted from the Trans-Atlantic (European) Slave Trade.

Ironically, every Ghananian we spoke with wanted to

105

go to the United States. We were coming and they wanted to go. We were like ships in the night, passing each other unseeing and uncaring. My story contrasts these with those realities of life on the other side. Brothers struggling to survive were being killed on a regular basis while driving taxis in New York City.

A few years before we repatriated to Ghana, two men held up my husband with a shotgun, while he was working his taxicab. When they entered the cab and sat down, the man with the gun, who spoke no English, put it to my husband's head, as the other man announced in broken English 'Dis es ah stickup, don' turn roun' or jew dead, Mon.'

They then tied and bound him, before throwing him in the trunk of the taxi. Riding around the Bronx and Manhattan they ended up dumping him on a dark street in the early morning. At a deserted Terminal Market in the Bronx, they ordered him to stay still and not move for 15 minutes. Thank God, he was unhurt that time, but what about next time? Certainly no one could doubt there would be a next time the way things were happening in New York City.

Children were being gunned down playing in the streets and in playgrounds. Safety was a problem even in the school system. These chaotic conditions, among other problems caused us to run like hell from New York, out of the United States and straight home to Afrika.

Here we found our family of four could live in comfort on my husband's pension from the New York City Fire Department. We set about pursuing economic empowerment for ourselves and the development and betterment of our Afrikan family on the continent.

However, since arriving here we have found that there are many jobs that are either reserved exclusively for Ghanaians or require certain monetary stipulations designed for big corporations. My husband, who owned and operated his own taxicab/car service in New York,

106

would have to have a minimum of 10 cars to go into the car service business here. If we could afford to purchase 10 cars, would we need to open a car service?

We owned our own Travel Agency in the United States but in Ghana we would have needed ($10,000.00) US Dollars operating capital and a Ghanaian partner, or ($200,000.00) U.S. Dollars to do it alone. In the absence of that kind of up-front cash, we have had to call upon our God given creativity. *Returning Home Ain't Easy* chronicles how we maintained ourselves, re-connected with our extended family, developed business interests to secure a good future for our families, while trying to make a worthwhile contribution to our community.

It has been ten years since our family returned to 'Mother' Afrika leaving behind mayhem, racism, creeping anarchy, bedlam, etc. (That's not to say things aren't far from or are perfect here in Ghana). We've been tricked, accused of being racist, called Obruni (White man and foreigner), but we've also been loved and welcomed home by many of our Ghanaian brothers and sisters. They are anxious to learn about us, as we are about them. Each of us wants to know who the other has become. Who, we have become while we were separated from our 'Mother' land.

This healthy exchange makes a stronger bond between us. Together we can set about correcting those wrongs committed against us and remember the strength and greatness of us as Afrikan people. Just as a two-chord rope is stronger than a one-chord rope, our knowledge of the truth of our separation from one another will enable us to go forward as a stronger, united Afrikan front, a power source to be reckoned with spiritually, economically and politically.

One of our great Afrikan Leaders and Statesman, the late Osageyfo Dr. Kwame Nkrumah, 1st President of the Republic of Ghana from 1957 to 1966 said, 'All peoples of Afrikan descent whether they live in North or South

America, the Caribbean or in other part of the world are Afrikans and belong to the Afrikan nation.'

That being so, it is with the blessing and fulfillment of Prophesy that we have returned home on the wings of the wind.'

Her experience, of course, contrasts sharply with that of other African Americans who have "returned home," to Africa, and who have lived in different African countries, including Ghana.

Some of them complain that they have been rejected or ignored by their brothers and sisters in Africa.

Others say 'all they want is our money, the dollar,' nothing else. 'We're nothing but bags of dollars for them,' as one African American woman who went to the Ivory Coast said.

They don't want to have anything to do "with us," as another African American woman, who lived in Ghana, reportedly said, as quoted by *The Wall Street Journal*, March 14, 2001. She got tired of the hostility and negative attitude towards African Americans and returned to the United States.

The story in *The Wall Street Journal* raises a number of questions, in a larger context, as to the relevance of what was reportedly said. Even if it is true that there were indeed some Ghanaians who were not very friendly with the African Americans quoted in the article, out of how many? Are most Ghanaians hostile or indifferent towards African Americans?

There are definitely those who are, just as there are other Africans who feel the same way in other African countries. But to tarnish the image of the entire country simply because some Africans feel the way they do towards black Americans in a negative way, is unwarranted. It also calls into question the motives of the writer. But that is typical of the Western media.

They love to portray Africa in a negative light. And

they hate to say anything good about the 'Dark Continent.' That would be too good to be true, is their attitude.

But if nothing good comes out of Africa, and if the vast majority of Africans are indeed hostile towards American Americans, it defies rational explanation why they keep on going there every year, and why many of them have even settled permanently in Africa. As Retha Hill, an African American, put it:

'A trip to Ghana is not just a vacation; it is a balm for a broken soul.'

African Americans are not the only ones who like going to Africa. Hundreds of thousands of whites from North America and Europe and other people also go to Africa every year, and definitely not to suffer.

However, those of us who were born and brought up in Africa and are members of indigenous tribes or ethnic groups should not deny the fact that there are some Africans who are either indifferent or hostile towards black Americans, for whatever reason or reasons. And even the few African Americans who complain about the negative attitude of some Africans towards them, should be taken seriously in order to set the record straight, instead of being ignored and dismissed as an insignificant minority." – (Godfrey Mwakikagile, *Relations Between Africans and African Americans: Misconceptions, Myths and Realities*, Dar es Salaam, Tanzania, Pretoria, South Africa: New Africa Press, 2007, pp. 141 – 149. See also Mwakikagile, *Africans and African Americans: Complex Relations, Prospects and Challenges*; and *Relations Between Africans, African Americans and Afro-Caribbeans: Tensions, Indifference and Harmony*).

It is a rocky relationship both sides must acknowledge is not as good as it should be. Had the two not been separated for centuries because of the slave trade, things would have been different.

There is no question that Europeans were the driving force behind the slave trade. But the role played by Africans, such as the Ashanti, in this diabolical traffic can not be ignored.

Still, it is important to remember that the Ashanti and other Africans did not enslave and sell their own people. They captured and sold members of other tribes whom they did not consider to be their people, although this may sound strange to African Americans and other people of African descent in the diaspora who simply see all blacks as one people – "we are the same people" – and even as "one tribe."

Yet the same societies of some of the Africans who were involved in the slave trade had redeeming qualities whose virtues even surpassed those of Europeans; one good example being the treatment of women.

When women were fighting for their rights in America and in many parts of Europe because of sexism, women in Ashantiland were enjoying theirs; a sharp contrast between the two. As Rita Muhammad stated in her book *At Home! Abroad*:

"One of the many mental illnesses we as Black people received from our enslavement and subsequent education in America is sexism. Sexism is simply discrimination based on gender. It is a practice of fear and insecurity. This was at one time unheard of on the continent of Africa, as noted by Dr. John Henrik Clarke, who once stated:

'In Africa the woman's 'place' was not only with her family; she often ruled nations with unquestionable authority. Many African women were great militarists and on occasion led their armies into battle.

Long before they knew of the existence of Europe, the Africans had produced a way of life where men were secure enough to let women advance as far as their talent

110

would taken them.'

That was the case with Queen Asantewa who was born in 1863 into a small, but proud Ashanti family and community in Kumasi, called Ejisu.

The Ashanti people have a strong sense of family and unity. To understand the people, you must know their history.

The Ashanti Kingdom in Ghana was founded in the seventeenth century by King Osei Tutu I. He was able to do this with the help of the Fetish Priest Okomfo Anokye. Tradition has also said that Okomfo Anokye conjured up the famous Golden Stool which fell from the sky and landed on the lap of King Osei Tutu, the first King of the Ashantis.

The Fetish Priest declared that the soul of the new Kingdom resided in the stool and the people must preserve and respect it.

The Ashanti people believe they will remain a united people as long as they retain possession of the Golden Stool.

It quickly became the supreme symbol of the sovereignty and independence of the Ashanti people." – (Ibid.)

It is also one of the symbols of Ghana's identity as a nation of strong cultural traditions.

Fante

The Fante are the second-largest group among the Akan after the Ashanti.

Like the Ashanti, they highly value their culture and traditions and have maintained their identity with pride in spite of external influence and modernisation whose effects have had a profound impact on many traditional societies not just in Ghana but across Africa.

The Fante are indigenous to the southwestern coastal part of Ghana but also live in neighbouring Ivory Coast.

The largest city in Fante territory in Ghana is Cape Coast. Its traditional centre is Mankessim which embodies the spiritual and historical identity of a people who migrated from the northwestern part of Ashantiland – what is now Brong Ahafo Region – to the Central Region. The town of Mankessim has a rich cultural heritage and a large market that is known throughout Ghana, attracting non-Fantes as well, although it is very much a part of Fante identity.

Like the Ashanti, the Fante are also matrilineal, a common feature among the Akan peoples. Although they are related, there was rivalry between the two, and the Fante resisted Ashanti encroachment and domination through the years before the advent of colonial rule which led to the establishment of the Gold Coast as a British possession. And they still retain their identity as a distinct ethnic group.

Their language, Fante, is the main language of the Central Region where they are the predominant group. It is also spoken in the Western Region and is one of the two main Akan languages together with Twi. It is very similar to Twi. It is spoken not only by millions of people in the southwestern part of Ghana and in the southeastern part of the Ivory Coast but also also in Togo.

One of the main characteristics of the native Fante speakers is the tendency to incorporate English words into their language and even anglicise some of the Fante words; a tendency that has drawn criticism from some people who say such a practice weakens and even erodes the language. Others contend that the adaptability of the language demonstrates it has withstood the test of time and even encourages native Fante speakers to learn English which is vital for communication in the global arena because it is the main international language.

The culture of the Fante is similar to those of other Akan groups and even other Ghanaians. Although they are mostly matrilineal, they are also patrilineal, and a close-knit society down to the family unit:

"Rural Fante occupy compounds consisting of rooms around a walled courtyard. Households may consist of kin groups related through either male or female descent; it is common for a husband and wife to continue living in separate homes after marriage.

The Fante have a dual lineage system.

Matrilineal descent determines membership in clans and their localized segments. Every lineage has a ceremonial stool in which reside important ancestral spirits, whose worship is a prominent feature of Fante religion.

Patrilineal descent governs the inheritance of spiritual attributes and also determines membership in the *asafo*, a military organization. Allegiance to the *asafo* takes precedence over that to the matrilineage.

The functions of the *asafo* are political (as the medium through which commoners express political sentiment and criticism of the chief), social (formerly as a cooperative labour unit and as guardian of the rights of its members), religious (in funerals and state ceremonies), and military (as the primary defensive unit of the state).

The head of each Fante state is the paramount chief, chosen from the royal lineage. Under him are divisional chiefs and subchiefs. The chiefs and representatives of the *asafo* function as advisers to the paramount chief.

The Fante states never united under a single chief; each remained autonomous and formed alliances only in times of war." – (Fante people, *Encyclopaedia Britannica*, 2017).

It was decentralisation of power which served many traditional societies across the continent very well before the imposition of colonial rule which led to concentration of power at the centre; a system that continued even during the post-colonial era in which almost all African countries had and still have highly centralised states with power concentrated in the hands of only a few people in the nation's capitals.

The Fante political system under which the leaders were accountable to the people was democratic even in its crudest or most elementary form. The people had the power to remove their leaders and replace them.

It is a system, like others elsewhere in traditional Africa where power was decentralised, that can serve as model for the modern post-colonial state to involve the people in the decision-making process all the way down to the grassroots level.

The Fante are also remembered in Ghanaian history for the role they played as middlemen between the British – as well as other Europeans – and the Ashanti in the trade in gold, slaves and other merchandise. Their early and long contacts with Europeans, because of their location as coastal people, also led to racial intermarriage between them. Some of the biracial men and women became prominent members of the Fante community.

In modern times, one of the most distinguished Fantes – in fact in the history of Ghana – is Kofi Annan who served as the first black African secretary-general of the United Nations. His father was half-Ashanti and half-Fante, and his mother was a Fante. But because the Fante trace their ancestry on the basis of matrilineal descent, as the Ashanti do, he was a Fante. He also came from one of the most prominent Fante families in Ghanaian history. As Marcus F. Franda states in his book, *The United Nations in The Twenty-First Century: Management and Reform Processes in a Troubled Organization*:

"Kofi Atta Annan...is the son of a prominent and wealthy family of hereditary paramount chiefs of the Fante people of Ghana. His father, Henry Reginald Annan (1904 – 1995), was half Asante and half Fante, his mother, Rose, was Fante....

Annan's family has been part of the country's elite for many generations, and in his immediate family, his grandfathers and an uncle were all tribal chiefs....

The Fante...acquired considerable international wealth before and during the British colonial period through trade, including trade in slaves and guns as well as gold.

The extent to which Annan's immediate family was involved in the slave and arms trade is a matter of dispute. Kofi's father worked for many years as an export manager for the Lever Brothers Cocoa Company, and upon his retirement was induced to enter politics, winning election as governor of the Ashanti province in the southern coastal region of the British colony of the Gold Coast.

Kofi – the word means 'Friday's child' – was born a twin in Kumasi...on April 8, 1938. His twin sister, Efua, died in 1991. Kofi grew up in a household where his father would hold mock court sessions after dinner in which he would 'try' his children for their misdeeds, testing how they would comport themselves and present their 'case.'

Kofi's elder sister recalls that the future (UN) secretary-general was a stalwart in these sessions, never hesitating and often collapsing the proceedings with a well-timed joke.

Kofi was taught by his father to have the bearing and manners of African aristocracy." – (Marcus F. Franda, *The United Nations in The Twenty-First Century: Management and Reform Processes in a Troubled Organization*, Lanham, Maryland, USA: Rowman & Littlefield Publishers, 2006, p. 73).

In spite of their early contact with Europeans and close business ties with them, members of Kofi Annan's family were proud of their identity as Fantes and as Africans. As Kofi Annan himself stated in his book, *Interventions: A*

Life in War and Peace:

"My father, Henry Reginald Annan, was not a rebel by nature. A Ghanaian executive of a European trading company, a Freemason, and a devout Anglican in a culture of tribes and ancestral worship, a hereditary chief in a time of radical change, he was not one to make a point. And yet he gave each of his children African names, a signal departure for a man of his background and position in the Gold Coast of the 1930s and 1940s.

To him there was no contradiction in being African in identity and European in outlook, a nationalist as well as a traditionalist, a proponent of political change and an upholder of those values of respect, dignity, discipline, and hard work that had sustained his own life and career. But by naming his five children Nana Essie, Essie, Kofi Atta, Efua Atta, and Kobina, he made an unmistakable wager on behalf of a proud and independent African future for his children.

To H.R., as he was known to friends and associates, crossing over – and back again – was inherent to his life, heritage, and political outlook. H.R. refused to choose – between radical change and the status quo, traditional and modern, tribal and national, Fante and Ashanti, African and European. Instead, he insisted that the only sustainable kind of change toward self-government was one that would honor the proud heritage of Ghana's people and ensure a balanced society able to stand on its own feet and make of independence a success. He managed to be both a pillar of society and a builder of multiple constituencies across tribe, class, and profession." – (Kofi Annan, *A Life in War and Peace*, op. cit., pp. 15 – 16).

He went on state:

"A business executive who who went to work in a dark suit and broken collar everyday alongside European

116

managers, he was also a traditionalist in his home, with his base being my grandmother's extended family in Kumasi. In a society where people identified closely with tribe and village, he was himself a product of a marriage between a Fante and an Ashanti, and among his wives were both Fante and Ashanti women. H.R. had four wives who bore him five children, including my twin sister, Efua, and myself.

My father worked as an executive of the United Africa Company, a subsidiary of Lever Brothers, the Anglo-Dutch multinational corporation that later became known globally as Unilever. His job kept us moving from city to city, town to town, throughout my childhood – from Kumasi to Accra and Bekwai, from Korfodua to Nsawan and Nkakaw – and in this shisfting panorama of home and belonging, no part of Ghana was foreign to us.

My own mother, Rose, lived in Cape Coast with my half-sister, Ewura Efua. My twin sister, Efua Atta, and I saw very little of her growing up, until we went to boarding school in Cape Coast in our early teens. Instead, a vital constant throughout this nomadic period was the family home in Kumasi to which we would always return, meeting with three generations of aunts and uncles.

At the many precarious moments of childhood, there would always be somebody to go to for guidance and love, when the subtle messages of traditional proverbs would be used. 'You don't hit somebody on the head when you have your fingers between his teeth' was one such proverb, a concept that reminded us that even when in dispute we remain bound to each other.

Everyday would bring a new face, a different language or tribal tradition into our home, and teach us a life lesson about the richness of the mix and mash of cultures and peoples. As a consequence, we were raised nontribal in a tribal society, political moderates in an era of radical activism, conciliators in a time of choosing sides.

This was the Gold Coast in the late 1930s and 1940s

117

where a small British colony in West Africa became consumed with the prospect of independence. Growing up in the twilight years of the Gold Coast – destined to become the first independent country in sub-Saharan Africa and to be renamed Ghana – was to experience a complete change in culture and society. By the time I was ten, in 1948, the independence movement was in full force, and as I came of age, so did Ghana as a free republic, in the vanguard of an African emancipation that would bring sixteen new African nations into the United Nations within two short years.

For Ghanaians, these were days of extraordinary hope and promise, the expectation that Africa was about to take off, and that we finally had an opportunity to create for ourselves all that we had accused the colonial power of denying us." – (Ibid., pp. 16 – 17).

It was the dawn of a new era for the entire continent.

The life story of Kofi Annan, a Fante, demonstrates that it is possible, and imperative, to transcend ethnic loyalties and differences for the sake of national unity. It has nothing to do with destroying your identity as a member of an ethnic group – Fante, Ashanti, Ga, Nzema, Ewe or whatever.

Among all the members of the indigenous groups, the Fante are also some of the most Westernised people in West Africa and on the entire continent because of their early contact with Europeans since the 1600s; a status that has played a role in the detribalisation of many members of this ethnic group who are equally proud of their ethnic, cultural and national identity as Ghanaians.

Akyem

The Akyem live mostly in the Eastern Region. They are matrilineal, a practice they share with other Akan groups.

And like the Fante, they fought to retain their independence and identity against encroachment by the Ashanti.

Kwame Okoampa-Ahoofe, whose highly controversial views include his hostility towards Dr. Kwame Nkrumah, stated on GhanaWeb that "the Akyem are also perhaps the only major Akan group that did not actively participate in the Trans-Atlantic Slavery; the colonial history of Ghana, the erstwhile Gold Coast, was not simply a rivalry between Asantes and Fantes over trade with Western Europeans. It is, indeed, not for no reason that today the Okyenhene is the only monarch in Ghana indisputably regarded as the co-equal of the Asantehene....The Akyem of the Eastern Region, headquartered at Kyebi (Kibi), were the most potent force that countervailed Asante imperialism."

The Akyem and the Eastern Region also stand out in one significant way in the history of Ghana. No other region can match their record in that respect. The largest number of the most prominent national leaders who campaigned for independence were Akyem.

They were Dr. Joseph Boakye Danquah, Ebenezer Ako Adjei, Edward Akufo Addo, and William Ofori Atta. And they all came from the Eastern Region. Together with Kwame Nkrumah and Emmanuel Obetsebi Lamptey, they constituted a group that came to be known as The Big Six and are acknowledged as the founding fathers of modern Ghana.

The Akyem have fundamental cultural similarities with other Akan groups including their conception of God, although with some variations and even differences in a number of areas. As Elias Yussif states in his book, *The Facet of Black Culture*:

"The spiritual, physical and philosophical sustenance of the Akyem people are derived from River Birim. While we do not worship the river *per se*, we do revere it as our

119

source of inspiration, (it) gives us life and strength, because the Akyems do not lack water or food in (their) existence.

The Akyem people use this to thank the creator (God) for blessing the land with such a magnificent river. The products from the land and the river become symbols for their thanksgiving whereby their ancestors are remembered for their struggles and perseverance to keep the society intact.

The descendants also pledge to continue the tradition – to keep Okyeman strong and free with peace and prosperity. They also pledge allegiance to the king (Okyehene) and his sub-chiefs and elders for their leadership and guidance.

The Ohun festival is celebrated in two parts: the Ohumkan and the Ohumkyire." – (Elias Yussif, *The Facet of Black Culture*, *Volume 1*, Bloomington, Indiana, USA, and Victoria, British Columbia, Canada: Trafford Publishing, 2013, p. 128).

The Akyem also stand out in the history of Ghana for being one of the first Akan groups to migrate south where they finally established permanent settlements.

Migration has been an integral part of the history of Africans across the continent. Oral tradition of almost all the ethnic groups includes tales of conquest and suffering, trials and tribulations, on the long journeys they made from their original homelands to where they finally settled after decades of traversing vast expanses of territory.

In the case of the Akyem, their origin – of other Akan greoyps as well – is north of present-day Ghana. According to the Okyeman Association of the Akyem people:

"Okyeman is a traditional area in the Eastern Region of Ghana. Historically, it has been attested that the Akyems were one of the first Akan tribes to migrate southwards

120

after the fall of the ancient Songhai Empire.

The Akyem states, commonly known as Akyem Mansa, consist of three main independent states, all grouped in the Eastern Region, with a common language, culture, customs and historical background.

The states are Akyem Abuakwa, the largest in terms of land, size, population and natural resources; Akyem Kotoku, the second largest; and Akyem Bosome, the smallest....

Akyem Abuakwa, like all Akan nation-states and tribes, inherit property and stools through their maternal clan, except where a personal will, affecting the person's personally acquired property, has been made in the presence of his family and a form of customary rites have been performed, before such a will is accepted as valid by the family. The practice excludes stools in any form in the Akan states.

The clan which has ruled and continues to rule in both Akyem Abuakwa and Akwapim paramountcy is the Asona clan of the ancestry of Nana Kuntunkununku I, Odiahene Kan (first king) of Akyem Abuakwa.

The Odwira festival is celebrated yearly in December or early January. The Odwira (purification) is a very important festival during which the whole state, symbolized by the stools, is purified of all its evils. The first stool to be purified is the Great Paramount Stool followed by the other stools, one after the other, until all the stools in the state have been purified.

In Akyem Abuakwa, the Okyeman Council has decided that the celebration of Odwira Kese should be at intervals of 5 or 10 years as the Paramount Stool and the Okyeman Council may decide. However, the Okuapimhene and the Amanokromhene, who took the Odwira festival to Akwapim, celebrate it annually in Akwapim with the Okyenhene or his representative attending.

Every year, unless decided by the Okyenhene and the Okyeman Council to celebrate it as Odwira Kese, the

121

festival is celebrated as an ordinary (Mpaegum) one with no fanfare. However, when it is declared as an Odwira Kese, all the chiefs in Akyem Abuakwa in their respective positions and paraphernalia, including the Okuapimhene and the Amanokromhene, are invited to attend the festival and pay homage to the Paramount Stool at Kyebi.

The term "Odwira" means purification of the state at the end of the Akan calendar year. During the celebration, digging and farming are prohibited. The celebration takes a week with various activities taking place each day, and on the final day, the Okyenhene sits in state to receive homage from his chiefs and people, as well as from firms and organizations in and outside Akyem Abuakwa state.

The Akyems give thanks to God for the blessed land with natural resources. There is a time of the year where the toil of the ancestors is remembered to make the Akyem land what it is. The festival celebrating this is the Ohum Festival. The Ohum festival is celebrated in Akyem Abuakwa in two parts: the Ohumkan and the Ohumkyire. They also pledge allegiance to their chief."

In spite of the impact of modernisation on their society, the Akyem are some of the most proud people on the continent who cherish their heritage and culture without compromising its essence. As Dr. Charlotte Kyerewaa Anokwa, an Akyem, stated in her book, *Hearing and Keeping – Remembering My Matrilineal Roots*:

"From the time I could engage adults in conversation – which was early for me – I had at least three homes. My immediate home was primary, but I knew I also had homes at Kyebi with Mepanyin and at Wirenkyiren with Papa's family.

People's culture sums up what the people truly are, what institutions guide their daily living, their language arts and craft, their foods, clothing, how they raise children, their thoughts on life, death and inheritance.

122

Growing up in my village and other parts of *Akyem Abuakwa*, I learned, first hand, the role that *Akyem* culture played in the normal life of the people. I could only do justice to the immense knowledge and learning that occurred, as I was growing up by sharing them as I experienced them daily." – (Charlotte Anokwa, *Hearing and Keeping – Remembering My Matrilineal Roots*, New York: iUniverse, Inc., 2006).

She went on to elaborate on her strong family ties and the cultural environment she was brought up in and which shaped her life as an Akyem:

"Papa was born and named Kwaku Ofosu in 1895 at Wirenkyiren. His father was Opanyin Kwaku Yeboa and his mother, Maame Kwaabea. He had one older brother, Opanyin Baa, and a younger sister, Maame Obeyaa. Later, when his mother remarried Opanyin Kwaku Dente, his other younger sister, Akua Hemaa and brother, Yaw Owusu, were born. He was the only one of his siblings that went to school, became a true '*krakye*' (educated male) and a Christian clergyman that his family and village kinsmen and kinswomen were very proud of....

(He) was quiet, a strict disciplinarian, yet spending about the same amount of time in his study as with his children. Not only was he a committed husband to Mama, he was a teacher and mentor. He loved children; he loved people in general. He would bring home to us unknown children from other villages so they could go to school under his supervision.

I remember he read a lot and was very time-conscious. So time-conscious was he that from time to time when he had quiet time with individual children he would draw their attention to the ticking of the clock with the reminder of how every second lost is never to be recovered – the moral being beware of procrastination!

He used this analogy regarding life: It is like traveling

123

in a group. If a member misses the right turn, it would be a lot harder for him or her to catch up with the others. Again, the moral was: some mistakes can cost dearly.

He was always dressed in suspended loose trousers with a long-sleeve shirt and full shoes, as the Mission expected of the clergy at the time. It was as though acceptance of the new faith came with disassociating oneself from one's traditions. Unlike many of his colleagues, in informal situations where the traditional cloth could be won, Papa never did."– (Ibid.).

She went on to state:

"Growing up, I was forever wondering how a '*krakye*' of Papa's type knew so much about the forests, the trees, bushes, roots, herbs and animals and even traps. As I learned later these were the survival techniques he learned from his parents and uncles. Before he entered the western-oriented world of the Christian mission he lived with his maternal uncles for a long time, and considered himself as having been raised by them. In a matrilineal heritage, it was not uncommon to have brothers helping to raise the children of sisters, because a man's sisters' children are like his own. It is through them that we fill the extended family house with youth...." (Ibid.).

One of the most prominent features of traditional societies across Africa is the extended family which is also an integral part of communal living, linking families with other families – including extended families – to form a stable, close-knit community whose members are interdependent. The Akyem are no exception.

What Charlotte Anokwa wrote about her people and her family, as caring members of the community who also cherish their heritage and culture, is common not only among the Akans but among other Ghanaians and other people all the way from West Africa to East and Central

Africa and Southern Africa.

She went on to explain other aspects of the Akyem culture and how her people define "family" when she wrote about her father's sister in the following terms:

"His sister from his mother's side, Obeyaa, must have died early in life since none of us heard much about her, but we did hear a lot about Akua Ohemaa and two sisters from his father's side, Amma Donko and Amma Otiwaa, even though they were actually his cousins. He loved them all dearly and we accordingly used he title *Mesewaa*, meaning my female father or my father's sister for all three of them. It was clear, as I was growing up, that there was no distinction between cousins and siblings, whether they had the same father or mother as he did.

So strong was the love between them that when Papa got married, two of them – Mesewaa Amma Donko and Mesewaa Amma Otiwaa – left all they were involved in and their own households to serve the newly-weds as 'househelpers' for three months. They wanted their brother's wife to have a stress-free start to the marriage! It did not stop there. They allowed their only son, Kwabena Bright, to be raised by Papa. It was an indication of how much they respected him. He was a role model and a mentor."

The strong ties family members have and the reverence they have for their culture is also demonstrated by the way they are named and whom they are named after; a practice common not only among the Akyem but among the members of other groups as well, not only in Ghana but in other parts of Africa. As Anokwa stated:

"There is every indication that Papa's family was closely-knit, judging from the way we, his children were named.
The eldest, my sister, Ellen Adwoa Kwaabea (Kyei),

125

was named after his mother; my brother, Fred Kwaku Yeboa (Okuro), after his father; my sister, Mary Abena Ayewa (Dankwaa, Afigyaase), after a female kin on his father's side; my brother, Clement Kwasi Danso (Abeam), after his maternal uncle; my sister, Theodocia Akosua Oforiwaa (Amamfo), after another maternal uncle; my brother, Eugene Kofi Amaning (Okumsika), after yet another maternal uncle. Hence my youngest brother is named Henry Richard Kwabena Ofosu (Kwabi, Adanwona).

As tradition demands, for me, his last child, my mother was humble enough to ask that I be named after her mother who, in Papa's eyes, was very deserving of the honour. And so I became Charlotte Lydia Amma Kyerewaa (Osiaboo, Awurukuo, Ampadukyere).

The Western names that each of us was given were also carefully chosen, as I later discovered, because Papa had a book of names with their meanings which became his reference when he had an addition to his family." – (Ibid.).

She further stated:

"As an adult I have had the opportunity to travel and see other lands and people and how they live. The one topic, which frequently comes up, is people's names. I learned that there surely is something in a name. For the *Akyems* and, indeed, all Akans, the day on which one was born is very important. It is a given and specific to one's gender. And then on the eighth day, at a naming ceremony, given names are announced and formalized. Equally important are the appellations that came with each given name.

In the names given above, these are indicated in brackets. Each simply gives further meaning to the name and reminds one of the virtues that those with that name stand for. Each time I hear mine, Osiaboo, Ampadukyere, it had a way of lifting my spirits.

126

I became even more interested in my name when an elder and a well-respected *krakye* at Kyebi further explained Akan naming and names as well as their importance. He explained, for example, the addition of 'a' or 'aa' to names to give feminine names like Okyere (masculine) and Kyerewaa (feminine) and paying special attention to the literal meaning of the names (*Osiaboo* – the one who stones, meaning strength)." – (Ibid.).

She also shed some light on the culture of the Akyem and some of the things she learned when she stayed with her mother after her father died, including natural cures and respect for nature, all central to the traditional way of life not only of the Akyem but of other Akans as well:

"My mother was born as Akosua Ntiriwaa, the second daughter to Opanyin Kwabena Oware and Maame Akosua Kyerewaa. She and her older sister, Menni Yaa Kwaamaa, lost their father early and were, in effect, raised by their stepfather, Agya Akomaning, before their only sibling and brother, Wofa Akomaning Asante, was born.....

Kyebi lies a few miles north of Wirenkiyiren and is Mama's hometown....As a family, we all ended up in Kyebi after Papa's retirement and death....

Literacy in the Twi language was as highly regarded as literacy in English. The *Akyems*, through local educational programs, had a well-developed written language....

We could tell from far away when our gang was already in the river, playing. I remember that the adults would warn us not to stay in the river for too long because it would make us sick. Perhaps the intense sunlight was the culprit, but we never really paid much attention to such warnings.

For our scorched skin we used the spitum from chewing palm kernel (*adwe*) or we would pluck lemons from nearby trees and use the juice as body lotion! Another 'bush' remedy we used was the juice of a

127

particular leaf, *afamma*, which we rubbed and squeezed into our ears in order to drain water from our ears when we overdid the swimming! (This plant is close to what is known as golden candle – *Pachystachys lutea* – except that what we used had pale green flower heads with small whitish bracts, not yellow).

Yet another remedy was a special leaf, *kwaseadua*, close to what is known as Angle's Trumpet (*Datura* or *Brugmansia x candida)*, the juice of which could stop bleeding when we got hurt from a bad accident. One of its large leaves, rubbed till soft, was our bandage!...

Generally, as children, we learned to respect all adults. We learned to revere God and praise and thank Him all the time. We learned to honour all living things. We dared not misbehave in the river such as relieving ourselves in the waters or over-fishing because the rivers were all deified. For instance, the river *Birem* had a God-given birthday, just as humans, and was called Abenaa (Tuesday-born female) *Birem*. So, on Tuesdays we were extra-careful in the river.

We learned to treat the trees respectfully as a way of getting them to give us their best. The forests, rivers and other things around us were used to put the fear of the Lord in us.

I remember one time my cousin, Kwabena Brako, brought home some poor newly-hatched birds. My uncle marched him off to put them back where he found them, saying, 'How would you feel if you were taken away from your mother?'

The two of them did not get back from the bush until quite late at night.

There is also the story of *'Kyekyere me ti ma me'* (Braid my hair). It teaches you should never stay in the river or stay nearby when it is dark because there is a ghost – female apparition – that would approach you, asking you to braid her hair."

Anokwa has provided profound insights into some very important aspects of Akyem – Akan – culture. It is a definition of the people and their identity and what makes them stand out among other ethnic groups in Ghana and even among the Akans themselves.

Had the Akyem – and other Akan groups who together constitute about 50 per cent of Ghana's population – not migrated south from the north and settled where they did, the history of what came to be known as Ghana would have been different; for example, there would have bee no Nkrumah or the Big Six. The same applies to all the other ethnic groups whose members migrated from different parts of West Africa and beyond and established themselves in the region that came to be known as the Gold Coast and finally as Ghana.

Akuapem

The Akuapem are Akans like the Ashanti, the Fante, the Akyem and other groups. They live in the Eastern Region in southern Ghana.

Formation of their identity is similar to that of other ethnic groups which absorbed other groups through the years. There are no pure tribes or ethnic groups. None has retained its original identity – "pure" Ashanti, "pure" Fante, "pure" Akuapem, "pure" Igbo, Yoruba, Maasai, Kikuyu, Zulu and rest. They all have absorbed elements from other ethnic groups. And that is the case with the Akuapem:

"The Akuapem people are an amalgamation of indigenous patriarchal, Volta-Camoe-speaking Guans and matriarchal, Kwa-speaking Akan people occupying the mountainous Akuapem Hills in the Eastern Region of Ghana.

(They)...were originally Guan speaking people (who)

include Larteh Guan...namely Larteh, Mamfe, Abotakyi, Mampong, Obosomase, and Tutu and the Kyerepong (Okere) Guan...namely Abiriw, Dawu, Awukugua, Adukrom, Apirede, and Abonse-Asesieso.

The Akan Twi-speaking towns include Akropong, the capital, and Amanokurom who are emigrants from Akyem and Mampong people who are also emigrants from Asante Mampong in Ashanti Region.

The name Akuapem was given to these multi-ethnic group by the famous warrior King, Nana Ansa Sasraku I of Akwamu. The name came from Akan Twi phrase 'Nkuu apem' which means 'thousand groups.' He gave them the name after the people overwhelmed his Akwamu invading army. The name 'Nkuu apem' got corrupted to Akuapem as we know them today." – (Kwekudee, "Akuapem People: Ghana's Ancient Guans and Akans of the Mountains," on "Trip Down Memory Lane," 11 September 2013).

He goes on to state:

"The Akuapem people are heterogeneous....They comprise both Akan and Guan communities.

The Guan Okere (Abiriw, Dawu, Awukugua, Adukrom and Apirede) who occupy the northern parts of Akuapem speak Kyerepong, whereas Late-Ahenease and Larteh-Kubease speak Larteh.

Both Larteh and Kyerepong Guan languages, unlike Akan Kaw language, belong to the larger Volta-Comoe group of languages of the larger Niger-Congo phylum (Dolphyne and Kropp Dakubu 1988: 77-79).

Akan Twi represent 51.6% of the population, 42.3% are of Kyerepong and Guan extraction while only 6.1%% constitutes Ewes, Northerners, Krobos and ethnic groups.

With Akuapem Twi spoken by almost all the residents in the Akuapem mountains, it could be said that the Twi language can be the most effective medium of mass communication and functional education as well as development information dissemination.

To illustrate this diversity further, the people of Abiriw comprise different ethnic origins among which are former Akan including Akwamu, Denkyira and Asante (Gilbert 1997: 511-512).

The Akan in Akuapem who speak Twi are the descendants of the Akyem people who live at Akropong and their relations at Amanokrom.

The people of Aburi are also remnants of Akwamu (Akan) and speak Twi but have intermarried with other ethnic groups.

The other southern Guan towns of Tutu, Obosomase, Mamfe, Mampong, Aseseeso, Abonse and Abotakyi are predominantly Guan with some Akwamu, who have assimilated different ethnic groups including Ewe and Krobo, who all now speak Twi.

There has also been a great deal of inter-marriage with Ga, Shai and former Ewe captives and several others (Gilbert 1997: 504) in the Akuapem towns. This mixed group of people lived in small independent towns ruled by priests until the Akyem arrived and were given the mandate to rule in 1733.

According to Prof. Kwamena-Poh, the recorded history of what is now Akuapem State goes as far back as the 17th century.

By 1646, the Guans who were living on the hill had come under the power of the Akwamus. According to the learned Professor, 'The Akwamu suzerainty witnessed a period of disturbed conditions among the Guan communities: incessant plunder, bad harvests … actions of cruelty.'

The atrocities of the Akwamus heightened to such an extent that it became unbearable. That and other factors became so crucial for the inhabitants to fight for their liberation. An appeal was therefore sent to the King of Akyem Abuakwa...to come and help...He also detailed his nephew, Ofori Dua or Ofori Kae or Ofori Kuma who later won the accolade, Safori, to come and lead them to fight against the oppression and suppression of the Akwamus....The Akwamus were defeated....

Safori and his people were made to live here with the Guans and as the political leaders of the new nation that had come to be known as the 'Akuapems', out of the Twi words, 'Kuw' and 'Apem' meaning, thousand groups." – (Ibid.)

He also states:

"The indigenous inhabitants on the Akuapem Mountains are the Guans...consist(ing) of Larteh (comprising Larteh, Mamfe, Abotakyi, Mampong, Obosomase, and Tutu) and the OKERE or Kyerepong (comprising Abiriw, Dawu, Awukugua, Adukrom, Apirede, Abonse-Asesieso)." – (Ibid.)

As a traditional kingdom, Akuapem today is only a shadow of its past in terms of power even in the realm of traditional authority. That is because traditional kingdoms and other centres of power which existed across Ghana during colonial rule and even in pre-colonial times were abolished by President Nkrumah who established a unitary state.

He felt there was an imperative need to strip traditional rulers of their power in order to create a united nation without competing interests – of local loyalties and allegiances – which would weaken the central government and even split the nation along tribal and regional lines.

He faced formidable opposition from tribalists and regionalists in different parts of the country when he campaigned for independence. As Professor Kwame Botwe-Asamoah states in his book, *Kwame Nkrumah's Politico-Cultural Thought and Policies*: *An African-Centered Paradigm for the Second Phase of the African Revolution*:

"Different kingdoms...were to serve as centers of opposition to and allies of Nkrumah's political policies.

The two Akyem Abuakwa paramount kings, Nana Ofori Atta I and II...were to become mistrusted, collaborators and stooges of the British Colonial Administration (Addo-Fening: 61). Therefore, when Nana Ofori Atta II and his royal family, including Dr. J. B. Danquah, of Kyebi became the strongest opponent to Nkrumah's CPP in the Eastern Province of the Gold Coast, the forces of Akyem Abuakwa, New Juaben, Kwahu, Krobo, and Akyem Kotoku rallied behind Kwame Nkrumah's nationalist agenda. Of particular importance was the Adonten in Akyem Abuakwa, Dr. J.B. Danquah's constituency, which became one of Nkrumah's strongholds in the region.

In Asante, the Asantehene, Nana Agyemang Prempeh II and the Ashanti Confederacy Council, were to form an ethno-regional political party against Nkrumah's unitary form of government in the 1956 general election (just before independence in March 1957). While Nkrumah's CPP was to enjoy strong support among the Ga-Adangbe groups, the Ewes in the Trust territory were also to form an ethnic-based political party in opposition to Nkrumah's CPP. Similarly, a parochial political party was to be built and based among the northern ethnic groups in opposition to Nkrumah's CPP." – (Kwame Botwe-Asamoah, op. cit., p. 93).

Yet traditional rulers and institutions of authority are highly cherished, especially in the traditional context, even if it is just for their symbolic and nostalgic value as symbols of ethnic identity and unity as well as a reminder and reflection of the past, a bygone era when they had real power before the modern unitary state was instituted after independence and centralisation of power became one of the primary goals of the new rulers.

That was the case not only with the Akuapem but with other traditional kingdoms and chiefdoms across Ghana and elsewhere in Africa where post-colonial rulers established highly centralised states. Even in Nigeria where they had a federal system inherited from the British colonial rulers, real power was concentrated in hands of a few people in the federal capital, Lagos, and was not effectively shared with regional governments.

Traditionalists across Africa remember those days with nostalgia when traditional rulers had real power. That is in sharp contrast with modernists and others who celebrate the emasculation and even the destruction of traditional institutions of authority because they see them as an obstacle to national unity and stability. You find both – modernists and traditionalists – in traditional societies across the continent including Akuapem.

Yet, in spite of all that, vestiges of power – however limited – including powerful symbolism reflected by traditional institutions of authority exist in some societies in Africa. Akuapem is one of them. As Professor Cati Coe of Rutgers University, USA, states in "Pedagogies and Politics of 'Culture': Chiefly Authority, the State, and the Teaching of Cultural Traditions in Ghana":

"The interaction of the traditional kingdom of Akuapem with the state began in the 1890s, as the British colonial administration became more powerful after the defeat of the Asante Empire in 1896, and colonial administrators were heavily involved in mediating chieftaincy disputes.

To this day, the modern nation-state coexists and overlays a traditional kingdom in which the 17 towns of Akuapem are organized into a hierarchical arrangement based on military formations, speaking to the importance of warfare in the past (Kwame-Poh 1973).

Although chieftaincy has lost its political power gradually since the beginning of the twentieth century, chiefs retain control over the sale of land and continue to be respected as 'custodians of culture' and spiritually powerful. They are not an independent authority set apart from the state. Rather, they are subject to the state's overtures and appropriations.

The national government of Ghana has consistently sought to use chieftaincy to cement its local legitimacy, at the same time as chiefs have sought legitimacy by bringing development funds to their regions (Dunn and Robertson 1973)." – (Cati Coe, "Pedagogies and Politics of 'Culture': Chiefly Authority, the State, and the Teaching of Cultural Traditions in Ghana," in E. Thomas Ewing, ed., *Revolution and Pedagogy: Interdisciplinary and Transnational Perspectives on Educational Foundations*, New York: Palgrave Macmillan, 2005, p. 91).

It is a reciprocal arrangement for mutual benefit, enabling both sides to benefit from the relationship between the traditional rulers and the national government.

But while it gives legitimacy to traditional authorities, although only for their symbolic value since they don't have real power anymore under the modern state, the government tries to tip scales in its favour by exploiting differences and rivalries among the local rulers. This has happened in Akuapem and elsewhere in Ghana through the years.

Modernisation – including education – has also played a big role in weakening traditional institutions of authority. It has also made the traditional way of life less attractive even to the rulers themselves who prefer to live in towns and cities away from the rural areas and traditional environment.

Cati Coe, who lived in Akropong, Akuapem, for one year from August 1998 to August 1999 and also visited the place for five weeks during the summer of 2002, goes on to state:

"Chieftaincy in Ghana is intensely factional, which the government exploits, supporting one chiefly candidate over another, at the same as it deplores the fissuring of traditional states – including Akuapem in the 1990s (Gilbert 1997) – as causing instability.

Most chiefs in Akuapem are members of the elite and professional class and live in the urban centers of Koforidua and Accra, returning on weekends for festivals and funerals. These are some of the ways that royal families attempt to use their educated members, whose money and influence give them access to the state, to promote the fortunes of their families and town.

The position of chiefs illustrates a point that is also true of the larger population in Akuapem; although people's loyalties and identifications revolve around their towns, rather than the traditional kingdom or the nation, Akuapem is dependent on its connections outside, to both rural and urban areas.

People in Akuapem wait for money from relatives working in in the cities of Accra, Tema, and Koforidua and are dependent on food from the valleys to the west or from food-producing areas even farther away.

It is caught in the middle of the urban-rural divide in Ghana, with the eyes of its youth turned to the cities and the old people remembering the ways of a hunting and farming life." – (Ibid., pp. 91 – 92).

As custodians of culture, traditional rulers play a very important role in the lives of the Akuapem people. Their culture is central to their life, as is the case among the members of other ethnic groups in Ghana and elsewhere in Africa; although some of them emphasise the importance of culture more than others do.

The Akuapem are among those who highly value their culture which includes festivals, rituals, artifacts symbolising very important aspects of life, customs and traditions which, altogether, give them a distinct identity as a people:

"A popular phrase refers to chiefs as the 'custodians of culture.' The chiefs, aided by the knowledge of their elders, are the ones who perform the rites that maintain good relationships with the spirits and ancestors of the town and family, one behalf of the whole community. Kwame Ampene, a retired teacher of Akan language and music, articulated this most clearly:

'The chiefs are custodians of our culture and the very embodiment of our customs and culture. They have retained our heritage from the ancestors. Ancestors founded the particular land, and they have to see the land is properly maintained and ruled, and the taboos kept, festivals observed, and to see that development is going on. (Ampene interview, March 3, 1999).'

The most powerful and sacred knowledge behind these rituals and festivals is considered secret. Just as chiefs are protected from the profane world by the mediation of their spokesmen (Yankah, 1995), so too are powerful objects and events kept hidden and protected by indirection. Even individual elders hold knowledge about different parts of a larger ritual, with few knowing the whole sequence of rites (Asiedu Yirenkyi, interview, March 26, 1999).

The secrecy of chiefly activities is accompanied by an aura of fear; many Akuapem people not connected to to royal families told me that they were too scared to go to the chief's court, telling me that they were afraid of making a mistake in etiquette. In the past, one might be executed for such an offense.

The secret nature of this knowledge is noted by authors in books that make cultural knowledge public. In a popular book documenting the various festivals of Ghana, A.A. Opoku wrote in the preface that it is difficult to give acknowledgments 'in a book dealing with what is sacred

137

and to some extent, secret in our cultural heritage' (Opoku 1970). In a review of two books documenting different Akan festivals, I.E. Boama wrote:

'Two Twi festivals which every Akan should try to watch are Adae and Odwira. But there are many people who even if they have seen these festivals, they have seen only a part. For only insiders have permission to see the true activities....If you are a child of a traditional state, buy these books to read, and once you know your nation's secrets, you won't avoid these festivals out of fear. (Boama, 1954, p. 12)'

Cultural knowledge, at its deepest or most true, is thus considered hidden and not accessible to outsiders; books documenting them violated that secrecy by describing rituals to non-royals and youth.

The secrecy of certain historical and cultural knowledge allows powerful elders to manipulate important decisions regarding property rights and political positions, which are entwined with family genealogy and local history. As William Murphy (1980) points out about secret knowledge in Liberia, the content of the hidden knowledge does not matter as much as the privileged society (in this case, of elders) the secrecy creates." – (Ibid. p. 93).

Elders are highly respected in the Akuapem society, not only because of the knowledge they have about the culture of their people; they are also revered simply because of their status *as elders* who deserve respect and who must be respected regardless of how much you disagree with them. It is the kind of respect elders are accorded in all traditional societies across Africa.

You are not going to find one traditional society, even in modern towns and cities, where young people do not respect older people even if they don't know them. If you find boys and girls who don't respect their elders, people

138

will tell you they were not properly reared or there is something wrong with them.

That is one of the big differences between Africans and Westerners. For example, it is not uncommon to hear American children tell their mother, "Don't be silly," "Shut up," or show disrespect in some other way. They may say they are just playing. And even some American parents – not all – may dismiss that as nothing. That's for them. There are things you just don't say to your parents or elders. They may be tolerated in Western societies but not in Africa – not in Akuapem, not in Ashantiland or in any other part of Ghana or anywhere else on the continent.

That's just out of the question.

In spite of the pride the people of Akuapem have for their culture and identity, their history also shows that they have been receptive to external influence in a way some groups in Ghana have not. They accepted Christianity and European form of education long before other people did. Yet they did not lose their culture, although such acceptance could have been interpreted as an abandonment of their traditional way of life.

Even their towns reflect adaptation to modernisation, although that is not unique to Akuapem. Other parts of Ghana have adapted to new ways of life in varying degrees.

It is an adaptation that has been demonstrated at the national level by the Japanese.

The Japanese did not hesitate to learn from the West. They absorbed all they could in terms of education, especially science and technology. Yet they did not compromise their identity or abandon their culture. Even the Japanese language is used in all areas of life. It is also the medium of instruction in institutions of higher learning.

They may be Westernised in terms of education but they have remained Japanese.

The capital of the Eastern Region where the Akuapem

and members of other ethnic groups – including other Akans as well as the Ga-Dangme, the Ewe, and the Guan – live also reflects modernisation in an area with a rich cultural heritage. The people have retained their ethnic identities and are proud of their heritage as Africans.

Other Akan groups which are smaller but no less important have their own attributes although their cultures are similar because they are an integral part of the Akan "nation."

The Kwahu, who live in the Eastern Region, share territory with the Akyem, the Adangbe-Krobo (who are also Akan) and with the Ewe who migrated to the region and are known for their fishing skills. The Kwahu are Ashanti in terms of origin but assumed their own identity after they broke away and went on to settle in their own area which also became the home of other Akans including the Akyem and other migrants from Ashanti.

The Wassa, whose homeland is one of the largest producers of gold in Ghana, are the only people in the Western Region who speak Twi as their native language. They are also the largest ethnic group in the region and occupy the largest area. Their land is equal to the entire Central Region in terms of square miles.

The Nzema who, like the Ahanta, were once a part of the Denkyira kingdom and then Ashanti, stand out in Ghana in one respect. The first president of Ghana and one of the most illustrious leaders Africa has ever produced, Kwame Nkrumah, was a Nzema.

Also, one of the leading philosophers in Germany in the 1700s, Anton Wilhelm Amo, was a Nzema. He was taken to Europe when he was only about four years old and later returned to his native land where he spent the rest of life and was buried there. He was the first African to attend a European university.

The Nzema also live in the Ivory Coast where they are known as Appolo. In fact, there is a rumour that has circulated for decades that Nkrumah's father came from the Ivory Coast. It may be true. Members of his ethnic group straddle the Ghanaian-Ivorian border, although that does not prove his father came from across the border. What may give the rumour credence is the credibility of the people in his home district who knew his family and said his father came from the Ivory Coast.

The Nzema are also known for their traditional calendar of seven days. And like other Akans, they are matrilineal. Their traditional festival, Kundum, which they share with the Ahanta, starts in the easternmost part of the Ahanta territory and then gradually moves southwest to coincide with the harvest period. It goes on for about four weeks.

There are other Akan groups which are no less important than the ones covered here. Suffice it to say they are all Akan but with differences among them. As Albin Akasanke states in his book, *Who Is the First-Class Ghanaian?: A Story of Tribalism, Religion and Sectionalism in Ghana and the Way Forward*:

"I moved to Birem in the Ashanti Region to attend my primary six there. In Birem I came to realize that ethnocentrism does not only exist for the Akans and for the northerners, but that also between the Akans themselves are in existence the beliefs of certain groups in their superiority.

The Akan itself is a large tribe made up of the Ashanti people, the Fantes, the Akuapem, the Bono people, the Ahafo people, the Nzema people, the Akyem, and many more. Although these Akan tribes have similar cultures and almost a similar language, there are still numerous differences that exist between them. Tribal comments levelled against one another are not only between the Akans and the northern tribes but between the Akans themselves, with each tribe claiming superiority over the others.

When it comes to electing a national leader, each tribe

would also like to have a representation, which is practically impossible, and is something that always causes great political tensions, although Ghana is considered to be the beacon of Africa's democracy." – (Albin Akasanke, *Who Is the First-Class Ghanaian?: A Story of Tribalism, Religion and Sectionalism in Ghana and the Way Forward* , Bloomington, Indiana, USA: iUniverse, Inc., 2013, p. 8).

He also explains why he wrote the book:

"My intention to produce this book came up first when I ran for the post of local National Union of Ghana Students (NUGS) secretary at the University for Development Studies (UDS), Tamale, Ghana, as well as during my subsequent contest for the position of general secretary at the national level.

Numerous issues arose during the campaign, especially at the local level. Although the election is supposed to concern student activism, many people were voting based on which part of the country the contestants came from. I am therefore not surprised when I see some of these tribal loyalties reflected in our national politics....

I hate politics of tribalism and discrimination, and that is exactly the status quo of Ghana....

As a proud northerner and later becoming adopted by my beloved new family of Akan descent, I spent much of my life with two different tribes. I have also spent time in the field as a result student, with rural people in the northern region when I was pursuing my bachelor's degree at the UDS....I believe my experience can take away some small percentage of doubt from folks who are ethnocentric in nature; we all pledge allegiance to one national anthem as Ghanaians, not as northerners or southerners. We should therefore embrace the things that unite us and keep us going as a nation." – (Ibid., pp. vii, ix).

It is a plea by a patriotic Ghanaian to save the nation's soul.

Non-one predicted Ivory Coast would degenerate into chaos, split between predominantly Muslim north and predominantly Christian south. No-one can predict, and be sure, it can never happen in Ghana, not necessarily between the north and the south but in different parts of the country because ethno-regional loyalties and rivalries fuelled by the Machiavellian politics of unscrupulous politicians.

And no-one can honestly say the Akan are the worst offenders and biggest threat to Ghana's territorial integrity. Gone are the days when the Ashanti wanted to have their own country, or an autonomous political entity, in post-colonial Ghana. And gone are the days when northerners harboured the same ambition.

They all have their own differences, among themselves, as Albin Akasanke testifies from experience living with the Akans.

But regardless of the differences Akan groups may have among themselves – and this is only one example – they are all united by a common ancestry which transcends whatever differences exist among them and form a single Akan communal entity which can be called "a nation within a nation" – without undermining the integrity of Ghana as a state and united political entity.

Ewe

The Ewe are the third-largest ethnic group in Ghana after the Ashanti and the Fante. They are also some of the most influential people in Ghana together with the Ashanti and the Fante. But they are not Akan. They have their own distinct identity, cultural and linguistic, as well as historical, which separates them from the Akan ethnic groups.

143

Their influence extends to the diaspora where remnants of Ewe culture, customs and traditions are found among some communities whose members are descendants of slaves taken to the Americas from what is now Ghana.

Most of the Ewe live in Ghana and Togo. But they also straddle the Togolese-Benin border. In Togo, they have close association with the Aja and the Fon.

In Ghana, they live mostly in the southeastern part of the country. They live mostly in the coastal regions of the countries where they are indigenous. They also live in Ivory Coast and in the southwestern part of Nigeria which is home to the Yoruba, one of the three largest ethnic groups in the country together with the Hausa-Fulani and the Igbo.

The Ewe are also found in large numbers in Accra, although they also live in other parts of the country where they have migrated.

They believe in God as the creator. They call the creator Mawu. They also have a large number of deities, or smaller gods, created by Mawu. These deities are believed to have direct influence on the lives of individuals, shaping their destiny. Mawu does not have such direct influence on the daily lives of the people the way smaller gods do. The Ewe believe the smaller gods have the power to cause harm or do favour to individuals. There are more than 600 of them.

They also honour their ancestors and believe in the existence of ancestral spirits.

The drum is a very important part of the spiritual and social life of the Ewe; so is dancing.

There are different kinds of dancing: to celebrate peace and hunting skills, honour ancestors, and mark funerals. Others are for religious purposes and entertainment.

Dancing, being an integral part of their daily life and traditional ceremonies, plays a very important role in strengthening social bonds among individuals and in the community as a whole.

Ewes who live in the northern part of Eweland use flutes and drums instead of singing, while those in the south sing. Yet both demonstrate the strong social bonds which exist among the people.

Social cohesion has always been a very important feature of their traditional way of life as is the case in most traditional societies across the continent. That is why it is very common to hear Africans talking about their extended family and communal living, be they East Africans, West Africans and the rest.

Unlike the Akan, the Ewe are patrilineal. And as in most traditional societies across Africa, land among the Ewe is inherited and is not sold. They consider it to be a gift from the ancestors who must always be honoured.

Traditionally, Ewe society has never been regimented. The people don't like centralised authority, with power concentrated in the hands of only a few people imposing their will on others. This spirit of independence also explains why they don't have group identity that is so strong among many ethnic groups in Ghana and elsewhere in Africa.

But lack of centralised authority has also led to disaster in times of crisis, especially during invasions making it virtually impossible for them to mobilise forces on a large scale and on coordinated basis for defence.

Yet they have also tried to build a common identity based on language and culture that transcends national boundaries and embraces all Ewes living in Ghana, Togo, Benin and even in Nigeria as well as Ivory Coast. But the bonds are tenuous in the case of the Ewe living in Ivory Coast unlike those in Ghana, Togo, Benin and even southwestern Nigeria where the Ewe straddle the borders of those countries.

Their history sheds some light on how they have organised themselves through the years to attain the distinction they have as a splintered entity – of separate, independent communities without centralised authority and institutions to keep them together as a cohesive unit – in spite of their common identity. As Jette Bukh states in her book, *The Village Woman in Ghana*:

"The Ewe-speaking people...were traditionally organized in a semi-segmental tribal society, organizationally very different from their strong centralized neighbours, the Ashantis to the West and the Dahomeans to the East.

The Ewes are supposed to have left the Northern part of Yoruba-land – Nigeria – about 500 years ago. They travelled to their present home in two movements, and stayed for about a hundred years in the middle of Togo-land near the town of Notise (now called Nouatya)....About 75% of them still live within the old Ewe land, today the Southern part of Volta Region in Ghana and Togo.

The Ewe's political organization has been described by Barbara Ward as a 'loose collection of independent sub-tribes,' and the 120 independent political chieftaincies had no common organization to defend their integrity against their militarily strong neighbours. 'The most that they ever attained in the way of concerted action seems to have been in the formation of alliances in times of war.' In contrast to their Akan-speaking enemies, the Ewe had no standing army.

The Ewes became the victims of numerous invasions and in consequence some of the sub-tribes made alliances with the neighbouring tribes during the 18th and 19th century. The Akwamus occupied the area for a hundred years from 1734 – 1833, and in 1868 – 71 the whole area was raided and plundered by Ashanti armies. The sufferings caused by repeated slave-raids stopped only with the final defeat of the Ashantis by the English in 1874....

Though the Ewe sub-tribes had never been one political unit, they perceived themselves as one nation with a

146

common language, history and culture. The colonial division therefore naturally provoked protests from them, and in the 1940's a political movement was formed to fight for the creation of a unified Ewe nation." – (Jette Bukh, *The Village Woman in Ghana*, Uppsala, Sweden: Scandinavian Institute of African Studies, 1996, p. 15, 18).

The fight for the creation of one Ewe nation led to the rise of an irredentist movement among the Ewe in British Togoland – also known as Trans-Volta Togo – seeking unification with their brethren across the border in French Togo which was only diffused by a UN-supervised plebiscite in 1956 in which the majority of the people in the territory voted to become an integral part of the new nation of Ghana – but with the majority of Ewes in the region voting against such integration. As Bukh states:

"A referendum was held in 1956 in the English administered half, Trans-Volta, for the people to decide whether they should join an independent Ghana the following year.
The final result was 61% for and 39% against, but the areas dominated by the Ewes in the South had an average of 58% against, some as high as 72% against (Ho District) and 66% against (Kpandu District).
The colonial governments did not consider the differences in the results and incorporated the whole of Trans-Volta into Ghana. Since then protests have continued in varying degrees demanding that the Ewe-population become unified under the same government." – (Ibid., p. 18).

It was those tendencies – among the Ewe, the Ashanti, the Dagomba and others – to divide the country along ethno-regional lines which made creation of a unitary state and centralisation of power an imperative during the early days of independence under Nkrumah who also survived many assassination attempts. As Lawrence E.K. Lupalo states in his book, *African Political Thinkers of Post-colonial Africa*:

"The plots to assassinate Nkrumah were attributed to his despotic tendencies, ethno-regional rivalries, foreign intrigues by Western governments and intelligence agencies especially of the United States and Britain; and his determination to establish a highly centralised state that was resolutely opposed by the Ashanti who wanted a federal system under which their kingdom would retain its status as a political entity and be recognised as an autonomous unit – Obote faced the same problem from traditional centres of power, especially from the Buganda kingdom, when he decided to establish a unitary state.

Like Nyerere in Tanzania and Obote in Uganda, Nkrumah knew Ghana would be fractured along ethnoregional lines if he did not centralise power under a strong unitary state. The country had well-established traditional institutions of authority which were regionally-entrenched and needed a political party whose nationalist agenda transcended ethno-regional interests.

Nkrumah was able to provide that kind of leadership when he formed the Convention People's Party (CPP) which mobilised the masses during the struggle for independence and became the ruling party after the country emerged from colonial rule. But it also galvanised its opponents – mostly regionalists – into action, determined to undermine Nkrumah in his effort to consolidate power at the centre. As Professor Kwame Botwe-Asamoah states in his book, *Kwame Nkrumah's Politico-Cultural Thought and Policies: An African-Centered Paradigm for the Second Phase of the African Revolution*:

'In Asante, the Asantehene...and the Ashanti Confederacy Council were to form an ethno-regional

148

political party against Nkrumah's unitary form of government in the 1956 general election (just before independence in March 1957). While Nkrumah's CPP was to enjoy strong support among the Ga-Adamge groups, the Ewes in the Trust territory were also to form an ethnic-based political party in opposition to Nkrumah's CPP. Similarly, a parochial political party was to be built and based among the northern ethnic groups in opposition to Nkrumah's CPP.' – (Kwame Botwe-Asamoah, *Kwame Nkrumah's Politico-Cultural Thought and Policies: An African Centered Paradigm for the Second Phase of the African Revolution, New York & London: Routledge, 2005, p. 93).*

As a nationalist, Nkrumah had many enemies to contend with....The military coup against Nkrumah was preceded by a series of assassination attempts on the Ghanaian leader which began as far back as 1955; threats which may explain why he took draconian measures – non-violent – to curb the opposition and protect himself. No leader takes such threats lightly.

The opposition comprised the National Liberation Movement (NLM), the Northern People's Party (NPP) and the United Party (UP)." – (Lawrence E.K. Lupalo, *African Political Thinkers of Post-colonial Africa* , Scotts Valley, California, USA: CreateSpace, 2017, pp. 88 – 89, 91).

Since the end of colonial rule, Ghanaians have been able to resolve their differences – and have even waged battles against each other in the political arena and beyond – in the context of a unitary state with little decentralisation the Ashanti, the Ewe and others tried so hard to achieve; at the very least, they wanted a weak centre with power devolved to the regions.

Although the Ewe are patrilineal, women play a major role in society because of their position as the main traders. This has enabled them to control markets and play

149

a big part in providing for their families. It is a common phenomenon in Ghana and in other parts of West Africa where women are known to be very active in business – in markets of all sizes, selling all kinds of merchandise.

The patrilineal system of the Ewe is socioeconomic, political and religious, and is extensive:

"Villages include several patrilineages, in which land ownership and certain political offices are vested; lineage members also share certain spirits ad gods. The lineage head, usually its oldest member, administers lineage property, settles disputes, represents the lineage in village affairs, and serves as a priest linking the living members to the ancestors.

Among most Ewe patrilineage is the largest important kinship unit; among the Anlo in coastal Ghana, however, the lineages are segments of larger, dispersed clans.

Clan membership is characterized by mutual help and friendliness, shared names, food taboos, and clan rituals. The introduction of a money economy, schools, Christianity, and government courts has weakened the corporate structure of the lineage....

Belief in the supernatural powers of ancestral spirits to aid or harm their descendants enforces patterns of social behaviour and feelings of solidarity among lineage members. In modern times many Ewe have become Christians." – (Ewe people, *Encyclopaedia Britannica*, 2017).

Although the majority of the Ewe are Christian, traditional beliefs are common among them even if such beliefs are against their Christian faith; a phenomenon prevalent in other parts of Ghana and elsewhere on the continent where even some of those who are supposed to be strong Christians still believe in the existence of ancestral spirits who provide them with guidance and interact with the living. The dead are not really dead. They have simply moved into another realm where they continue to live as spirits capable of communicating with the living.

This syncretism has led to the emergence of religious movements in some parts of Africa which defend traditional religions while at the same time embracing Christianity. The two complement each other, thus giving legitimacy to African religious beliefs which are dismissed and denounced by many Christians as satanic.

Modernisation has played a major role in weakening and even in destroying traditional ways of life in Africa. And the replacement of traditional institutions of authority by the modern state – colonial and post-colonial governments – has virtually sealed their fate. The Ewe are some of the people who have been affected by these developments although there is still reverence for traditional leaders, especially chiefs. As Amara Esinna states in "The Ewe People: Ghana Culture in Perspective":

"In modern times, chiefs are generally elected by consensus and get advice from elders.

There are a number of guidelines regarding the behaviour of chiefs. They are expected to keep their heads covered in public, and are not to be seen drinking. The people see the chief as the communicator between the everyday world and the world of the ancestors.

The chief must always keep a clear mind.

Traditionally, chiefs are also not to see the face of a corpse. They may take part in the funeral, however, once the corpse is buried or inside the coffin, (but) they are not to have any contact with the corpse.

Extended families are the most important units of Ewe social life. (The) Ewe ha(ve) never supported a hierarchical concentration of power within a large state." – (Amara Esinna, "The Ewe People: Ghana Culture in Perspective, " *The Guardian*, Lagos, Nigeria, 6 June 2016).

151

The Ewe are also some of the people who have had a major impact on life outside the continent through the centuries. A large number of people of African descent in the Americas, especially in the Caribbean, have Ewe ancestry.

Ga-Adangbe

The Ga-Adangbe is a collection of different groups whose members share a common identity as an ethnolinguistic and cultural entity. But they are distinct groups. In fact, there are at least 12 different subgroups within the Ga-Adangbe community each with its own dialect.

Their fused identity as Ga-Adangbe is similar to that of the Hausa-Fulani of northern Nigeria who are also considered to be "one tribe" or a single ethnic group in spite of the fact that they are different people with different identities but united by a common culture, religion and even history although one of conquest; with the Fulani being the conquerors and rulers of northern Nigeria before the advent of colonial rule.

However, in the case of the Ga and Adangbe, there are scholars who contend that the two ethnic groups have the same origin. As Steven J. Salm and Toyin Falola, both professors in the United States, state in their book, *Culture and Customs of Ghana*:

"The Ga-Adangbes most likely traveled along the coast from Nigeria. Oral tradition tells a story of leaving Yorubaland because of political strife....The Ga language shares some structural similarities with Yoruba, supporting those ties.

Similarities in language, circumcision rites, in the importance of priests in state affairs, and in child naming patterns suggest that the Ga and the Adangbe were originally one group." – (Steven J. Salm and Toyin Falola, *Culture and Customs of Ghana*, Westport, Connecticut, USA: Greenwood Press, 2002, pp. 7 – 8).

Every Ga community has a number of cults and gods as well as several festivals held annually.

The Ga-Adangbe live mostly in three regions: Greater Accra, the Eastern Region, and the Volta Region, stretching inland along the Volta River.

The Ga are dominant in the greater Accra Region. The largest and most important urban centre in the Ga community is the nation's capital itself, Accra. The Adangbe dominate the eastern part of the Ga-Adangbe community in the coastal areas, while the Ga are mostly in the west.

These coastal areas, home to both ethnic groups, are located west of the Volta River:

"The Ga inhabit the stretch of coast from Accra to Prampram, below the Akuapem escarpment, between the Laloi lagoon on the east and the Densu river on the west, in the Greater Accra Region. The Ga are a fishing and farming people organized into seven main towns: James Town, Ussher Town, Osu, La, Teshie, Nungua, and Tema. The oldest parts of Accra, James Town and Ussher Town, are largely Ga neighborhoods, and up to 75 percent of the Ga reside in coastal urban centers.

Like the Fante, the Ga had extensive contact with Europeans before the colonial era and entered into political alliances with them. The declaration of Accra as the colonial capital in 1877 further ensured that it became a center of learning and trade that attracted, and continues to attract, migrants not only from other Ghanaian towns but from all over West Africa.

Returnees from the New World, mainly Brazil, also settled in the Ga urban complexes. Many of these migrants were absorbed into Ga society, but, because of its urban nature, the Ga language and culture also demonstrate a willingness to absorb external cultural traits." – (Ibid., p. 8).

Women play a major role in the Ga community. As in the Ewe community, women control commercial activities. Almost all commercial transactions are managed by women. This is partly explained by the nature of the organisational structure of the Ga society. It is both matrilineal and patrilineal. Property and positions of authority held by women are inherited by women; those held by men are inherited by men.

Living arrangements are also based on gender. Even when women are married, they continue to live with their mothers and children in women's compounds, while men live together in men's compounds.

The prominent role women play in the Ga-Adangbe society also coincides with their status as bearers of children, which is directly linked to the importance of children. The more children a family has, the better it is for the family and by extension for the community. It is a common belief in many traditional societies across Africa, the Ga-Adangbe being no exception. As the late Professor John A. Arthur of the department of sociology and anthropology at the University of Minnesota – he was a Ghanaian and died on 31 March 2016 at the age of 58 – stated in his book, *African Women Immigrants in the United States: Crossing Transnational Borders*:

"In traditional African cultural systems, a high premium is placed on children. There is a conscious desire on the part of families to have many children. This pronatal culture is pervasive in rural and urban parts of Africa.

Children are seen as blessings from the ancestors. When children are born, elaborate festivities and rituals –

154

popularly known as outdooring or child-naming ceremonies – are performed to symbolize the continuity of life and to solicit the prayers of the departed ancestors to ensure the survival and prosperity of the new-born and their family.

These outdooring or child-naming ceremonies are sometimes lavish. Women clad in white sing and dance to pacify the soul of the newborn. In some societies, the celebrations assume pomp and pageantry when the first born is a son.

In the Ga-Adangbe nation in Ghana, elaborate celebrations await those women who have their twelfth child. The mother's status is elevated in the eyes of her peers and community of kin group. A sheep is slaughtered in order to symbolize her feat.

In the northern tier regions of West Africa where Islam is the dominant form of religious practices and orientation, very large families are also the norm. Household sizes are large, and male children often spend their time herding cattle and cultivating the land, growing millet, rice, and sorghum. Literacy levels remain very low despite mandatory laws requiring parents to send their children to school. The infrastructure remains poor or nonexistent; so are standards of living that continue to lag behind the southern regions of West Africa." – (John A. Arthur, *African Women Immigrants in the United States: Crossing Transnational Borders*, New York: Palgrave Macmillan, 2009, p. 167).

Many Africans with large families also see their children as a source of labour. In African societies, child labour does not carry the stigma or draw condemnation the way it does in industrialised countries whose production methods are capital-intensive without relying on underage children to work the way they do in Africa, especially in the rural areas where they are an integral part of the labour force, working on farms.

Professor Arthur explained the traditional system in African societies with regard to children in the following terms:

"Within the traditional system, the more children families have, the more they command respect and prestige. Status in the community and the number of children one has sired is an affirmation of power and virility.

At the economic and community organization level, children are considered assets. They are incorporated into the system of division of labor and provide assistance to their families. At an early age, children who live in the rural and agricultural areas assist parents with weeding farms, hoeing, planting, and harvesting of crops. Family size may also influence the acreage or hectares that a family is able to bring under cultivation. Children are integrated into social and economic production.

In the urban centers, children assist family members in trading at the markets, engage in head-portage retailing, or provide care for elderly parents and grandparents. Some of the children earn wages, which they contribute toward total household income.

These income-generating activities are sometimes performed in addition to attending school." – (Ibid., pp. 167 – 168).

The Ga-Adangbe are an integral part of this social structure so common across the continent.

The Adangbe live mainly in the coastal areas and in the interior along the Volta River. They also have a much larger population than the the Ga. In fact about 70 per cent of the land in the Greater Accra Region is owned by the Adangbe.

In terms of social organisation and inheritance, the Adangbe are patrilineal, unlike their relatives, the Ga, who are both patrilineal and matrilineal. But both have a clan system. Clans are composed of lineages in both ethnic groups.

Their festivals are similar. But while the major festival among the Ga is Homowo, marking the beginning of the planting season and in remembrance of a famine that once devastated their community, the Adangbe celebrate two major festivals. One is Asafotu to remember their fallen warriors and the victories they won. It is also the time when young men become men by being initiated into manhood as warriors. The festival also marks the harvest season.

The other festival is Ngmayem. It is held to celebrate harvest and lasts for one week.

Like in all the other traditional communities across Africa, traditional dances are an integral part of social and spiritual life among the Ga-Adangbe, strengthening family and communal ties.

Although they are mostly Christian, many of them including Christians still adhere to their traditional religious beliefs; a common practice among other ethnic groups across the continent.

Mole-Dagbani

In the northern part of Ghana are the Mole-Dagbani, one of the largest groups in the country. The largest ethnic group in the Mole-Dagbani family is the Dagomba.

Northern Ghana is sharply contrasted with the south in terms of culture and geography; a division similar to Nigeria's in fundamental respects.

Both countries are divided by geography and religion. The northern part of Ghana is mostly Muslim; so is Nigeria's. It is also a dry region in terms of climate; so is Nigeria's northern part. And the people in both parts, northern Ghana and northern Nigeria, lag behind their southern counterparts in terms of education and development; a disparity that has led to friction in both countries and in the case of Nigeria to outright conflict.

The disparity has to do with history. It was the people in the southern parts of both countries who had the earliest contact with Europeans, enabling them to get formal education and other benefits from Western material civilisation and intellectual development. In the case of Ghana, contacts with Europeans were established very early, centuries before they were in Nigeria. The Portuguese established their presence in what is now the coastal area of Ghana in the 1400s.

The contrast between northern and southern Ghana is striking. As Steven Salm and Toyin Falola state in their book:

"The northern third of the country is largely savanna and open woodland, but overgrazing by livestock and increased cultivation are gradually depleting the natural vegetation and the region is beginning to resemble the arid lands of the Sahel to the north....

The northern savanna area is hotter and drier, with daytime temperatures in the 90s for much of the year. In the northern savanna, there is only one rainy season lasting from May to October, with the most falling in August and September, and one dry season.

The period of the harmattan involves cold and dusty northeasterly winds that come down from the Sahara Desert, limiting visibility and decreasing the temperatures slightly, especially at night."– (S. J. Salm and T. Falola, *Culture and Customs of Ghana*, op. cit., pp. 3, and 4).

They go on to state:

"About 70 percent of Ghanaians live in the southern and central areas of the country. The triangular-shaped region bounded by Tema and Accra to the east, Sekondi-Takoradi to the west, and Kumase to the north has the highest density, estimated at more than 200 persons per square mile. This area also contains the bulk of Ghana's mineral deposits, the main cocoa-producing regions, and all the major port facilities.

The Northern, Upper West, and Upper East Regions, despite occupying more than 40 percent of the country's surface area, contain only about 25 percent of the population.

Variations in culture and economic development coincide with the population disparities. Groups in the southern and central areas have had a longer history of contact with Europeans. They are more likely to be Christian, to have had greater access to formal education, and to have greater interest in Western goods.

Islam, on the other hand, has a long history in the northern areas, and its influences there are more pervasive in everyday life. There are, of course, variances. Christian missionary groups continue to convert northerners, while branches of Islam, especially the Ahmadiyya movement, have established a presence in some of the southern regions. Indigenous religions prosper throughout Ghana, and often coexist with Christianity and Islam.

Ghana is a highly multicultural and multiethnic country. There are about one hundred ethnic divisions characterized by linguistic and cultural differences. The large majority of Ghana's population today, however, can be classified into five major groups: the Guan, the Mole-Dagbani (with the Gonja), the Akan, the Ewe, and the Ga-Adangbe." – (Ibid., pp. 4 – 5).

As a cluster of different groups like the other major ones, the Mole-Dagbani have a collective identity characterised by unity in diversity among the groups within in terms of culture. They also have a regional identity that is recognised by the rest of Ghanaians:

"The two most populous groups in the northernmost

159

states of Ghana are the Mole-Dagbani and the Gonja. Ghanaians often refer to the Northern, Upper East, and Upper West Regions as 'the North,' suggesting some degree of homogeneity of the geography and the people that differentiates them from the rest of the country.

In contrast to the more forested and tropical south, the northern regions are situated in the hotter and drier Sahel, where vegetation is less dense. The peoples of these regions also rely on different food crops, such as yam and millet, and show a greater influence from Islam.

The Dagomba, the Nanumba, the Mossi, and the Mamprusi fall under the umbrella of the Mole-Dagbani group." – (Ibid., pp. 5 – 6).

The Mole-Dagbani who live in the northern regions of Ghana – Upper East, Upper West and in the Northern Region – are the largest Muslim group in the country. They are a meta-ethnic group of four major components: Dagomba, the largest; Mamprusi, Nanumba, and Mossi. Other groups in the Mole-Dagbani family or who are related to them include the Bulsa, Dagaaba, Frafra, Gurni, Kusasi, Wala also known as Waala as well as a number of other smaller ones.

Altogether, the Mole-Dagbani constitute the dominant group in the northern part of Ghana which is about 16 per cent of the country's population.

They have a common ancestry. And their cultures and languages are similar. Although they speak different languages, their languages are collectively known as Gur. They are also united by a common religion, Islam, which gives them an additional identity among Ghanaians. It is a common assumption that when a person comes from the northern part of Ghana, he/she is most likely a Muslim. In most cases, that is true.

Also, the term "northerner" may be misleading. A true "northerner" is someone who comes from the Northern Region, although geographically, this region is not quite

160

northern Ghana.

Geographically, a "northerner" could be someone who comes from the Upper East and Upper West Regions. But because there is also the Northern Region, the people from these three regions are collectively identified as "northerners," which may be confusing and even offensive to some "northerners" – whoever they are.

The Dagomba are the largest group in the Mole-Dagbani family. There are about one million of them. They are indigenous to the Northern Region. They speak the Dagbani language which is mutually intelligible with Mampruli or Mampelle spoken by the Mamprusi in the northern parts of the Northern Region.

The Dagomba are related to the Mossi who are also a major ethnic group in neighbouring Burkina Faso. They have a strong oral tradition articulated by griots and accompanied by singing, drumming and poetry to tell a story – of philosophical and moral relevance –and explain history.

Islam has played a major role in their lives for centuries and their culture has a strong Islamic imprint, although it is not entirely divorced from its African roots. But there is no question that Islam penetrates every social fabric and has a profound impact even on political life in a society where it continues to grow. The Dagomba and their brethren in the northern part of Ghana are some of the most Islamised people in Africa.

Their society is patrilineal. And traditional festivals such as the Damba and Bugun are very important to them. Equally important, if not more so in some cases, is Eid Al-Fitr, an Islamic festival celebrating the end of a month of fasting known as Ramadan.

The nucleus of the Dagomba community is Tamale, a city where Islamic influence is evident everywhere. It is also the capital of the Northern Region. Their entire homeland is known as Dagbon, once a traditional kingdom founded in the 1400s in the northern part of what is now

Ghana. It covered the Northern, Upper East and Upper West Regions and still exists today but without political power which it lost when the country became independent. Its role is mainly ceremonial, upholding customs and traditions, honouring traditional rulers – the king based at Yendi, chiefs and others – and holding the community together through festivals and other events including traditional ceremonies.

The traditional pattern of the Dagomba is also reflected in the way they organise their communities and villages. Their houses are built in such a way that the house or hut of the chief or the elderly man in charge of the community is in the centre surrounded by other houses and huts. He is symbolically and practically the heart and soul of the community, holding it together.

Closely related to the Dagomba are the Nanumba. They are indigenous to the southeastern part of the Northern Region. Their language is Nanun, also known as Nanuni. In terms of population, they are a small ethnic group of about 80,000 compared with one million Dagombas. But they are an integral part of the Mole-Dagboni meta-ethnic group; their status enhanced by being closely related to the largest Mole-Dagboni ethnic group, the Dagomba. Still, they have their own cultural and linguistic identity. They are also closely related to the Mamprusi. The Mossi – some of whom live in Ghana, mainly in the north, and are the largest ethnic group in neighbouring Burkina Faso – are also their relatives but not close.

The traditional ruler of the Nanumba is called Bimbilla Naa, a paramount chief. And their capital is Bimbilla.

Although chiefs no longer have political power in the modern state of Ghana, they are recognised under the constitution as authorities in traditional matters and constitute a House of Chiefs.

Like the Dagomba and members of other northern groups, the Nanumba are overwhelmingly Moslem. There are only a few Christians among them and they are mostly

Catholic. But even they, together with their Muslim brethren, have not completely abandoned their traditional religious practices although not all of them observe them.

The Nanumba celebrate traditional festivals, one of the most important being Bugum Chugu.

The festival is dedicated to remembering the search for a son of a king in ancient times. The son was lost and a search was launched to find him. The Nanumba still commemorate the search with fire which perhaps symbolises a torch light used to look for the lost son.

Being predominantly Muslim, the Nanumba also celebrate Islamic festivals including Eid al-Fitr and Eid al-Adha.

Their cousins, the Mamprusi, are considered to be the first of the Mole-Dagbani groups to settle in Ghana, while the Guans – among whom are the Gonja – who are a separate group and are not related to the Mole-Dagbani, are believed to be the first among all the ethnic groups to settle in the area that came to be known as the Gold Coast and later Ghana.

The Mamprusi society has some characteristics that are common in most traditional societies across Africa. The majority of the Mamprusi come from polygamous families, a traditional practice so common on the continent and which is – in the case of the Mamprusi – further validated by the Islamic faith which allows men to marry more than one wife. Traditional religious beliefs are also practised sometimes along with Islam as is the case with many Christians in Ghana and elsewhere in Africa.

There is also flexibility in the way the Mamprusi name their children. Despite their adherence to Islam in most cases, they still use traditional names, and Arab names – so-called Muslim names – when they name their children.

The Mamprusi speak a language known as Mampruli, a branch or variation of Gur.

They have a very strong oral tradition which has played a major role in recording and retaining, orally, their

163

history. And as in most traditional societies across Africa, the Mamprusi are patrilineal; and it is the elders who settle disputes.

Their society is structured this way:

"The social structure of this group is patrilineal and acts as the basic unit of structure for society. A person's right to inheritance, property and privileges are defined through this structure.

Perhaps the most distinctive feature of Mamprusi society is their political system which is known as the *Nam*. This political system is constructed through a complex hierarchy of chiefdoms.

The term *Nam* means office or political authority. When a new officer is installed it is said that he eats the *nam* signifying the incorporation of the *nam* with the physical person.

Office eligibility is determined through the gate system. This gate system refers to the family lineage and signifies those who are eligible for chiefdom.

Competition for office is held on two levels, first between gates in Gbewa's lineage as well as between members of the same gate.

Once installed the chief will have final say in all disputes, including marriages, witchcraft trials and succession. Chiefs are regarded as protectors of the Mamprusi." – ("The Unique People of the Northern Part of Ghana: Mole-Dagbani," 20 September 2013, on aswelive.wordpress.com).

Another Mole-Dagbani group is the Dagaaba. According to historical accounts handed down through generations by oral tradition, the Dagaaba are an offshoot of the Mole-Dagbani. They have therefore developed their own identity although still inextricably linked to the Mole-Dagbani as a collective entity. And they have lived in their present native homeland for about 300 years.

164

Their combined population in their traditional homeland of northwestern Ghana and in southwestern Burkina Faso – they straddle the border between the two countries – is more than two million. But the majority live in Ghana. They also live in the Ivory Coast, especially in Buna and Bonduku districts, but in smaller numbers than those who live in Ghana and Burkina Faso.

Although, in the case of Ghana, the vast majority of them still live in their native area in the North West Region, a large number of them have migrated to other parts of the country, especially Brong Ahafo Region. Many have also migrated to towns and cities in the southern part of Ghana.

This migration started during pre-colonial times, continued during the colonial period as the colonial rulers sought labourers in the south, and accelerated in the 1980s, mainly for economic reasons in search of better opportunities, to the point where the Dagaaba are now found almost in all parts of the country.

The name of their language, Dagaare also known as Dagare among other names, is sometimes used by non-Dagaaba to identify them; they speak Dagaare, or Dagare, and are therefore Dagaare or Dagare – or Dagara.

But they are mostly called Dagarti by outsiders; a term introduced by the British colonial rulers. It is a corruption of the original name of the people, a practice so common in all colonial territories where Europeans could not correctly pronounce local names. For example, Kilimanjaro is not the original name of the highest mountain in Africa. It is a corruption and an "anglicised" version of the local name, Kilima Nkyaro, given by the Chaga people who are indigenous to the region where the mountain is located in northeastern Tanzania. Europeans could not pronounce *Nkyaro*, changed it to *Njaro* and fused Kilima and Njaro into Kilimanjaro.

In the case of the Dagaaba, some of them prefer "Dagara" as the right term to identify the people and the

165

language they speak. Their homeland also is sometimes called Dagara country.

Since pre-colonial times, the Dagaaba have organised themselves into small social units without centralised authority and have relied on farming as the foundation of their economy. A group of families – or households – constitutes the basic unit, a subclan. There is a shrine and a priest in every one of these communities. The priest has traditionally been the elder and leader of the community. There is also a council of elders and a custodian overseeing the shrine.

Traditional religious beliefs are still practised along with Islam and Christianity.

The Dagaaba are both matrilineal and patrilineal, depending on which group the members belong to. Those in the eastern part are patrilineal and those in the west are matrilineal.

They also have the distinction of being the last people in West Africa who still use cowrie shells as currency, although they also use Ghana's national currency, the *cedi*. The cowries also enable them to carry on commercial transactions across national borders with their kinsfolk divided by colonial boundaries; something they can not do with the national currency which is not accepted in another country without being converted and without complying with other rules and regulations.

Like the members of other ethnic groups in Ghana and other parts of West Africa, the Daggaba have a very strong oral tradition as a way of preserving their history, customs and traditions, and proving education to their children and other people in their communities. Religious oral texts are also an integral part of this oral tradition.

Their traditional religious beliefs also play a major role in strengthening communal bonds to keep the people united as solid communities which are organised in compounds.

The Catholic Church has the largest number of

members among all Christian groups in Dagaabaland. Catholics first went into the area in 1929 and made a great impression on the people when they helped them to fight disease, administering medicine the indigenous people had never used or heard of. This encouraged them to convert to Christianity, with higher numbers of them becoming Catholics in the 1930s. As Anthony Y. Naaeke states in his book, *Critical Essays on Dagaaba Rhetoric*:

"The dominant tribes (in the North West Region) that have embraced Christianity are the Dagaaba and the Sisaala. These two tribal groups share many common cultural practices and religious beliefs, as Edward Tengan so clearly explains in his book, *Land as Being and Cosmos: The Institution of the Earth Cult Among the Sisaala of Northwestern Ghana* (Tengan 43). The Manlaale, Birifor and Chakale dialects (of the other three ethnic groups in the region) are closely related to Dagaare....

Dagaaba social organization is characterized by a low degree of role and institutional specialization. Apart from a few specialized roles, such as, *diviner*, people generally learn to do whatever is necessary for the upkeep of the family or community.

Tradition is cherished, and elders have the responsibility to protect the time-honored axioms and mores (Mendonsa, 36) of past generations.

In this region, unilineal descent groups are widely dispersed among peoples of different language and social organization. Compounds are scattered unevenly across the countryside in such a way that it is difficult to tell where one settlement ends and the next begins (Goody, 17).

The two main tribes, which were the original focus of missionary activity from 1929 until recently, when parishes were opened among the Birifor and Chakale, were the Dagaaba and the Sisaala. Some amount of study

167

on the social and religious world-view of the Dagaaba and Sisaala has been done by expert ethnographers, anthropologists and theologians, such as Henri Labouret (1931), Robert S. Rattray (1932), L. Girault (1959), Jack Goody (1967), Bruce Grindal (1972), Eugene Mendonsa (1982), Edward Kuukure (1985), Edward Tengan (1991), Paul Bekye (1991), Alexis Tengan (2000) and Eugene Suom-Dery (2000)....

Geographically, the land occupied by the Dagaaba is flat with low trees. The year is divided into two distinct seasons – dry and wet – the latter lasting from late April through October. Temperatures range between 20 (68°F) and 35 (95°F) degrees Celsius.

The people who live in this area are mainly subsistence farmers. They derive their livelihood from cultivating the land and rearing animals. Farming is done by means of a hoe, although animal traction has been introduced by agricultural projects funded by government and the Catholic Church.

Cereal crops, such as guinea-corn, maize and millet, and shoot crops, such as groundnuts and yams, are cultivated. Livestock include cattle, sheep, goats, dogs, chickens and guinea fowls. Fruits include dawadawa, baobab and sheanuts. Sheanuts are particularly popular because they contain oil, which is easily extracted for domestic use.

For art and craft, some people weave baskets using reeds picked up along the riverbanks.

Others engage in blacksmithing and still others make xylophones or carve wood. Some women make clay pots and brew beer (*pito*). – (Anthony Y. Naaeke, *Critical Essays on Dagaaba Rhetoric*, New York: Peter Lang Publishing, Inc., 2010, pp. 5 – 6).

He goes on to state:

"Before the advent of the British colonizers, the

Dagaaba were not organized as a political society in the same way that other African societies, such as, the Asante in Southern Ghana, were. Chieftaincy among the Dagaaba was, therefore, a political imposition by the British colonial masters. The Daggare word for chief, *naa*, means 'either a chief or wealthy person' (Angsotinge, 102).

The chiefs were responsible for enforcing the law imposed by the colonial administration in their respective villages and also for collecting taxes from the people for the colonial government.

Prior to the advent of the colonial administration, the main source of traditional authority was the *tendaana* or *tengan sob* (custodian of the land) and village elders.

The *tendaana* and village elders wielded socio-religious power and authority.

The *tendaana* or *tengan sob* is usually chosen from the clan that first settled in an area. Among the Dagaaba, the *tengan sob* is a priest or custodian of the shrine that is dedicated to the spirit of the earth.

Because the Dagaaba did not have an organized political system does not mean they were a lawless people. Dagaaba society is organized around the clan.

Clan members are those who share a common birth-origin. They trace their descent to a common male ancestor whose name may even be lost to surviving members. The whole clan is a family, and members have reciprocal responsibilities toward other members of the clan.

In clanship relations, seniority by age is the general rule in the exercise of authority. Decisions are usually reached through discussion and informal consensus among the elders." – (Ibid., p. 7).

Traditionally, in terms of religion, the Dagaaba have an elaborate system of worship, marriage, funerals and other ceremonies which give them a distinct identity different from the groups they are related to – the same applies to others in the Mole-Dagbani family – although modernisation has had a profound impact on the way the people live even in traditional settings. But they do have those traditions and customs, rites and rituals, without which they would not legitimately claim to be different or unique in many respects as an ethnic group. As Professor Sidonia Alenuma-Nimoh states in her paper, "The Dagaare-speaking Communities of West Africa":

"Dagawie (as Professor Sidonia Alenuma-Nimoh calls the land of the Dagaare-speaking communities) is inhabited by various Dagaare-speaking communities that form a continuum both of dialect and of culture. However, within this cultural uniformity, there are certain local variations.....(Yet) the Dagaare-speaking communities are, to a considerable degree, a unified cultural group....

Also...Dagaare-speaking communities are in some ways different from and in other ways similar to their neighbors – the Wala, Tallensi and Sisala.

There is no accepted name for the inhabitants of these Dagaare-speaking communities (who I refer to as the Dagaaba, although others like Somé, 1994, refer to them as Dagara). They are a people without a specific tribal designation but who, from the standpoint of their culture, are a relatively homogeneous community.

Although most Dagaare-speakers tend to focus on the differences between them and the other communities, the resemblances are certainly more numerous.

The Dagaaba gain their livelihood through cultivation by hoe of guinea-corn (sorghum), maize, millet, groundnuts (peanuts), cowpeas, and root crops such as cassava, sweet potatoes and yam.

Cattle, sheep, goats, dogs, chickens, and guinea-fowl are kept as livestock, and food supplies are occasionally augmented by the flesh of wild animals, fish, oysters, and turtles from the rivers and pools, and by wild leaves and fruits, especially those of the dawa-dawa, the baobab, and

170

the shea (noted for its oil-bearing nut).

Until recently, all Dagaaba were farmers and hunters. In addition, some men specialized in black smithing, others in playing and making xylophones, still others in divination and other activities of a magico-religious nature. The only full-time specialists, mostly traders, were to be found in the villages or quarters of foreigners that were distributed along the main trade routes.

The inhabitants of these were mainly Moslem, and their relationships with the indigenous peoples were limited to the market place.

The compact villages of foreigners stood in great contrast to the dispersed settlements of the indigenous people, whose houses are scattered unevenly over the arable land, fifty to a hundred yards apart." – (Sidonia Alenuma-Nimoh, "The Dagaare-speaking Communities of West Africa," *Journal of Dagaare Studies*, Vol. 2, 2002, p. 3).

She goes on to explain some of the "commonalities and differences among the Dagaaba" and states:

"From one Dagaare-speaking community to another, there are various differences and similarities. There is a certain homogeneity of culture over the whole area, but it is only relative; for customs change gradually from settlement to settlement. For example, the dialects of the language seem to be drifting apart, especially those divided by the political boundary between Ghana and Burkina Faso.

The differences that exist among the Dagaaba are as concrete as those that exist between the Kachin and the Lakher. These differences have been substantiated by intensive field observation, and confirmed by both local usage and the opinion of other observers.

The inhabitants of these communities, the Dagaaba, do recognize the cultural and linguistic differences that obtain

171

in the area, the local variations that exist within a considerable degree of cultural uniformity, and refer to them by placing particular customary practices in relation to certain categories..., a practice which, as Jack Goody correctly observes, resembles the English use of 'Westerners' and Easterners'....

Being a native Dagao (singular of Dagaaba), I hope that my perspective will blend well with that of the outside observer to produce new insights into the Dagaaba culture." – (Ibid.)

The differences which exist among Dagaaba communities may be complex and subtle. This does not mean calling the people a collective entity is meaningless. It simply shows that any generalisation about their identity does not correspond to reality.

Each community has its own identity, attributes and characteristics. Yet they are all united by a common identity as Dagaaba. In some respects, the differences among the Dagaaba communities may be analogous to differences among siblings. They are members of the same family; yet each member has his/her own personality, character and characteristics, interests and preferences; and a name, of course. As Alenuma-Nimoh states, in pointing out differences between and among Dagaaba communities:

"For example, although the staple dish among the Dagaaba is *saabo*...,the constitution/texture of this millet, sorghum or maize-based meal may vary from one community to the other....

In addition, from one Dagaare-speaking community to another, funeral xylophones may sound different both in terms of the tunes and the tempo of the music. During the funeral celebration, people may be required to run and wail as they approach the funeral ground, in other cases, they may be required to simply wail as they get closer to the funeral home." – (Ibid., p. 4).

She goes on to explain kinship ties whose nature may not be comprehensible to most people in Western societies and others but whose relevance could be continental in scope especially in traditional societies across Africa. It is not uncommon for many Africans – I am one of them – to call cousins "brothers" and "sisters"; the children of their relatives as their children.

There is not even a term for "half brother" or "half sister," or "step brother" or "step sister" in many African languages. Such a relationship simply does not exist in many – if not in most – traditional societies on the continent. The Dagaaba community is one of them:

"Kinship terms can be confusing to the casual observer of the Dagaaba. The terms 'brothers' and 'sisters' do not only refer to people one shares parents with but also to all cousins. There is no Dagaare equivalent of the term 'cousin.'

Similarly, wives of males of the same descent may refer to each other's children as 'daughters' or 'sons.'

There is no such word as 'step-child' although children generally know who their real mothers are and women may sometimes treat step-children differently from the way they treat their own children.

Another confusing term is *n pog*, my wife, used by both males and females, in reference to a brother's wife. There is usually a joking relationship between people and their brothers' wives. A woman pretends to be a man when cracking jokes with the brother's wife, hence the use of 'my wife' or 'n pog,' which she may also used in everyday language outside the joking context.

N pog may also be used by a grandfather in reference to a granddaughter and *n seere* (my husband) used by a grandmother in reference to a grandson." – (Ibid., p. 5).

173

There are other ethnic groups in Africa where that is also done: for example, a grandson being described as his grandmother's "husband." One example is the Nyakyusa of southwestern Tanzania.

Fathers tell their sons in the Nyakyusa language (Kinyakyusa) *nkasi gwako*, meaning "your wife," in reference to their paternal grandmother.

The meaning of such references is hard and even impossible for outsiders to understand, including the paradoxical nature of the statements. If a son is a "husband" of his paternal grandmother, then his father is "a son" to him. It can be understood only in the cultural context of the Nyakyusa and members of other ethnic groups who have such relationships.

One of the most strict taboos among the Nyakyusa has to do with daughters-in-law and fathers-in-law. A daughter-in-law is not allowed to look at her father-in-law at all. She must look down at all times in his presence. When he is talking to her, she must answer in very low submissive tones, almost inaudible. She is also not allowed to mention his name at all, anywhere, anytime.

The Nyakyusa also have a joking relationship with the Ngoni, members of an ethnic group related to the Zulu and the Nguni, who migrated from Natal Province in South Africa to what is now Tanzania – also to Nyasaland (now Malawi), Mozambique and Northern Rhodesia (Zambia) – between 1820 and 1840 and settled in the southern part of the country.

They had a reputation as fierce warriors and, together with the Matumbi, formed the backbone of the Maji Maji resistance against the Germans in Deutsch-Ostafrika (German East Africa) – renamed Tanganyika and now mainland Tanzania – from 1905 to 1907 because of the brutal oppression they suffered at the hands of the colonial rulers. Fighters from 20 ethnic groups fought the Germans and about a quarter of the country in the southern half was engulfed in the conflict.

Before the country became a German colony, the Ngoni tried to invade Nyakyusaland but were repelled by the Nyakyusa fighters who themselves had a reputation as fierce fighters even in the mines of South Africa – as well as Northern Rhodesia and Southern Rhodesia (Zimbabwe) – where many of them went to work between the 1930s and 1950s.

The joking relationship between the two has roots in those bloody encounters when the Ngoni attempted to conquer the Nyakyusa ansd seize their land. The Ngoni call the Nyakyusa *watani wetu*, a Swahili expression meaning "our joking partners." The Nyakyusa also call the Ngoni *watani wetu* in acknowledgement of this reciprocal relationship between the two ethnic groups whose homelands are 300 miles apart.

In the context of the Dagaaba, Alenuma-Nimoh explains how social ties and interactions facilitate bonding among family members and members of the community as a whole and what kind of differences exist between Dagaaba sub-ethnic groups and some of their neighbours:

"Grandchildren and grandparents usually have a joking relationship that facilitates a special type of bonding, making it easier for the old ones to impart their knowledge and wisdom on the little ones.

The above joking relationships are different from what exists between all Dagaaba and one of their neighboring groups – the Frafra – which is referred to as *loloroung*.

The Frafra are *lolorobo* or joking partners of the Dagaaba and this has nothing to do with the *denie* or play that exists between kinsmen as exemplified above.

In some Dagaaba communities, a considerably settled agriculture and inheritance of rights of tillage by a close agnatic kin leads, after a number of generations, to the formation of a group of compounds inhabited by males descended from a common patrilineal ancestor and constituting a unilineal descent group with specific

175

genealogical connections.

In these communities, inheritance is within farming groups. Such a group consists of brothers and their sons, where the surviving full brother or senior son will become farm-owner after the death of a family head. This successor must provide land for his dead brother's children when they desire to farm by themselves.

Among the Dagaaba, most houses are made of mud and/or cement with either thatched, laterite or aluminum roofs. They are usually a cluster of compounds inhabited by several nuclear families of the same descent. A typical patrilineage inhabits some seven large compounds situated about a hundred yards apart from each other." – (Ibid.)

She also explains how the Dagaaba view incest. In some traditional societies, it is not taboo in all cases. Relatives-in-law – but not blood relatives – can marry each other without being sanctioned or ostracised. It is not prohibited.

Also, among the Dagaaba, some blood relatives are not allowed to marry each other. But there are those who allowed to do that:

"Incest taboo is observed in all the Dagaare-speaking communities of West Africa. In some cases, the slightest indication of a blood relationship, no matter how distant, is enough reason for a prospective couple not to be allowed to proceed with their marriage plans.

In other cases, matrilateral cross-cousin marriages are permissible and encouraged. Among the LoWiili, a woman's first-born girl is encouraged to marry (and sometimes, as an infant, betrothed to) her maternal uncle's son (i.e. marriage between the children of a sister and a brother). This is supposed to strengthen the relationship between a woman's patrikin and her husband's kin, who are now her kin due to the marriage.

Such matrilateral cross cousin marriages may also

involve a woman's sons and girls from the woman's patrikin. These kinds of marriages give parents the peace of mind (knowing who their children are getting married to) and also help establish satisfactory relations between the in-laws." – (Ibid., p. 6).

She goes on to state:

"Marriage, among most Dagaaba, is virilocal. A woman has to leave her own father's house and join her in-laws/husband's patrikin. Until death or divorce, she lives away from the main body of her agnatic kin. Due to the general lack of transportation, the need to keep in touch with one's patrikin, attending every funeral, visiting the sick, etc., girls are encouraged not to marry men from villages that are not a walking distance (seven miles or less may be considered as the preferred distance) away from their agnatic home.

Similarly, since in-laws are expected to attend each other's relatives' funeral ceremonies, parents are particular about how far away their sons go to seek marriage partners." – (Ibid.)

Arranged marriage is still practised by the Dagaaba, although it is frowned upon by most young people in Africa today because of rapid changes and social transformation as a result of modernisation, a term synonymous with foreign, especially Western, influence:

"In fact, all the kinsmen of a young man of marriage age keep their eyes open for the suitable would-be bride and may make suggestions to the young man as to who is available and ready for marriage in the nearby villages.

In some cases, the selection of a wife and all marriage arrangements are made without the in-put of the groom. The groom is supposed to take their word for it, when his kinsmen bring home a lady and say, 'this is the best woman for you.'

According to the Dagaaba elders, an ideal bride is one that is hard-working, physically fit and strong enough to be a *pog kura* (female farmer, capable of all performing such activities as sowing, carrying large loads of firewood, giving birth to as many boys as possible, etc.), and comes from a family with good health and conduct." – (Ibid., p. 7).

Although most young people, both men and women, across Africa will probably not accept arranged marriages, there are those who do for a number of reasons including convenience – not having enough time to find a bride or a husband, or simply not being able to meet someone who is interested in marring him or her.

Another reason is ethnic preferences and loyalties. Many people even today, educated and uneducated, Westernised or not, prefer to marry members of their own tribe. Therefore, there are those who agree to have their parents and relatives as well other people help them find "wives" and "husbands" from their tribes and even from their home areas, within the same village, or not far from where they come from.

Another "old-fashioned" practice that is still accepted by some people across Africa is elopement. In fact, it goes on even today in modern or in so-called civilised societies in the West, not just in traditional ones in the Third World countries of Africa, Asia and elsewhere.

Also, some people elope because parents and other relatives may not want their son, daughter or relative to get married for different reasons: they don't like the prospective wife or husband; they don't like their future relatives-in-law or believe they are just bad people; or they think their son or daughter or relative who wants to get married is simply not ready for that.

Among the Nyakyusa of southwestern Tanzania, although elopement is almost unheard of nowadays, the

178

young man who wants to get married – together with his relatives and friends or alone – "kidnaps" his future wife while the girl pretends she does not want to go and even cries when she is "grabbed,", yet puts up little or no resistance at all as she is taken away. Her parents also pretend they don't want their daughter to be taken away "against her will," while they at the same start making plans for the wedding.

It is interesting that such reactions are not isolated; they are common – where elopement takes place – in communities which are thousands of miles apart, in East and West Africa, in Central and Southern Africa; the Dagaaba in Ghana and the Nyakyusa in Tanzania being two examples of some people on the continent who do almost exactly the same thing when elopement takes place in their communities.

In the case of the Dagaaba, Alenuma-Nimoh states the following, as if she is writing about the Nyakyusa (faraway in southwestern Tanzania in East Africa) and other ethnic groups elsewhere on the continent, in explaining what happens when a couple decides to elope:

"Another type of arrangement for first marriages is elopement, which occurs at the age of puberty. The girl is persuaded to leave with her admirer to his home or she may be seized by his kinsmen/colleagues at a dance, market place, or while sleeping at night and forcibly brought to her would-be husband's home.

Although elopement is usually done with the girl's consent, she is expected to resist and scream the loudest possible to show that she is up-right, morally, and not a bitch. Similarly, although some of the girl's relatives may have been aware of the plan to elope, they may express anger publicly.

The resistance to elopement marks the beginning of a period of intensive interaction between the girl's filial and conjugal ties, within which the necessary steps are taken to finalize the courtship and marriage process.

Other marriages may have less dramatic beginnings. After a young man declares his interest in a girl, his kinsmen accompany him to present his proposal formerly to the kinsmen of the girl. During this period of courtship, the kinsmen of the young man are expected to shower gifts in the form of *pito*, kola nuts and money on their in-laws each time they make a trip to the girl's village. When both parties are satisfied with the way issues have been handled during the courtship period, a day is fixed for the bride wealth (*kyeru*) to be brought to the girl's family.

After the transfer of bride wealth has taken place, the girl (who carries with her a number of accessories including calabashes, bowl/basins and baskets) is accompanied by her kinsmen to her husband's home. This is known as *pog bielle*." – (Ibid.)

She goes on to state:

"Although all marriages among the Dagaaba involve courtship (*pog bo*) and the transfer of bride wealth/kyeru, the details of what goes on during courtship and what constitutes the bride wealth vary from one community to the other. For example, Goody (1967), reported that among the LoWiili, the bride wealth is not accepted on the first day it is presented. It is only on the third occasion that the bride wealth is finally accepted as being the accurate amount required. This is not the case among other communities like the Sapaare and the Jiribale.

However, as to what constitutes a bride wealth, these two communities tend to differ. For example, the amount of bride wealth required for a wife from Sapaare will be insufficient to obtain a wife from a Jiribale community.

In general, bride wealth among the Dagaaba usually involves some amount of cowries, cash, and livestock. The proportions of these various items may vary but will almost always involve a number of cowries. The cowries

180

and/or cash portion is referred to as the *pog libie*. Among the LoWiili, the bride wealth consists of a cock and guinea-fowl to the in-laws, and the *pog libie*, a sum of approximately 20,000 cowries, usually, the same amount that was paid for the girl's mother.

Various rituals accompany the counting and transfer of bride wealth by the groom's family to the bride's agnatic home. Once the patrikin of the bride receive the bride wealth, they also perform a number of rituals during the counting, distribution and storing of it.

In general, the bride wealth received for a daughter is used to get a wife for a son. Whereas paying the bride wealth of a young man's first wife is the obligation of his family elders, if he wishes to become polygamous, he will generally be solely responsible for paying the bride wealth of these subsequent wives." – (Ibid., p. 8).

The amount of bride price paid, and this is not unique to the Dagaaba, depends on how much the girl is worth in terms of honesty, faithfulness and so forth:

"The various rituals performed during the counting and transfer by the groom's relatives as well as those that go on during the counting and acceptance of the bride wealth, are tied to the fertility and fidelity of the bride.

If some of the rituals are not well done, the woman could have difficulty bearing children during the marriage. It is also believed that once those rituals have been performed and the bride wealth accepted, then any infidelity on the part of the woman could result in her death if she does not confess immediately and go through purification rites/rituals." – (Ibid.)

Rituals play a very important role in the lives of the Dagaaba in other areas as well, not just in marriage. That is true of other traditional societies in Africa. Even where Christianity has penetrated and taken root, many people

181

still follow their traditional beliefs while professing to be Christians. There is a link with the past, the spirit of the ancestors, which nothing seems capable of breaking.

There is also the African psyche, Africanness, the spirit of being African and of being determined to remain African that nothing from Europe or anywhere else can erode or destroy. Even some of the most modernised Africans have remained loyal, sometimes fiercely loyal, to their roots and heritage. Rituals are at the core of their very being, heart and soul, and survival. In the case of the Dagaba:

"Until recently, rituals have played a dominant role in the lives of Dagaaba. Although they are no longer as pervasive, they still occur to a considerable degree. Being hunting and agricultural societies, the Dagaare-speaking communities have animal ceremonialism (or rituals around slain animals) and a calendar cycle of rites around crops.

The subsistence work (activities like farming and hunting) links humans together while rituals link them to gods or God.

The role of rituals among the Dagaaba can best be illustrated by this brief exchange between Somé (1993) and his grandfather.

Somé: Why do people do rituals?
Grandfather: Do you know why you go to the bathroom? Do you know why you urinate?
Somé: Of course I know. I can't help it.
Grandfather: Well then, you know why we do rituals.

Most Dagaaba were, and some still are, like the parents of Somé (1993), for 'at least once a day we had something to say to our ancestors. At least once a day a word is addressed to the shrine of Nature, be it at home before undertaking a journey to the farm or to another village, be it in the farm before working at it.'" – (Ibid., pp. 8 – 9).

Without performing or following rituals, life itself is empty and in danger. The people have to appease the gods. They have to live in harmony with nature. Don't do anything to disturb or upset the equilibrium or offend the gods.

Rituals are a way of ensuring that everything is in order and atonement for any wrongdoing is done – and it is done the right away. There is no ritual that is performed without a reason. It must be done to achieve something. As Alenuma-Nimoh states:

"Most of these Dagaaba will agree with Somé that 'visible wrongs have their roots in the world of the spirit. To deal only with their visibility is like trimming the leaves of a weed when you mean to uproot it. Ritual is the mechanism that uproots these dysfunctions. It offers a realm in which the unseen part of the dysfunction is worked on in ways that affect the seen.'

Every ritual is performed for a purpose. It may be a ritual performed in order to cure/prevent a wrong or to celebrate an event. It is therefore not unusual to perform some rituals at an individual's birth or death, at a harvest or at an initiation. Although the purpose and nature of each of the various rituals may have a general point of agreement, the details of these rituals tend to vary from one community to the other." – (Ibid., p. 9).

People in different societies differ on how they view life and death and how they perform funeral ceremonies. There are those who, when they mourn the dead, believe life is over. "We will meet in heaven." All communication ceases. In fact, it is impossible to communicate with the dead. That is the Christian belief, and possibly other religions. The dead know nothing.

That is in sharp contrast with traditional African religions in which rituals and beliefs are based on

183

continuity of life. Death is only a transitional phase from this world to the next. Those who die go on to live with the ancestors. It is often called – especially by Westerners – ancestor worship. That is the wrong term to describe it.

The people do not worship their ancestors who are on the other side in another world. The ancestors, who are now spirits and who can appropriately be called spirits of the ancestors, only act as intermediaries between the living and the gods or between the living and God, the Supreme Being and Creator. And how funerals are conducted is a manifestation of the reverence the people have for those who have just passed away.

In some societies funerals are very expensive and highly elaborate. It is a way of honouring the dead on their journey to another world, the spirit world, of the ancestors. Specific and appropriate rituals are performed to accomplish the task. The Dagaaba are some of the people who perform elaborate funeral ceremonies:

"Funeral ceremonies are the most elaborate of the ceremonial occasions of the Dagaaba, be it in terms of attendance, time taken, or emotion generated.

There is a general belief in life after death, and funeral ceremonies are the means by which the actual passage of a human being from the Land of the Living (*tengzu*) to the Land of Dead (*dapaarewie*) is effected.

Additionally, ancestor reverence and respect for the belief in the ability of the ancestors to protect, guide, and offer showers of blessing to the living, may be considered as the most important aspect of the relationship between the living and their supernatural agents.

The ancestors are never dead. They merely continue to live in the other world of spirits and serve as media between their relatives and the spirits and gods.

All funeral rituals among the Dagaaba involve musicians, mourners and the assembled villagers and guests from neighboring villages. The music group usually

184

consists of xylophonists, drummers and singers. The singers improvise, recreate and reproduce through their songs the history of the family up to the death that resulted in the separation. The theme of the songs is a combination of the deeds and sorrows of the family.

The best singer is one who can stir the maximum level of grief in the chief-mourners (*kotuodeme*, the closest relatives of the diseased) by his choice of words. The effect of the words of the singers is echoed and amplified by the tunes of the xylophones and the sounds of the drums, moving the community to grieve freely. Wailing, screaming, groaning, running, jumping, dancing and singing are all acceptable ways of expressing grief.

Shedding of tears is highly recommended and admired. The *kotuodeme* are expected to shed a lot of tears and behave in a way that stirs sympathizers to share the grief to the fullest by shedding as many tears as possible." – (Ibid., pp. 9 – 10).

Funerals among the Dagaaba are also highly complex, full of emotions, and may be even shocking to outsiders, especially the way the mourners handle and display corpses:

"The dead person, dressed in ceremonial outfit, is seated on a high wooden stool called *paala*, and surrounded by her/his valuable possessions. The stool is constructed from a special kind of tree. The singers, drummers and xylophonists are usually not far from the corpse and the entire funeral area is marked by turmoil and turbulence, as people act out their grief while others try to control themselves in order to calm down some of the *kotuodeme* from time to time.

The *kotuodeme* are tagged with ropes (much like leashes) for identification purposes and for easy control by people who may want to calm them down by holding on to the rope....

A well-attended funeral is an indication that the household has a high social reputation. The length of funerals varies between one to five days. The final day is marked by the burial of the dead person.

There are usually designated grave diggers and specially trained people who do the actual burying, for it is believed the dead is capable of preventing one from exiting the grave once the burial procedure is about to end.

Renowned witches and medicine people are particularly notorious for challenging the under-takers. In such instances, only equally toughened witches or medicine people who have been trained to bury the dead will be entrusted with the task at hand.

Highly respected elders are usually buried in the middle of the family compound or in front of the family house rather than in the cemetery. This is to keep them close to the family who are constantly being watched over by the dead elder or ancestor. From time to time, libation may be poured and sacrifices made on the grave.

On other informal occasions, the grave may serve as a resting place for naps and for relaxing and chatting. The elders do not play an important role only after their death, but also while they are alive." – (Ibid., pp. 10 – 11).

In terms of political organisation, the Dagaaba have traditionally lived under a decentralised system without a state – institutions of authority which wield power over a defined area inhabited by one or more groups.

One of the best examples of such a community without a central government are the Igbos of Nigeria unlike their counterparts, the Yoruba and the Hausa-Fulani, who traditionally have had highly organised institutions of authority under kings (obas) in the case of the Yoruba and emirs in the case of the Hausa-Fulani.

Yet the decentralised nature of the Dagaaba political system does not mean they were disorganised:

186

"Inferring from Yelpaala's (1992) article, the political organization of the Dagaaba was, until the imposition of colonialism, decentralized in its general structure.

From the outside, it might have appeared amorphous and not easily susceptible to analysis, for its organization and institutions were not defined in terms of the total territorial unit but in terms of sub-territorial areas (of) *teni* (villages) referred to by Goody as parishes, and by Fortes in his study of the Tallensi as settlements.

The political organization of each *teng* (village) exhibited a certain degree of centralization of authority with a very limited vertical structure.

The central authority was cross-hauled from the elders (*ninbere*) of different kin-based groups within the territorial area. This body was the basic institution dealing with most issues of general community interest. All elders with the exception of the custodians of the land (*tendaana*) in certain cases, were theoretically co-equals in all deliberations.

However, in matters that related to the *teng* and the land deity (*tengan*), the *tendaana* was the final authority. Thus depending on the issues involved, the central authority was either circular with its functions based on consultation and consensus, or unidirectional, from the *tendaana* downwards to the rest of society." – (Ibid., p. 11).

Alenuma-Nimoh points out that each village was independent from the others. She goes on to state:

"In every village (*teng*), this basic structure more or less replicated itself. Each teng however, enjoyed an independent autonomous existence from the others. Therefore, the society was at the same time centralized at the unit level and decentralized at the total societal level. Centralization within the small units provided the useful check on the abuses or excesses in the use of centralized political power.

On very important and broader cultural or extraterritorial issues involving non-Dagaaba, such as warfare or resistance against slave raiding, these centralized institutions would coordinate, cooperate or deliberate as a larger central unit.

However, these higher level organizations did not appear to involve the total territorial area of the Dagaaba.

Yet, taking any territorial unit as a starting point, that unit was linked separately to all other contiguous units by a chain of common culture, common descent, and political or legal cooperation. Each of these other units was also separately and similarly linked to yet other contiguous territorial units until the chain of interlocking linkages involve the entire Dagawie.

Depending on the issues at stake, contiguity, consanguinity, historical ties and the level of sophistication in the native art of diplomacy, cooperation or integration between different territorial units was great or small in amplitude.

The basic philosophy which guided the interaction of all central authorities at the larger unit level was equality. All component units functioned as co-equals, for the Dagaaba say that *doo bii pog ba gangna o to* (i.e., no man or woman is superior to their peer). This then, has been and continues to be the basis of egalitarian thought among the Dagaaba, what is called the traditional level. Within the national political structure, Dagaaba political thought, like all other traditional systems, is relegated to an inferior status." – (Ibid., pp. 11 – 12).

Moral values and teaching have played a critical role as a foundation for societies throughout man's history. That is why some Biblical commandments and other religious texts have been codified into secular laws in many countries founded or ruled by Christians. Predominantly Muslim countries also have laws derived from the Koran;

so have others based on their religious teachings.

Pre-colonial Africa also had its own morality, laws and values. They formed the foundation of African societies, shaped and regulated behaviour, and were used to sanction individuals and families whose conduct violated the norms of society.

Christianity and Islam did not introduce Africans to morality; their moral teachings only complemented what Africans already knew and practised as a way of life and as the basis of their societies. That is why there was so much revulsion at any reprehensible conduct and against those who violated basic norms of society.

That was the case among the Dagaaba who had their own religious beliefs but who are now also Christian unlike some of their neighbours such as the Wala who are predominantly Moslem but also traditionalists in terms of religion:

"Until recently, theft was a rare occurrence among the Dagaaba. It was taken as a very repulsive and anti-social act condemned by all, including the spirits and the ancestors who could be invoked whenever necessary to punish a thief severely.

Theft is so much looked down upon that it is not uncommon to hear a person trying to prove her/his integrity, say that (s)he does not steal or rob – *N ba zuuro, n ba faara*. In a society where houses have virtually no door panels nor locks, there is understandably a general need for trust and social cohesion.

In Dagaare, the term *iibo* signifies the general normative value system covering established and accepted norms, principles, practices, procedures which govern life in general and disputing in particular.

It is when a specific conduct is in conflict with the Dagaaba *iibo* that one may be characterized as deviant. In light of this concept of *iibo*, therefore, the Dagaaba may be viewed as a unified group, vis-á-vis other non-Dagaaba, including their neighbors." – (Ibid., p. 12).

The role of modernisation and its negative impact on the traditional way of life can not be underestimated. It has happened all over the continent. Alenuma-Nimoh has observed the following in the case of the Dagaaba:

"Being a native Dagao, one of the questions that was of interest to me, as I researched on the Dagaaba, include how the contemporary situation is different from the reports of earlier ethnographic studies. Just like any other culture, the Dagaaba culture is not static, and must be changing at some pace.
When Jack Goody visited Birifu after more than a decade since his field study, he was struck more by the continuities than the changes.... When he attended a funeral, he observed that the standing, dancing, contributions, mourning behavior, all seemed much as he had known them thirteen years earlier. Jack Goody attributed the apparent stand-still to the absence of any important cash crop and the emigration of the educated youth to the cities (in other words, the low literacy rate).
Jack Goody may have overlooked another cause for the unchanging nature of the funeral ceremony: the therapeutic nature of the ritual.
It is not accidental that one of the things that has remained considerably unchanged is the way funeral rites are performed. Funeral rites have proven their therapeutic worth to the people over the years and the people have responded by protecting them from change.
Although, at a first glance, the funeral rites may seem too 'primitive,' too elaborate and bothersome (in the eyes of an outsider or an alienated native like me), one only needs to lose a close relative while away from Dagawie to truly appreciate the significance of those elaborate funeral ceremonies and the role of ritual in general.
I could not agree more with Somé (1993), when he says

that the loss of a cultural practice like the loss of initiation in the traditional culture opens a psychic spiritual hole that is rapidly destroying the soul of his people (Dagara, a dialectal variant of what I refer to as Dagaaba).

The introduction of formal education and Christianity has resulted in cultural discontinuity, creating a condition that traps people in a meaningless and wayward life pattern. For example, something that used to be an uncommon sight – cases of theft – is now frequently being reported in remote villages every now and then.

The trust that used to exist in many Dagaare-speaking communities is gradually being eroded. It is now possible to find doors with sophisticated locks as opposed to days of gaping doors.

Some changes that I consider positive include the decrease in incidences of a customary practice usually referred to as clitoridectomy. I look forward to the day when the practice will come to a complete end. I also hope that the cultivation by hoe may be improved one day to increase the chances of commercial farming rather than the subsistence farming that is still the norm." – (Ibid., pp. 13 – 14).

After Professor Sidonia Alenumah-Nomoh read my work which has benefited from her extensive research and scholarly insights into the Dagaaba, she said it would be appropriate to clarify one thing. And I have incorporate her remarks into the book:

"Given that the work was published in 2002, and given that the focus was on a partial or a mere cursory coverage of the culture of the Dagaaba of West Africa, I suggest that you prefix any reference to my work as one that was meant to fill a vacuum but has outlived its significance over the years. The focus was on culture and culture is not stagnant. So a lot has changed and will continue to change over the years."

191

Her research and profound analysis have been invaluable to completion of my work, nonetheless.

Africa has undergone a lot of changes through the centuries. Foreigners have had a profound impact on the destiny of the continent from the first time they arrived there, mainly as conquerors.

It all started with the conquest of Africa by Europeans and even by Arabs in some parts of the continent. Africa has been on a downward spiral since then in her struggle to maintain her identity. There are Africans who have lost their true identity. They have lost their African-ness. Some of them are even proud of that. They are glad they are no longer "natives," no longer "African." They have lost their soul, as Africa continues to struggle to remain Africa in essence.

So, all is not lost among the Dagaaba and other Africans. It is a struggle between modernity and tradition. Modernisation has its consequences, brutal in its impact. It also has its benefits. Africa's traditional past, which is still very much present especially in the rural areas, also has its consequences even if not as brutal as the impact of modernisation on Africa's identity and wellbeing. And both are here to stay.

The real struggle for Africans is to strike a medium between the two, modernisation and tradition, knowing what to accept and what to reject, being fully aware of Africa's place in the world as an integral part of the global village from which she can not and does not want to escape. Africa can interact with the rest of the world, and benefit from this interaction, without compromising her essence.

The Dagaaba have witnessed modernisation and its destruction including the accompanying loss of their values among some members of their society. But tradition, sustained by a spirit of resilience, also abounds amidst forces of destruction. Therein lies the hope for

Africa.

Another ethnic group in the Mole-Dagbani family are the Gurunsi. They include the Frafra who are also known asa Fare-Fare. The Frafra live mostly in the northeastern area of the Upper East Region.

The Gurunsi, who are also known as Grunshi, also live in the southern part of Burkina Faso. They speak related languages collectively called Gur; they are Gur languages, not Gur language. There are at least 70 languages in the Gur family spoken mainly in southern Mali, northeastern Ivory Coast, Burkina Faso, northern parts of Ghana and Togo, southwestern Niger, northwestern Togo, and in the farthest corner of northwestern Nigeria.

Besides the Frafra, other Gurunsi groups in Ghana include the Kusasi, Talensi, Kassena, Nabt, and Nankani.

Cultural similarities among these groups, especially in terms of social structures and traditional religious practices as well as economic activities, have been used as criteria to describe them as a single entity.

The Gurunsi are one of the most prominent groups in the Mole-Dagbani family, a status enhanced by the nature of the group's composition as a collection of smaller groups which are also unique in their own ways, for example, the Frafra, giving the Gurunsi its identity as a collective entity.

The Frafra (Farefare or Fare-Fare) are a cultural and linguistic unit with a common history and political organisation. They are the largest of the Gurunsi sub-groups. The second-largest are the Kusasi, and the third-largest, the Nankani.

The political system of the Frafra is not based on class or centralised authority. Traditionally, elders make final decisions affecting their community. Besides settling disputes and making decisions on other matters affecting the wellbeing of the community, the elders – who are the oldest members of the community and collectively constitute a council of elders – also play a very important role as historians; they are responsible for keeping the history of their people alive and passing it on from generation to generation.

There are no chiefs. But religious leaders do have some authority. They are responsible for upholding morality and laws which govern their community with the help of the council of elders. Religious leaders are also responsible for apportioning land and determining the cycle for farming and planting crops.

They have a pre-Christian and pre-Islamic belief in the existence of a Supreme Being as the Creator. Christians and Muslims did not teach them that; they already knew God exists. There is a shrine in every village for worshiping the Creator.

Their traditional religious beliefs include interacting with the forces of nature through magical objects kept by every extended family. The objects are handed down through the generations from the ancestors and serve as guardians of the family, protecting family members from evil forces. The reverence for these ancestral objects also serves as a binding force to keep families together as stable and cooperative units. They also make a variety of other objects including wooden stools to honour the spirits of the ancestors with whom they interact when they perform religious rites.

The Frafra are mostly farmers. The vast majority have remained in their native land. But some of them have migrated to cities and towns, especially the nation's capital Accra and other large urban centres such Kumasi, Tamale, Cape Coast, Sekondi and others forming communities in which they are united by a common identity as Frafra. They are known for their products such as baskets and other items popular with tourists as well as other people in urban centres.

They also travel a lot in search of work, including menial jobs, in the southern coastal towns and elsewhere, especially during the dry season when conditions are harsh in the northern part of Ghana where they live.

The north-to-south migration by the Frafra and other people from the north is also a product of history, dictated by colonial bias against the north with its small population and poverty.

Religion also played a major role in neglecting and marginalising the north. Islamic influence was strong in the northern regions. The colonial rulers were Christian and based mostly in the south. They were not interested in developing the north or integrating it with the south in areas where the two parts of the country could have moved forward together even if at a different pace, with the south already having advantages over the north.

It is a pattern that was common in many parts of colonial Africa where some regions were favoured over others, with areas where a significant number of whites had settled having advantages in educational opportunities and other fields.

Usually, it was the missionaries who first built schools and played a major role in converting the people in those areas to Christianity with all the benefits such a conversion entailed. It happened in Nigeria – North versus South; it happened in Kenya, Tanganyika (now Tanzania), Uganda and in other colonial territories. And its impact is still felt today, especially in the area of education and employment requiring high academic qualifications and skills.

The people who have the highest level of education come from regions which were favoured by the colonial rulers, giving them advantage over other groups even today in many areas of life, not just education and employment; a disparity which caused tensions among different ethnic groups, sometimes leading to violence.

In Ghana also, even today, the northern part lags behind the south and other parts of the country in terms of development. The people themselves are considered to be "backward," especially by their southern counterparts who have had the benefit of education and Western material civilisation for more than one hundred years contrasted with the northerners. As Martha Adimabuno Awo states in her work (it was her doctoral dissertation later published as a book), *Marketing and Market Queens: A Study of Tomato Farmers in the Upper East Region of Ghana*:

"The two regions (of) Upper East and Upper West have less than 20% urban population. The high poverty level also has historical roots in colonial times namely, the influence of the Trans-Sahara slave trade, slave raids and biased colonial administration.

Sociologists and anthropologists have often explained the low educational levels and general under-development in these contexts (Perby, 2004; Konings, 1986; Bening, 1990; Plange, 1978/79 and Luabe, 2005). Relics of the slave trade can still be seen at the slave camp in a community called Nania in the KND (Kassena Nankane District in the Upper East Region).

During the British colonisation of the Gold Coast – now Ghana – the Northern part of Ghana was excluded from development plans and rather reserved as a labour force for the Southern parts, the seat of the colonial administration. Educational and economic policies were deliberately structured to neglect the region and to ensure continuous migration of the labour force to the South. 'Kumedsro (1970) found that the low population growth of the Kassena Nankana District between 1948 and 1960 is attributable to the emigration of about 26,000 people, i.e. '...almost 20% of all people born in the district" (Laube et al, 2008: 9).

However, people later began to migrate voluntarily for various reasons....

The colonial masters did not only refuse to establish schools in the North as was the case in the south but prevented missionaries from doing so.

The region's religious roots in Catholicism date back to the 20th century, symbolised by the building of the cathedral in 1909 in the district (KND). Yet, during the time, the missionaries who introduced Christianity were restricted in the implementation of their development plans. This was done to retain high levels of illiteracy so as to guarantee the availability of unskilled labour, particularly as the need for military recruitment became apparent.

These processes created vast inequality in terms of development between the Southern and Northern sectors of the country. The lack of education for the people in the region has become a blemish which the people have to deal with to this day. The Southerners have a perception of superiority so look at Northerners with scorn. The poor education of the people limited their participation in the country's politics and administration (Saaka, 2001). This offered an opportunity for the political elite to continue to be biased against the North in terms of their development policies.

The region has, since Independence, remained the poorest in the country. According to the 2000 census figures, the three regions located in the Northern part of the country have the highest rate of illiteracy with the Upper East being the worst with 76.5%. Greater Accra Region has the lowest illiteracy rate of 18.4% followed by the Western Region with 41.8%, Central 42.9%, and Brong Ahafo 48.5% (GSS, 2002).

However, the region is famous for its rich historical and diverse cultural background....This part of the country is well known for its handicraft industry producing straw hats, baskets, traditional textiles and leather goods which are fast gaining a place on the international market. In addition, the region's architecture – round huts built from mud – is very attractive and quite different from other structural designs in the southern parts of the country. This design is not only very suitable for the extreme weather conditions but has, for generations, created a special identity that is traditionally and culturally unique to the

197

people." – (Martha Adimabuno Awo *Marketing and Market Queens: A Study of Tomato Farmers in the Upper East Region of Ghana*, Bonn, Germany: Center for Development Research (ZEF), University of Bonn, 2010, pp. 21 – 22).

This unique northern identity, derived from the traditions, history and unique culture of the people including art and architecture, is an identity that has also been reinforced by the north-to-south migration of northerners. The migration has been going on for so long that it is automatically identified with northerners and has become a part of their identity – social identity, how they are perceived in society – in spite of the stigma attached to it.

The migratory pattern is also a reflection of the impact of modernisation on the Frafra society – as well as others in the north – and demonstrates the vital link between urban Frafra dwellers and their kinsfolk in the rural north; a relationship that is reinforced by the interdependence between the two and the profound impact they have on each other in life. As Marshall Sahlins states in his chapter "Reports of the Death of Cultures Have Been Exaggerated" in a work edited by Howard Marchitello, *What Happens to History: The Renewal of Ethics in Contemporary Thought*:

"Modernization has not been the only game, even in the town. The inverse effect, the indigenization of modernity, is at least as marked – in the city and country both.

In the complex dialectics of the cultural circulation between homelands and homes abroad, customary practices and relations acquire new functions and perhaps new situational forms....

Wealth from the city subsidizes relationships in the village, while relatives in the city organize migration from the village.

198

In perceptive and prescient researches undertaken in the 1960s, Keith Hart was able to show that the integration of rural and urban Frafras – Tallensi and related peoples of Ghana – was largely effected through their classic lineage system.

From this Hart concluded the necessity of a new anthropological perspective, one that would transcend the correlated oppositions of the modern and the traditional, townsman and tribesman, urban and rural. He spoke rather of an 'expansion of the horizons of the community':

'This expansion of the horizons of the community, in terms of the physical distribution of those who claim membership in a socially defined aggregate such as a lineage, makes it no longer easy to dichotomise, at least spatially, the traditional and the modern or even the rural and urban in Frafra life today. The world of the migrant and that of the homeland are not separable entities....

The difficulty of separating the old and the new in the analysis of present day Frafra society, either in the national context of modern Ghana or even in the local context of the home tribal area, is illustrated by the simultaneous participation by most Frafras in both cultures, the exchange of personnel on a reciprocal basis between the home compound and southern city, the internal urbanisation of the Frafra district itself, the pervasiveness of the market economy, and especially the ease of communication between all parts of the country.

When the discontinuities between town and village life have been diminished, what meaning can we legitimately give to types such as 'townsmen' and country men'?'

I hazard a few generalizations on the structure of these translocal systems as described by Hart, Hau'ofa, and many others.

Culturally focused on the homeland, while strategically dependent on the peripheral homes abroad, the structure is asymmetrical in two opposite ways.

Taken as a whole, the translocal society is centered in and oriented toward its indigenous communities. The migrant folk are identified with their people at home, on which basis they are transitively associated with each other abroad.

These denizens of the town and the larger world remain under obligation to their homeland kinsmen, especially as they see their own future in the rights they maintain in their native place. Accordingly the flow of material goods generally favors the homeland people: they benefit from the earnings and commodities acquired by their relatives in the foreign-commercial economy. As one researcher put it, the village succeeds in reversing ' the parasitic function traditionally ascribed to cities' (Hugo, "Circulation,"264).

In such respects, the indigenous order encompasses the modern." – (Howard Marchitello, *What Happens to History: The Renewal of Ethics in Contemporary Thought*, New York: Routledge, 2001, pp. 200 – 201).

In the case of the Frafra, this has been demonstrated not only by the interdependence between their urban dwellers mostly in southern Ghana and their rural kinsmen in the north – as well as the migrants who move back forth in search of jobs in the south during the dry season – but also by their achievement in the area of education as some of the most educated people in the northern part of Ghana.

Another Gurunsi group is the Talensi (Tallensi), an offshoot of the Frafra. Like most Africans, the Talensi are patrilineal. Because of their patrilineal heritage, it is very important for a man to have a son who will inherit what he left behind and carry on the family's name.

That is sharply contrasted with a daughter who, once married, "belongs" to her husband – and will never carry on her father's name even if she is never married because she can not succeed her father; only the son can and will later be accorded the status of ancestor once he is gone and joins his ancestors in the world of spirits.

Once the father dies, the eldest son becomes the head of the family. He is responsible for performing rituals including making sacrifices to the ancestors. The ancestors include his own father who has just died and has now joined them.

Taboos are also very important in Talensi society. They regulate behaviour, reinforce and enforce morals and values, strengthen social bonds and hold families and the community together.

Their traditional religion which involves honouring ancestors is known for its shrines whose significance goes beyond religious worship. They also have highly symbolic value as an embodiment of the identity of the people and their culture.

Polygamy also is widely practised by the Talensi; a practice justified on cultural grounds in many traditional societies across Africa. Prestige is one of the reasons given to justify polygamy; the larger the family, the more respected you are as a man.

There are other cultural reasons as well which are given to justify polygamy or simply having large families even in monogamous contexts besides economic considerations, especially the need to have enough children to help work on the farm and perform other duties. Among the Talensi, there is also an emphasis on the importance of having first-born children; a point underscored by South African anthropologist Meyer Fortes:

"The reason for this strong emphasis on having a firstborn son or firstborn daughter is that a person can never achieve the fulfillment necessary to become a revered ancestor after death if he or she does not have children to carry on rituals.

The birth of a firstborn son or firstborn daughter makes a man truly mature and fulfilled, and it represents his

ascendance to the highest position in the society." –
(Meyer Fortes, 1969, quoted by Charles Wundengba, "The
Talensi People," northerngh.com, 21 April 2016. See also
Meyer Fortes, "The First Born," *Journal of Child
Psychology and Psychiatry, 15*, 1974; and M. Fortes, *The
Dynamics of Clanship among the Tallensi*, London:
Oxford University Press, 1945; and Meyer Fortes, *The
Web of kinship among the Tallensi*, London: Oxford
University Press, 1949).

Although they are well-organised as a society, they
don't have a centralised political structure. The highest
symbol of authority is the chief, although without
executive authority. Chiefs are symbols of unity. Yet there
is a way traditional "laws" are enforced: by moral sanction
even without institutional power.

The Talensi are bound by moral obligations to ensure
social stability and cohesion; also as a form of sanction
against wrongdoers who may incur the wrath of the
ancestors not just of the community. Every member is
responsible for the wellbeing of the community by
fulfilling his/her responsibilities.

Related families maintain strong ties and live close to
each other. As in most traditional societies on the
continent, family members identify themselves as brothers
and sisters even if they are cousins. This is not only
tradition; such identification helps to reinforce family ties
among relatives. Talensi communities are established on
this basis. They are communities, or villages, of related
people. And they collectively constitute the Talensi ethnic
group.

Another Mole-Dagbani group is the Wala or Waala.
They are not a cluster of sub-ethnic groups.

They are one of the the main ethnic groups in the North
West Region together with the Sisaala (or Sissala) and the
Dagaaba who are predominantly Christian, unlike the
Wala who are mostly Moslem.

The other ethnic groups in the North West Region are the Birifor, Manlaale and Chakale. And the main languages in the region are Dagaare, Sisaali and Wali.

The Wala, who speak Wali, founded the town of Wa which is now the capital of the Upper West Region.

Wa has several impressive mosques and other buildings reflecting heavy Islamic influence. It also has a palace of the traditional ruler of the Wala, made of mud bricks, and is one of the most impressive buildings in the town in terms of traditional architectural splendour and historical significance.

Although their culture is similar to that of other groups whose members speak related Gur-languages, the Wala have their own identity which distinguishes them from the other groups; their Islamic faith being one of their most distinctive attributes.

Their land also has shaped their "national" character as a people and how they have adapted to the environment in terms of survival and even how their traditional religious beliefs have evolved. For example, there would be no Mount Kenya mentioned in the traditions, customs and religious beliefs of the Kikuyu in Kenya had there been no such mountain in the area where they settled; best exemplified by Jomo Kenyatta's anthropological work, *Facing Mount Kenya*.

The Kikuyu name for the mountain is Kiri Nyaga. In their traditional religion, they believe the mountain is God's terrestrial throne.

In the case of the Wala, Professor Ivor Wilks states the following in his book, *Wa and the Wala: Islam and Polity in Northwestern Ghana*:

"The climate is unreliable, the soils indifferent, and disease rife. There are, however, its people. Wala is, because people at some point in time decided that it should be and at other points in time took further decisions to ensure that it should continue to be.

People made Wala, but, to use one of Karl Marx's memorable phrases, they did not make it under circumstances of their own choice. The very indifference of the environment meant that their strategies for survival were often more in the nature of gambles than of calculable expectations.

Wala is an antique land....No one can say how often, over that span of time, older peoples have been displaced by the newer, or have been overrun and assimilated without a trace.

Today, despite the seemingly inexorable forces that are impelling people to congregate in towns with or without any obvious means of support, the majority of the Wala remain rural. They live in family 'compounds,' some with a hundred or more members, which are often grouped to form larger or smaller villages.

In the less densely populated areas, fallows are long. In the more densely populated areas, particularly around the town of Wa, continuous cultivation has become usual.

The soils in the more northern and western parts of the region favour cereal cultivation, and in the more southern, yam.

Livestock never quite flourishes, but the more northerly the location the better it does. Cattle are reared for local slaughter and for sale at more distant markets. They are also a mark of wealth. They are used for marriage payments and for procuring political support, and are sacrificed on festive occasions. Few herds number more than 200 head, and rustling is not uncommon.

Vegetable gardening is everywhere a necessity; hunting is now little more than a gainful sport." – (Ivor Wilks, *Wa and the Wala: Islam and Polity in Northwestern Ghana*, New York: Cambridge University Press, 1989, p. 5).

It is an environment that is not very much different from other parts of northern Ghana some of which have tested even some of the most hardened souls.

Professor Wilks goes on to state:

"The town of Wa has long enjoyed the status of a central place. Until the end of the nineteenth century it was indeed the capital of the small but independent Wali polity. The first agent of the Government of the Gold Coast Colony to visit the town testified to its distinctive appearance. 'Wa is not a walled city,' wrote G.E. Ferguson in 1894, 'but the flat roofed buildings and date palms present it with an eastern appearance. It is the capital of Dagarti." It was quite apparent that the town was a seat of authority." – (Ibid., pp. 5 – 6).

It is still the seat of authority, but this time of the North West Region, with the additional distinction of being the most urbanised centre in the northwestern part of Ghana. It is also the capital of Wala District of the Wala people.

Wilks also sheds some light on the concept of ethnicity in the context of the Wala:

"The concept of ethnicity was much in vogue in scholarly circles in the 1950s and 1960s, and an enumeration by 'tribal divisions' was attempted, avowedly 'to give the research worker in the social sciences – especially the sociologist – a few basic data on population groups which are distinguished by certain characteristics and are generally referred to as tribes or tribal groupings'....

To be Wala, it might be said, is an achieved rather than an ascribed status, though it is clearly not one which all those historically within the political ambit of Wa have sought. Some Dagaaba have aspired to become, and succeeded in becoming, Wala. Some – indeed, the majority – have successfully resisted assimilation.

In question are processes of acculturation that can only be investigated in an appropriately extended framework of time. Key to any such inquiry is the three spheres of·

traditional authority....That based on access to the Earth-god is referred to in Walii as *tendaanlun*, and that based on the control of the instruments of coercion as *nalun*. The third is Islam." – (Ibid., pp. 14, and 17).

Traditional authority among the Wala has been supplanted by – or has been subordinated to – Islam in some areas because of the prevalence and the nature of the Islamic faith as a way of life. But it still exists although in a modified form since the advent of colonial rule. And because the Wala are overwhelmingly Muslim, there may be even some Islamic adherents in Wala who may want to transform their homeland into a theocratic "state" – in no way comparable to Boko Haram in Nigeria – but know the limits of such authority in a secular state that is Ghana.

The traditional way of life which existed long before the introduction of Islam also continues unto this day because it is very much an integral part of the identity of the Wala as a distinct group. It is embodied in the institutions of traditional authority encompassing religious beliefs and socioeconomic and political matters. As Wilks states:

"Through the exercise of *tendaanlun*, the community obtains the favour of the Earth-god and seeks to avert the disasters that occur when the Earth-god is offended. The Earth-god is omnipresent, but certain natural features – often rocks, trees, pools and the like – are designated as its shrines, *tengani*. Each *tengani* has its priest, the *tendaana*. It is, then, the *tendaana* who has *tendaanlun*.

The most ancient units of organization for production in Wala are the *ten* (singular, *teng*), a word often translated (into) the English 'parish.' Few if any of the *ten* survive in anything like their original form in Wala, newer structures of chieftaincy having been superimposed upon them....

The original *ten* were self-sustaining and self-reproducing communities. Their autonomy was defined not politically but ritually. Each was a tract of arable, fallow and waste land capable of sustaining the people, the Tendaanba, who lived on it. Each had a *tengani* or shrine through which its *tendaana* interceded with the Earth-god on behalf of the Tendaanba.

It was the responsibility of the *tendaana* to ensure that the Tendaanba observed the norms of communal life. If they did so, the Earth-god would in turn ensure the harvest, on which the very survival of the community depended. If they did not do so, then drought crop diseases and a host of other afflictions might result.

The *tendaana* was therefore the locus of authority, that is, of *tendaanlun*, in the *teng*, though he would act in consultation with the heads of the various lineages farming the land. Ultimately, however, whether in the allocation of land, the resolution of disputes, the punishment of those who violated social mores, the marketing of any surpluses, and so forth, it was the *tendaana* who was responsible for the well-being and indeed the very reproduction of the *teng* and its people." – (Ibid., pp. 17 – 18).

It was a way of life that was profoundly affected by the imposition of colonial rule which distorted and destroyed traditional institutions of authority and social organisation. And it is a way of life that continues to be affected in this era of modernisation and centralised authority of the post-colonial unitary state.

As northerners, the fate of the Wala is in many ways inextricably linked with the fate of other northerners who feel marginalised and ignored by the government and even despised by a large number their fellow countrymen, especially southerners.

There is a serious economic and social imbalance between the north and the south. It is a disequilibrium that can be rectified through equitable distribution of wealth and provision of economic and educational opportunities to northerners including building infrastructure in the northern part of the country.

Migration continues to have an impact on the people of northern Ghana because of the magnetic pull of the south with its economic opportunities. Some of the people in the north who have experienced the highest rate of migration are the Sisaala. About 20 per cent of them have migrated south.

The imbalance in economic and educational opportunities and in infrastructural development between the north and the south will continue to have a negative impact on the north unless it is redressed for the sake of equality, unity and stability of the country as a whole. Otherwise it is a recipe for disaster.

Guan

The Guan are one of the major ethnic categories in Ghana. There are more than 20 ethnic groups which collectively constitute the Guan meta-ethnic group. They are found in all parts of the country.

One of them is the Gonja, the most well-known subgroup in the Guan family. The Gonja live mostly in northern Ghana. They also live in the Brong Ahafo Region in large numbers.

Although they share cultural and linguistic similarities, there are some differences among them because of the different historical paths they took, settling in different parts of what is now Ghana.

This diverse settlement pattern also had an impact on their identities which evolved through the years, influenced by the environment and by the people they found in – or who came into – the areas where they settled and who became their neighbours.

One of the biggest impacts of this settlement pattern and migration was on language an cultural practices. The languages of their neighbours and their cultures had an influence on Guan cultures and languages in a profound way. The Guan also had significant influence on their neighbours. The result was assimilation.

Even some of the people who are native to the areas where the Guan settled have Guan ancestry because of the intermingling and intermarriage which took place through the years. They include some people in the Greater Accra Region such as the Kpeshie; the Ahanta, the Sefwi and the Nzema in the Western Region, among others.

There are at least five Guan groups in the Eastern Region, including the Kyerepong, the Okere and the Boso; and more than six in the Volta Region, including the Buem, Lolobi, Logba, Nkonya and Akpafu. Gonja groups in the Central Region include the Awutu, the Efutu and the Senya.

The Guans are considered to be the first people to settle in the area that became Ghana. And because of that, many groups in the country trace their ancestry to the Guan settlers. They include a number of Fante groups. As Professor Kwamina B. Dickson of the University of Ghana states in *A Historical Geography of Ghana*:

"The earliest...peoples in the country were the Guan. They may have been widely distributed throughout the whole of the southern half of Ghana, as is suggested by the oral tradition that nearly all the aboriginal peoples inland from, and along the whole length of, the coast 'belonged to the Guan, Kyerepong, Le, and Ahanta tribes, speaking different dialects of the Ahanta, Obutu, Kyerepong, Late (Le) and Kpesi languages,' all of which are related.

Indeed it would not be far-fetched to suggest further the possibility that the Guan, in view of their possible countrywide distribution, could have been direct descendants of the Neolithic population. Neither would it be out of place to speculate on the possibility of the Guan having introduced or acquired iron technology before the Akan arrived, for it may not be for nothing that Gua, a senior god of the Kpesi (Guan) in the Accra Plains, is the blacksmith and thunder god.

It is thus probably incorrect to restrict the original home of the Guan to the 'eastern forest and adjacent plains,' which they are supposed to have infiltrated and settled after having migrated from Mossi, the whole process of migration and settlement stretching over a period of some two hundred years, beginning from A.D. 1000." – (Kwamina B. Dickson, *A Historical Geography of Ghana*, London: Cambridge University Press, 1969, p. 19).

Professor Dickson goes on to state:

"There is no doubt, on the other hand, that the areas where Guan is spoken today in one form or another lie within a stretch of territory which extends along the Black Volta, through the Afram Plains and the Volta gorge and swings westward to the coast beyond Cape Coast, after skirting the eastern margins of the Closed Forest.

On the assumption that the Guan once occupied the forest country, spilling over into the parkland zone immediately to the north of the Black Volta, the distribution of present Guan-speaking areas could be accounted for by postulating absorption of the Guan by later groups of Akan-speaking peoples who infiltrated into Guan territory from the Ivory Coast and fanned out in all directions.

Thus the circumferential distribution of Guan-speaking areas with respect to the forest area would indicate, not the route for Guan migration, but remnants of Guan people displaced and engulfed by new comers from the west. The operation would have taken many centuries, beginning from about the end of the twelfth century, if not earlier." – (Ibid., p. 20).

Although Guans are found in other parts of the country,

they have a significant presence in five regions: Northern, Brong Ahafo, Central, Eastern, and Volta. And although they speak their own languages, they also speak the main languages of the people in the areas where they live.

The Gonja, who live mostly in the Northern Region of Ghana, are one of the main subgroups among the Guans.

But they did not retain their original identity because of the heavy influence that was exerted on them by the Akan, the Mande and the Hausa. However, they did have an impact on the northern part of what came to known as Ghana when they established the Gonja kingdom in the region and traded with the Akans and other people farther afield.

They were also heavily involved in the slave trade which formed the basis of their economy.

Another item that was a major part of their economy and commercial transactions was kola nuts.

The Gonja traders were mostly Muslim, Islam having made inroads into the kingdom long before Christian missionaries tried to penetrated the region. There were also animists in Gonjaland.

The Gonja have a long history which has been passed down through the generations by oral tradition; a common practice among many ethnic groups in Ghana and elsewhere in Africa. As Solomon Salifu Tampuri, a Gonja who is also a lawyer, states in his book, *Gonja, the Mandingoes of Ghana*:

"This book tells the story of the people of Gonja, who refer to themselves as *Ngbanye*.

The Gonjas are a tribe in the Northern Region of modern-day Ghana and one of the Guan-speaking groups in the country. The people should not, therefore, be confused with the town or people of Gonja in the region of Kilimanjaro in Tanzania, East Africa....

The Gonjas are the only known Guan-speaking tribe in the Northern Region of Ghana, and probably the last to arrive in that territory.

Gonja was once an important kingdom before the land mass known today as Ghana was colonised and brought under British rule. This book traces the tribe's journey from their original home in the ancient Songhai Empire to their present location in the Northern Region of the Republic of Ghana. The people of Gonja have a massive and intricate history, which, until the twentieth century, was written in Arabic or handed down by word of mouth....

Answers as to where Gonjas actually came from, how we ended up where we are now, and how we got our name *Gonja* are relatively unknown to many of my kinsmen in the diaspora. Part of the problem has to do with our educational system in Ghana, which teaches the Eurocentric version of our history.

Most history books about Ghana either focus on the Ashanti kingdom and how the Ashantis bravely stood up against the Europeans or begin and end with the British colonisation of the country and subsequent granting of independence. However, more than twenty other important tribes are in the country, and their history and stories have, if anything, been relegated to the background – to oral histories and anthropological research material at various universities.

Perhaps this is because most of these other tribes and clans did not have any direct or dramatic dealings with the Europeans, such as did the tribes of the coastal states and Ashanti.

The outside world has always viewed Ghana with admiration, perceiving Ghanaians as peace-loving, warm, and welcoming people. Anyhow, underneath this warm, receptive nature lie some ethnic rivalries that go back centuries. For example, not until long-standing grievances over landownership and the carte blanche of chiefs resulted in a full-blown war between the Konkomba tribe and the allied tribes of Nanumba, Dagomba, and Gonja –

212

which claimed more than 2,000 lives and displaced another 150,000 people in February 1994 – did people show interest in the social organisations of Northern Ghana's tribes." – (Solomon Salifu Tampuri, *Gonja, the Mandingoes of Ghana*, Bloomington, Indiana, USA: Xlibris, 2016).

He goes on to state:

"I particularly feel quite privileged to have listened to my father proudly and passionately tell the story of the Gonjas, our struggles, and our achievements and his hopes for the tribe's future. As a Gonja of royal blood, I feel it is only morally right that I make available such little knowledge I have of my people to as wide an audience as I can reach. If the Gonjas of this generation who speak and understand the customs and practices of the tribe have no grasp of our history, then what will become of our children and those who shall come after them?...

I visited Bole, my hometown, and had the opportunity to rummage through my late father's file of papers and documents going back six or more decades. It was then I stumbled upon a handwritten manuscript titled *The History of the Gonja*. He had handwritten it himself, albeit without references.

I had no way of establishing the veracity of his story. However, knowing how diligent and robust my father could be when it came to facts and figures, I am certain he went to great lengths in putting together his little manuscript about the history of his people. Perhaps it was his own way of documenting the history of his people as it was handed down to him." – (Ibid.)

Tampuri also sheds some light on Gonja customs and kinship ties when he states:

"The older generation still say they do not differentiate

or discriminate between a sibling's children and their own children, so the word *cousin* doesn't seem to exist in Gonja; a cousin is simply referred to as 'sister' or 'brother.' This echoes the popular Gonja phrase *Anye le kanang konle na* ('We are one family'). This is rightly so, despite the fact that Gonja has three social segments, consisting of the ruling estate (*B'wura*), the Muslims or priestly clan (*Nkaramo*), and the commoners (*Nyemasi*). They lack a detailed and documented genealogy of the tribe." – (Ibid.)

He further states:

"The people refer to themselves as *Ngbanye*, which means 'brave men,' and rightly so, because they are a warrior clan, descendants of Mandingo warriors.
The word *Gonja* comes from a corrupted Hausa phrase, *Kasan Goron-Ja*, which literally means 'the land of red kola nut.'
The kola nut is a caffeine-containing nut grown in the thick Akan forests. Often red or yellowish in colour, it has a bitter flavour; people from many West African cultures chew it. Kola nuts are also used as a religious object and sacred offering during prayer, ancestor veneration, and significant life events, such as naming ceremonies, weddings, and funerals.
The kola is probably the most important nut to Gonjas. To formally invite a person to an important life event such as a funeral, wedding, birth, or chief installation, a kola nut is first presented before the news is delivered." – (Ibid.)

Tampuri provides a historical context – in which the Gonja evolved as a nation – linked to contemporary times:

"Before British colonial rule, Gonja was an important kingdom situated where the savanna met the thick Akan

214

forest. It was also a centre for north-south, east-west trade with very strong links to Hausaland in present-day Northern Nigeria, Mali, and other trade centres in the West African subregion. At the time, articles of trade included kola nuts – from which came the name Gonja – hides, gold, and slaves.

In modern times, many Gonjas live in towns and villages....The Gonja word for 'town' is *Kade*, or *Nde* plural. However, a Gonja will rather refer to his village or town as *Epe*, which means 'home.'

The importance of a Gonja village or hometown cannot be overemphasised. It goes beyond a mere haven of shelter and security. It is the centre of his world, which he will do anything to preserve, and rightly so, because many battles have been fought, won, and lost in Gonjaland.

The most significant thing within a Gonja village or town is one's compound or household, locally referred to as a *langto*. This will usually comprise a group of individuals who are all directly related to each other by ties of kinship. Often, this includes a man, his wife or wives (because Gonjas widely practise polygamy), and his children but may also include foster children, his sisters and brothers, and their wives and children.

Every Gonja household or compound has a recognised head, usually the oldest man. He is often referred to by his name or title, if he holds one. In some cases, this could refer to the nature of his business or trade. Every compound is thus a named unit and provides a point of reference within the village or town. The compound head is often called *langwura* ('chief of the house'). The compound head represents his family unit in dealings with the village elders and chief. He sees to his immediate family's welfare and settles disputes within his own compound." – (Ibid.)

Respect for elders is a very important part of culture among the Gonja as is the case in *all* traditional societies

215

across Africa; so are rituals which play a vital role in keeping family members and the community together:

"By custom, all adults in the compound must greet the family head in the morning and evening. In this way, he keeps in touch with their affairs. They inform him of any new developments in the compound or family (as some families have more than one compound). They will bring developments such as illnesses, pregnancies, births, and disputes to his attention. They will most likely seek his permission for most things, including betrothals and journeys that members of the compound contemplate.

The compound head leads his family in performing certain important rituals, such as naming ceremonies for newborn babies, funeral rites, or supplications for dead parents or grandparents. The remembrance and supplication of dead parents (*nyina*) are important parts of Gonja custom.

Such rituals often bring an entire family unit together. They will kill an animal, such as a cow or sheep, and use the meat in preparing food, which members of the family unit share. Prayers are said for the dead, usually by an imam. The living may also perform certain rites directed to their own souls (*akalibi*). Despite the influence of the Islamic religion, Gonjas believe in reincarnation, and divination is widely practised." – (Ibid.)

Compounds are the basic units of Gonja society. Collectively, they constitute larger settlements whose members are linked by kinship, unlike those in a number of traditional societies on the continent where even non-relatives can establish a village, although even in some of these societies, members of related families also form villages. Tampuri states the following about Gonja compounds:

"Several compound units form a village or town.

216

Therefore, to a Gonja, his village people are not only his neighbours but his kinsmen or wider family. Similarly, groups of villages will form divisions within the Gonja political system. Therefore, one's village and both parents' villages form the main points of orientation for a Gonja.

Prominent Gonja towns include Bole, Busunu, Daboya, Damongo, Buipe, Laribanga, Kalba, Kandia, Kabalma, Kong, Kpembe, Kusawgu, Mandari, Mankarigu, Mankuma, Mpaha, Nakwabi, Nyanga, Salaga, Sawla, Soma, Sonyo, Tuluwe, Tuna, Yipala, and Yapei.

At present, there are no cities in Gonjaland, but that hasn't stopped many Gonjas from clamouring for their own region in recent times." – (Ibid.)

Solomon Salifu Tampuri's book was published in 2016. He also describes his homeland in terms of geography and climate in the following terms:

"Geographically, Gonjaland, as most Gonjas refer to their land, is located in the northern part of Ghana. The area is much drier than the southern areas of the country due to its proximity to the Sahara Desert. The vegetation consists predominantly of grassland, especially savanna, with clusters of drought-resistant trees, such as baobabs....

Temperatures...can vary between 14°C (59°F) at night and 40°C (104°F) during the day." – (Ibid.)

He goes on to state:

"Most houses in Gonjaland villages are made of adobe and have thatched roofs. Those are the materials found in the immediate area, and those are the materials that most of the people can afford, anyway....

The main occupations in Gonjaland include farming, fishing, hunting, weaving, and trading. There are also a few blacksmith and white-collar jobs in the larger towns and villages.

Gonjas have a patrilineal or agnatic society, and they widely practise polygamy, although, in recent times – and due to the influence of Western education and culture and economic reasons – there is a gradual shift in favour of monogamy, especially among the educated elite and those living in urban centres." – (Ibid.)

As in other traditional societies in Africa, transformation has taken place through the years and has in some ways even changed the original cultural identity of the people in those societies.

Very few, if any, have remained as they were in the beginning. There have been some changes in language and culture because of the influence of other ethnic groups, interacting with them; sometimes because of conquest. In the case of the Gonja, Tampuri states:

"Although the main language spoken in Gonjaland is Ngbanyito, it may not be the same as the original Mande language spoken when they first arrived. The original dialect would have undergone some significant transformations due to the Akan's language influence while they sojourned in Bonoland and later due to vanguished tribes' languages. In fact, according to Ward (1948):

The only theory I can suggest to reconcile these facts is that the oldest inhabitants of the country were Gonja speaking; that at a later date there occurred a gradual, and probably peaceable, infiltration by Vagale-speaking clans so the two lived side by side; and that when the recent invasion from the West took place, the small party of men happened to marry Gonja-speaking, not Vagale-speaking, women so that the Gonja language became associated with the conquerors and became the language of the ruling class' (p.123).

Ward has stated that the Guan language in that region is not the language of the masses but of the ruling class. The masses speak languages akin to Moshi:

218

The Gonja-speaking class state that they found the Ashanti settled in the country when they arrived, and they married the Ashanti women. This they gave as the explanation of the resemblance between their language and Ashanti.

I suppose Ward is referring to the Akan people of Bono Manso, who still remain the closest neighbours of the Gonjas to the south, not Ashanti. It is also true that the Mandingo expedition that left Mande came with very few women perhaps to assist care for wounded fighters and other domestic chores. In any event, Gonja men are known to have a reputation for their amorous adventures.

The Mandingoes were described as tall, masculine and light in complexion while the inhabitants in the Akan area were said to be short, dark in complexion and hairy." – (Ibid.)

Gonja does not exist anymore as a kingdom as it once did. Even its remnants may not reflect the glory of its past.

It was one of the most successful states in precolonial Africa; its people today, together with the Akans and other Ghanaians as well as other Africans, a reminder of what Africa once was, in terms of social and political organisation, a continent with a glorious past in spite of its shortcomings in many areas; the brutal institution of slavery as one of the foundations of some of the kingdoms such as Gonja being the most tragic.

But, besides that and other deficits in a number of areas, it was a past to be proud of, with vibrant cultures and institutions as well as spiritual and moral values which were, to a large degree, destroyed by the invaders from Europe when they imposed imperial rule on a people who never wanted to be brought under colonial tutelage.

They were independent before Europeans came, and they wanted to remain independent, preserve their cultures and institutions which reflected and defined their identities as a people. As Nkrumah stated in his speech on the Motion for Ghana's Independence to the Gold Coast Legislative Assembly on 10 July 1953:

"Throughout a century of alien rule our people have, with ever increasing tendency, looked forward to that bright and glorious day when they shall regain their ancient heritage, and once more take their place rightly as free men in the world....

There comes a time in the history of all colonial peoples when they must, because of their will to throw off the hampering shackles of colonialism, boldly assert their God-given right to be free of a foreign ruler. Today, we are here to claim this right to our independence....

In the very early days of the Christian era, long before England had assumed any importance, long even before her people had united into a nation, our ancestors had attained a great empire, which lasted until the eleventh century, when it fell before the attacks of the Moors of the North.

At its height, that empire stretched from Timbuktu to Bamako, and even as far as to the Atlantic. It is said that lawyers and scholars were much respected in that empire, and that the inhabitants of Ghana wore garments of wool, cotton, silk and velvet. There was trade in copper, gold and textile fabrics, and jewels and weapons of gold and silver were carried.

Thus may we take pride in the name of Ghana, not out of romanticism, but as an inspiration for the future. It is right and proper that we should know about our past. For just as the future moves from present so the present has emerged from the past. Nor need we be ashamed of our past. There was much in it of glory.

What our ancestors achieved in the context of their contemporary society, gives us confidence that we can create, out of the past, a glorious future, not in terms of war and military pomp, but in terms of social progress and of peace. *For we repudiate war and violence.* Our battle shall be against the old ideas that keep men trammelled in their own greed; against the crass stupidities that breed hatred, fear and inhumanity.

The heroes of our future will be those who can lead our people out of the stifling fog of disintegration through serfdom, into the valley of light where purpose, endeavour and determination will create that brotherhood which Christ proclaimed two thousand years ago, and about which so much is said, but so little done....

Were not our ancestors ruling themselves before the white man came to these shores?...

The strands of history have brought our two countries together. We have provided much material benefit to the British people, and they in turn have taught us many good things. We want to continue to learn from them the best they can give us and we hope that they will find in us qualities worthy of emulation....

In our daily lives, we may lack those material comforts regarded as essential by the standards of the modern world,...but we have the gifts of laughter and joy, a love of music, a lack of malice, an absence of the desire for vengeance for our wrongs, all things of intrinsic worth in a world sick of injustice, revenge, fear and want.

We feel that there is much the world can learn from those of us who belong to what we might term the pre-technological societies. These are values which we must not sacrifice unheedingly in pursuit of material progress....

We have to work hard to evolve new patterns, new social customs, new attitudes to life, so that while we seek the material, cultural and economic advancement of our country, while we raise their standards of life, we shall not sacrifice their fundamental happiness. That has been the greatest tragedy of Western society since the Industrial Revolution." – (Kwame Nkrumah, Speech on the Motion for Independence, the Gold Coast Legislative Assembly, 10 July 1953, reprinted in George Padmore, *Pan-*

Africanism or Communism? The Coming Struggle for Africa, London: Dennis Dobson, 1956, pp. 400, 406, 409, and 412).

Fihankra

FIHANKRA is a community of Africans from the diaspora, mostly African Americans, in the Volta Region.

As descendants of African slaves "returning home" to the motherland, they may be described as an ethnic group united by their common diasporan identity in a country where ethnic identity is determined by a common history, a common culture and a common language as is the case in other African countries and elsewhere.

Africans in the diaspora have a common historical experience of being descendants of Africans who were uprooted and forcibly taken away from their motherland centuries ago during the trans-Atlantic slave trade. They were stripped of their African identities. They share a common culture of Euro-American domination. And they speak a common language the same way members of indigenous ethnic groups speak their native languages.

All these attributes collectively constitute an ethnic identity – of the descendants of African slaves who have "returned home" – that is unique in the African context but an ethnic identity nonetheless.

In the Ghanaian context, the black returnees or settlers from the diaspora who have settled at Fihankra are Fihankrans, probably one of the most well-known groups of the descendants of African slaves in modern times who "have returned to the motherland."

But not all African Americans who live in Ghana are members of the Fihankra community. Only a few of them are.

Fihankra was supposed to form a nucleus of the ethnic group of the descendants of African slaves who "have returned home," to Ghana, and who want to reconnect with their brothers and sisters, the indigenous people, in a way that would make them not just some people who want to live in Ghana but who want to be an integral part of society as Africans and no longer as Americans or Britons or whatever they were before in the countries where they were born and brought up as Africans in the diaspora.

Not all African Americans or other diasporans of African descent who live in Ghana have organised themselves and formed a community the way Fihankrans have tried to do. Many of them live in Ghana simply as individuals and not as a members of any community. Also, many of them don't want to renounce their American or British or Jamaican citizenship; the list goes on and on. They want to remain Americans – or whatever they are – with the intention of returning home, some day, to the countries where they were born and brought up.

And there are those who are in Ghana only for a specific period of time, unlike the few members of Fihankra who are there to stay for the rest of their lives. Fihankrans have bought some land and have even sought atonement from the indigenous people for the role their ancestors played in capturing and selling some of their people into slavery and whose descendants have now "returned home."

The Fihankra community was supposed to attract a significant number of African Americans – and Afro-Caribbeans as well as others – through the years and would have earned its place in Ghana as a distinct and viable settlement of diasporans had it not been for the mismanagement that took place in the new ethnic enclave. It ended up being mired in controversy. Only a handful of people settled there. The founder and his family were said to be the source of the problem.

They were accused of taking full control of the land. The land that was given to the diasporans by the chiefs in the area was 30,000 acres. But only about 300 acres were acquired for the Fihankra settlement.

The land was given free. Instead of giving it free to diasporans who wanted to settle there, the founder of the Fihankra community reportedly claimed he bought it from the chiefs of the area for $300 and started selling it to those who wanted to build houses on the property.

Members of the Fihankra community were embroiled in financial conflicts with "the royal family" – Nana Kwadwo Oluwale Akpan and his wife Majewa Adoujokroke Akpan – who ruled Fihankra and accused them of taking their money without even giving them the land they paid for.

Others complained the founder and his wife charged them too much money for the land they bought or wanted to buy.

Some of the people who had already paid for the land said they could not even get their money back from "the royal family." They said they were swindled.

Another major complaint was that Kwado Akpan claimed he was the chief of Fihankra although he did not have the legal right to claim the title.

The disputes at Fihankra escalated and even led to murder, with local elements – some people indigenous to the area – added to an already highly combustible situation. According to a report, "Ex-Detroit Activist, 75, and Her Sister Slain in Ghana," in the *Detroit Free Press*:

"Inspired by the social movements at the time, Jeannette Salters of Detroit got involved in the early 1970s with African-American and feminist causes, helping lead a

225

black women's group.

That led her to discover her roots in West Africa, where she eventually settled in Ghana, changing her name to Mamelena Diop. Her journey to Africa was part of a movement of Detroiters who sought to reclaim their ancestral roots during a revival of black nationalist movements.

Diop loved it there, say friends and family. But this week, her body, along with that of her sister, Nzinga Janna, was found near their home in Ghana in what may been killings in a dispute over land. She was 75 and her sister was 60 at the time of death, according to reports in a Ghanaian online news site and family members. Two men have been arrested, according to the Ghanian news report and family members.

'I feel terrible about what happened,' said her son, Greg Salters of Detroit. 'It's a tragedy. Words can't even explain how I feel about my mom being taken away from her home, murdered and put in a shallow grave 300 feet from her home.'

Salters said his mother and aunt were killed by people who wanted land she had legally acquired from the government in Ghana.

'Some locals decided they wanted to take the land from them,' he said. 'My mom went to court over that' and won.

'I guess the locals decided they were going to take matters into their own hands,' he said. 'And they decided to abduct and murder them.'

A report on MyJoyOnline.Com said the sisters 'had gone missing and a search in their room Tuesday afternoon revealed blood on the floor and a bloodstained cudgel, believed to have been used to hit them.'

Her dogs had been poisoned several weeks ago, said family members and the media report.

The report said the dispute also may have been over who has the authority to be a chief, with others trying to say that the sisters could not legally be chiefs. But family members in metro Detroit say that story doesn't add up since the sisters could not be chiefs in that area because they were women.

Friends and family of Diop mourned her loss, saying it was a tragedy for her to die in a land she loved so much. Diop had moved back and forth between Detroit and Ghana over the years and was a dual citizen of the U.S. and Ghana. She was last in Detroit two years ago for the funeral of a relative.

'She loved that place,' said Diop's daughter Cheryl Salters. 'She loved Africa. The people were nice.'

A family member or friend of Janna could not be reached for comment.

Diop's close friend, Thea Simmons of Grosse Pointe Park, was in shock when she heard about the deaths.

'My mind went blank ... I shed some tears,' she said. 'It's beyond a travesty that she should lose her life in her adopted homeland. She loved Ghana. And she loved the Ghanian people.'

Family are now trying to get her body back into the U.S. The U.S. Embassy has contacted them to notify them of the deaths of the sisters, said family members.

The family is trying to raise money through GoFundMe to ship the sisters' remains back to Detroit.

Diop was originally from Cleveland, but moved to Detroit as a young woman, said Simmons. She 'became involved in radical politics ... social movements' in African-American and women's movements.

In 1973, she helped set up the Detroit chapter of the now-defunct National Black Feminist Organization. She was also a social worker and counselor, said family members.

Several years later, she traveled to West African countries, the land of her origins. She settled in Ghana, getting involved with helping people, said family members. She was also into eating organic and using natural herbs.

'My mother was very articulate, very into herbs and holistic medicine, eating natural,' said Cheryl Salters.

A grandson, James Salters, said that Diop was involved with helping Ghanians with education, water systems and affordable housing.

He said: 'I feel sad that someone would actually target an older woman when she's over there trying to do good for that country.'" – (Niraj Warikoo, "Ex-Detroit Activist, 75, and Her Sister Slain in Ghana," *Detroit Free Press*, 8 May 2015).

According to another report, "Autopsy Report on Murdered Women Ready," in *The Ghanaian Times*:

"The autopsy report on the two murdered African Americans, Mamelina Diop and Nzinga Jaana, at Fihankra, near Akwamufie, has been concluded.

The Director-General of the Criminal Investigations Department (CID), Commissioner of Police (COP) Prosper Kwame Agblor, who disclosed this to *The Ghanaian Times*, however, declined to give details.

He explained that the CID was awaiting the official report from the medical doctor who performed the post-mortem examination, for onward submission to the Attorney-General's Department for advice.

COP Agblor said once the autopsy had been concluded, their bodies would be released to their families or representatives.

Meanwhile, he said, his outfit was still investigating whether other people were involved in the crime.

COP Agblor said as directed by the court, Nana Obiri Yeboah, one of the accused in the case, had been sent to the Accra Psychiatric Hospital for examination following his mannerism which compelled the court to take the decision on his examination.

An Accra Magistrate's Court, presided over by Veronique Manford, has remanded in police custody, six persons arrested in connection with the murder, explaining that it was to enable the police to conduct further investigations into the matter.

They include, Anokye Yaw Frimpong, a driver, Nana Appia-Nti, Chief of Appiakrom, and Nana Obiri Yeboah, a farmer, all Ghanaians.

The rest, all African-Americans, are Brenda Kareema Mohammed, a female pensioner, Yazid Alazim Mohammed, a businessman, and Mensah Kamauogogo, a surgeon assistant.

Assistant Superintendent of Police (ASP) Stephen Kwame Adjei, the prosecutor, told the court that the deceased, Mamelina Diop, 75, and Nzinga Jaana, 69, were pensioners from the American Civil Service and lived at the Fihankra settlement, near Akwamufie.

He said in 1997, some African-Americans in the diaspora decided to settle at Appiakrom and therefore acquired 218.5 acres of land in the town, which is now called Fihankra.

ASP Adjei said the group, in an agreement, reached with the people, promised to provide the community with schools, a hospital, a stadium, potable water and other basic amenities.

He said the leader of the group, Olumale Kwadwo Akpan, who installed himself chief of the area, started issuing indentures and collecting annual rent for lands allocated to the residents.

After his death in May 2009 (2008), his wife, Majewa Adoujokroke Akpan, his son, Goloi Osakwe Dwamena Akpan, and the two latest deceased persons, took over the management of the fund.

However, the three accused African-Americans revolted against that arrangement, and accused the Akpan family and the two deceased persons of fraud and mismanagement.

That resulted in the creation of a website where the Akpan families and the deceased were maligned to the diaspora, leading to a confrontation and a threat to the lives of the two by the accused persons.

The prosecutor said in 2003, the Appia-Nti family filed a civil suit against the Fihankra community at the Koforidua High Court over the acquisition of the land, for not fulfilling the arrangement.

The three accused African-Americans and others yet to be arrested, threw their support behind the Appia-Nti family.

According to ASP Adjei, they (African-Americans) held a meeting with Nana Appia-Nti III, one of the accused persons, and his elders to find a way of evicting the Akpan family from the community.

Last month (April 2015), the three African-Americans, and others now at large, met with Nana Appia-Nti and his elders to remind them of their earlier agreements and promised to have better negotiations with them and also build a storey building as palace for Nana Appia-Nti if their opponents were evicted.

ASP Adjei said the three African-Americans conspired with Anokye Yaw Frimpong, Nana Appia-Nti and Nana Frimpong, now at large, to move into the community to monitor the activities of the Akpan family and the deceased.

For that purpose, the accused rented an apartment for Anokye Yaw Frimpong, Nana Obiri Yeboah and Nana Frimpong, into which they moved about nine months ago.

He said on May 5, Mamelina Diop and Nzinga Jaana were reported missing and a report was made to the Akosombo Police.

A search led to the discovery of a fresh grave about 150 metres to Anokye's maize farm. On May 6, an order was obtained from a district court at Akosombo, and the spot was dug under the supervision of a medical officer from the Volta River Authority (VRA) Hospital at Akosombo.

He said, the bodies of the two women which were found in a shallow grave, were exhumed and deposited at the Korle-Bu Teaching Hospital mortuary in Accra for autopsy.

ASP Adjei said investigations led to the arrest of the accused, and Anokye Yaw Frimpong confessed to the crime, while the others denied their involvement." – (Francis Asamoah Tuffuor, "Autopsy Report on Murdered Women Ready," *The Ghanaian Times*, Accra, Ghana, 21 May 2015).

A family member of one of the women who were killed, who also lived at Fihankra, blamed the police for the murders. According to a report on a Ghanaian radio station website for Citi 97.3 FM, "Police Caused the Death of Two African Americans – Family":

"The family of one of the two African Americans who were killed in Akwamu is blaming the Police in the Eastern Region for the murder.

According to Majewa Akpan, sister to one of the deceased, the Police could have prevented the murder of the two traditional leaders of the African American community in Fihankra if they had been proactive.

She claimed that they sought the help of the Police on several occasions when their lives were being threatened but they were not assisted in any way.

Majewa Akpan narrated, saying, 'we went there on numerous occasions to report threats and misbehaviour on the property and when the Minister sent two of the accused men to occupy our building…we asked the Police to come and assist us in getting them out and they said they wouldn't do it.'

Two African Americans; Mamelina Diop, 75, and Nzinga Jaana, 69, were found dead on May 6, 2015 after being kidnapped.

The incident happened a year after the two sued the Chieftaincy Minister for 'unlawfully' confiscating and declaring the Fihankra stool and skin as vacant at a press conference.

The women accused the Chieftaincy Minister's support for one Osofo against the African American community.

So far, six people have been arrested and processed for court and they were subsequently remanded.
One of the six suspects, Anokye Yaw Frimgpong, a driver, was charged with murder.

The rest, Nana Appia-Nti III, a mechanic, Yazid Alazim Mohammed, a businessman, Mensah Kamaugogo Muata, a surgeon assistant, Nana Obiri Yeboah, a farmer, and Brenda Kareema Mohammed, a pensioner were charged with conspiracy to commit crime to wit murder.

According to the statements by Majewa Akpan, about six complaints of harassment by one Osofo and his allies were ignored by the Police as well.

According to reports, there were times when Osofo and his group broke in the house of the murdered African Americans with the claim that they had the permission from the Chieftancy Minister, Alhaji Seidu Danaa.

The US embassy in Ghana has expressed its condolence to the families of the deceased and has said it is confident in Ghana's rule of law to find the culprits.

The African American Community was set up as the physical first step to the reintegration of African American who wanted to come back home.

A stool and skin was created with the support of the National House of chiefs and government as a symbol to get other blacks in the diaspora to return." – (Betty Kankam-Boadu, "Police Caused the Death of Two African Americans – Family," Citi 97.3 FM, citifmonline.com, Accra, Ghana, 13 May 2015).

One Fihankran, Curtis Murphy, an African American, had this to say – quoted verbatim – about Fihankra in an interview, "Fihankra: The Way Forward":

"I didn't know about Fihankra then. It's a brother who I

232

helped raise...he told me, he said, had I ever heard about Fihankra? His name is Tony Marshall. I said, 'No.' He said, 'They've got a thing, some land that was supposed to be for the Africans to come to. So I came here to see.

The Akwamu people gave the land because back during slavery, they had a fight over chieftaincies. And in their fight, the clan that lost, it was 400 members of them, and they gave them to the white folks to just get them out of here, and that village is down here.

So, they gave the 30,000 acres of land, was for the 400 people of their own clan to make amends; that's what was about. So, then, when these people from Detroit, Gerald Simmons, he sort of hatched a scheme to say the land was for him, he paid, he tried to say he paid $300 for all the land and then he started selling it to the people in the diaspora.

So, as we go, you see these houses...mostly all of them vacant now. You're looking at one right there....

Most of the ones involved now are up in age. So if the young people don't get involved....

You're going to scam your own people for what?....

The land was given from the Akwamu people for free, and then, the first one that got here started saying they was going to sell it.

Supposedly, the money, was supposed to be – a palace built. And people from the diaspora was sending money – it's a twisted scam. But when diasporans were sending money, under the pretext that there was some land for all of us, then they was taking the money and trying to use it for themselves. And that caused, eh, there was a lot of deceit at that point....

The stool and skin (symbols of chieftaincy and royalty) was taken from them the last year (2014) and so we are in the process of forming a gazette committee to re-stool it. We are right now in the nomination process for Queen Mother and Fihankahene. So we got a constitution now....

We requested it (to take back the stool and the skin), I

233

am one of the ones that requested it....The national police arrested them....

The national director for culture and chieftaincy affairs he (asked) the Ghana government to bring the national police to arrest them and take it from them. That's how the stool got took from them....

We first came with a petition from the court and asked them to turn it over. And then they wouldn't. In fact, she (Kwao Akpan's wife, Majewa) threw it on the ground, like, 'forget the court'....

They asked them several times...So they took it from them, the police took it from them....

They have done a lot of damage with the scamming and they had a negative connotation, Fihankra had a negative connotation even to the diasporans because if you don't know what's going on when you come here, you really don't put in a lot of energy in trying to find out what's going on....

When the national police took the stool and the skin, then the Akpans filed a suit against the Ghana government....

The National House of Chiefs created the stool. It is the property of the National House of Chiefs. If they bestow it on Fihankra, when they say turn it back in, and you give it back to them....

The palace that is up there on the hill was – the money that was taken from the diaspora was supposed to be for the Fihankra palace. Then they scammed it and said it belonged to him (Kwadwo Akpan and his wife)....

So all this game playing has been that.

So when the people went to the Akwamu palace, the Akwamu said we didn't sell them the land. And if the land was going to be sold, then they want part of the money for it being sold....

There is no administration for the Fihankra stool and skin now. That's what we are in the process of doing, that's why we wrote the constitution. We follow the

234

directions from the National House of Chiefs on what we need to do to re-establish the Fihankra administration. So that's the process that we are under now. And once that's done, then this matter, how we are going to deal with this land, the houses that's vacant, stuff like that, all that will come up and a decision made from the administration.

It ain't settled; just like he's talking about, he's talkin' about the dude Osakwe, Now, his daddy was Gerald Simmons. I'm not even sure that's his real name, Akpan, because Akpan wasn't his real name, his real name was Gerald Simmons from Detroit, Michigan.

So, they took the name Akpan from here. But when you see, after the murder shows up in a Detroit paper, it didn't show up as none of the names they was using here....

The Ghanaians created the stool, not us. This is not from the USA. This is the Ghanaians to make amends for the involvement that the chiefs had in slavery. After the ceremony in '94, then they gave, this was the first land, it's supposed to be land given to Fihankra in each region. So, in this region, it was supposed to be 30,000 acres....

So,...from them creating the stool and the skin, then Akpan, who was a part of the guardian mission, he was acting as a custodian. He never got gazetted. In other words, nobody never chose him, nobody from the diaspora chose him to be no chief for us.

Then he took it, that he was the chief.., he started telling them that the Ghanaians may tell the people in the US that the Ghanaians made him chief for the diasporans. And us not knowing nothing about how the syst.., how this society works, we just took the word. And then, he told the Ghanaians that the ones in the US made him chief. So he played both sides....

But nobody chose him to be chief. The Ghanaians didn't chose him nor did diasporans. He was taken (sic) the title, and then when he got arrested he tried to say he didn't say he was a chief. But when we came here in 2011, and we did the investigation, we videotaped it too, with him, they saying he was the chief.

They didn't know that we was part of the investigation team that was chose from RTA to come and investigate what was the deal with Fihankra; you see, because even before I knew what was going on, we got a letter to our group that said we was, that diasporans was going to lose the land because of non-payment of taxes.

So, we started raising money to pay the taxes. And the process of raising the money, the people who had got scammed, who had already been here, they was arguing with us that don't give them nothing. It was..., we started to have a big fight about raising money to give to the Akpans, and the people who had already been scammed was definitely opposed to it.

So, we said, OK, the ones who had never been here, we said OK, we will go to the Ghana government and find out what the truth is. We won't give no money to them.

And so then, Imahkus from One Afrika, said, well, we don't need your money, and we ain't gonna lose the land. So then we started reversing the Paypal back to the people who had sent the money. And then some of them said, well, no, take the rest of the money, go do the investigation and find out what was the truth. And so we did that....

There is a list, we have about 200 people who had already gave their money for land here but never got the land. So, how to satisfy them first; we want them to care too, we don't want just..., some of them gave almost their life savings, and we don't want them to lose." – (Curtis Murphy, "Fihankra: The Way Forward," on Breaking the Chains: Repatriation Journeys, published on youtube.com, 17 July 2016).

Complaints from other Fihankrans, mostly African American, include the following:

"Many people have heard about Fihankra over the

years and while many have come forward to 'claim' their free land, many do not really understand what Fihankra is.

The term Fihankra is a Ghanaian expression which means, 'When leaving home no goodbyes were said.'

Fihankra, then, refers to all Africans from the Diaspora who are descended from the trans-Atlantic slave trade. That comprises some maybe 300 million people. That's just a guess 'cause these figures could never be totally accurate.

The skin and stool of Fihankra are physical symbols which were purified to represent the apology given by several Ghanaian elders and the welcoming home of those of us out in the Diaspora. This was done in December 1994. It was considered an historic event and everyone was optimistic about the possibilities of joining the entire African family once again.

The land that many people refer to as Fihankra is really called Yeafa Ogyamu and is only one of many parcels of land that were offered, but few know this fact.

The land was a 'gift' of the Akwamu people to represent their own personal atonement (for slavery). The land was given for all Fihankra, in other words, all of us descendants of the slave trade.

The original people who made up the group given the land promised development of many kinds, including, fire station, police station, health facility, schools and various businesses.

One family eventually usurped not only the land, but the stool and skin of Fihankra. They call(ed) themselves the 'royal family'. How this happened is not really clear.

Some of the key figures are no longer on this plane and cannot answer that question. The man/chief's name is down on the indenture as CUSTODIAN for the skin and stool of Fihankra.

What should have been an opportunity for African descendants to resettle became a personal business enterprise for one man.

The fee for land started at $3,500 for one plot (100ft x 100ft), at a time when plots were leasing for approximately $200 with a 50 year lease. I never really understood whether a person who chose to have 5 plots would have to pay $17,500 or the same $3,500.

With stool land, the general procedure for acquiring land is to negotiate with the family chief, agree on a price, have the land surveyed and have the land registered. Then you are expected to pay a 'land rent' every year, half of which goes to the district assembly and half goes to the chief. This process ensures that each succeeding chief benefits a bit from the original land deal.

For further clarity and information, the land rent today, after years of increases, on 6 plots of land is just under $100. On a new acquisition, the land rent on the same six plots may be only $30 (this is every year until an increase).

Back to Fihankra.

Around 2003 the tactics changed. The usurper decided that it would be better to charge a yearly fee and started with a fee of $100. By 2004 it was $200/year and recently we were told the fee was $800/year.

The original usurper (Nana Kwado Akpan, formerly Gerald Simmons, from Detroit) died in 2008 and many thought that the politics would change and become more favourable and just.

Well, it seems we were completely wrong. Now the 'royal family' has decided that this land is their private property and that any others who try to do anything on the land are trespassers!!!!!!!

The 'royal family' claims that one of the original custodian's sons is the heir and successor and therefore it is his land. The landlord (an Akwamu chief) is not in accord with any of this and is working to remove that 'royal family' from the land.

We live ½ mile down the road from Yeafa Ogyamu so we have seen quite a bit in the almost 12 years we have lived here. Some of the things that we have witnessed include:

People pay their yearly fee to secure their plot. When they arrive to commence building they are told they have to pay infrastructure fees (which we are told are $800 per room) and until that is paid they cannot build.

People are not being showed where their plots are unless they pay the infrastructure fee.

The security guards are not allowing workers on the site, blocking any building from going on.

One sister sent close to $20,000 to have her home built and when she arrived all she found was a load of sand, and didn't get her money back.

One sister paid for 3 plots for herself and 3 plots for her son – at the time the yearly rate was $200. When her husband went to clear the land, some men came at him with rifles and told him he had no business to build there.

One man paid an astronomical amount for an incomplete building and when he wasn't paying the agreed monthly payments, one of the 'royals' broke in and took all his legal documents.

Despite collecting yearly fees, the land rent was left unpaid for several years until one land 'owner' paid all and started to keep decent records.

One family has been taken to court for trespassing, even though they are land owners. They wanted to have a small business and it was opposed by – Yes, you guessed it, the 'royal family.'

Many people have been turned away from acquiring land based on the fact that the 'royal family' feels they don't have 'what it takes' to build.

Who are they to judge?

After about 18 years of having the land, the only people who are living at Yeafa Ogyamu other than the 'royal family' are two families.

Another brother has stayed there for a length of 6 months so is basically living there also.

After 18 years I would hope that a lot more families would have taken advantage of this gift from the chiefs.

From what we know, we have close to or more than 10,000 people living in Ghana from the Caribbean and the United States. 10,000 people and only 8 people are living at Yeafa Ogyamu.

We have tried to stay out of this issue but it's difficult to watch such injustice occurring and not react.

The question is, what to do and how to 'free' the land so that interested parties can come and develop their homes and/or businesses. We are putting this out so that the truth can be known and the correct people come forward to assist in this freeing. Many blessings." – (Black Star Lions, "The Fihankra Controversy," Facebook, 24 October 2013).

The Fihankra controversy took another turn when Majewa Akapan, the wife of Kwadwo Akpan, was arrested in October 2014. According to a report by Nathan Gadugah, "Chieftaincy Minister Sued Over Akwamufie 'Chieftaincy Tussle'," on a television and radio news site *MyJoyOnline*, Accra, Ghana:

"The Chieftaincy Minister has defended a decision to arrest some persons claiming to be Chief and Queen mother of an African-American community at Akwamufie in the Eastern Region.

Dr Seidu Danaa said the arrest of the claimants to the Fihankra Stool is to restore lasting peace to the area and to ensure that 'the right thing is done.'

Goloi Osakwe Akpan and his mother, Majewa Akpan were arrested over the weekend for allegedly creating a near chieftaincy crisis in the area.

A third suspect, said to be the leader of a group of African- Americans who settled in Akwamufie in the Eastern region in 1997 was also arrested but granted bail.

Erna Terefe-Kasa, an aunt to one of the arrested

persons has challenged the basis for the arrest of the three.

She told Joy News' Dzifa Bampoh the suspects were arrested for holding themselves out as chiefs, something they never did.

She explained her nephew's father had been enstooled as chief in 1997 but after he died the nephew became the 'custodian of the stool and skin.'

She said at no point did her nephew call himself chief of the area.

Erna Terefe-Kasa has filed a suit against the Minister of Chieftaincy as well as the Attorney General, seeking justice for what she says is the bad treatment being meted out to her family.

But the Chieftaincy Minister told Joy News the conduct of the suspects is reprehensible and if action is not taken the situation could take a turn to the worse.

Dr Danaa told Joy News nobody can hold himself out as chief 'when you are not qualified to do so.'

He said 'if you acquire land, that is good but acquiring a land does not give you a right to be a chief.'

According to him, the names as given by Osakwe Akpan and his mother Majewa Akpan are not recognised in the register of chiefs.

The decision to arrest the three is to bring peace to the area, he insisted." – (Nathan Gadugah, "Chieftaincy Minister Sued Over Akwamufie 'Chieftaincy Tussle'," *MyJoyOnline*, Accra, Ghana, 13 October 2014).

The idea of acquiring some land in Ghana where African Americans could settle was the brainchild of some African Americans in Detroit, Michigan, USA, especially of one individual known as Nana Kwadwo Oluwale Akpan who was simply called Kwadwo or Kwadwo Akpan.

They were members of the Pan-African Congress-USA, an organisation that was formed in Detroit in 1969 to foster black solidarity and propagate and implement the ideals of Pan-Africanism. It was founded by Ed Vaughn and Kwame Atta, formerly Riley Smith, who was a close friend of Malcolm X. Born on 16 December 1933, Kwame Atta passed away in Detroit on 20 November 2005.

The leaders and members of the organisation were inspired by Marcus Garvey, Malcolm X and four African leaders: Dr. Kwame Nkrumah of Ghana, Mwalimu Julius Nyerere of Tanzania, Ahmed Sékou Touré of Guinea, and Patrice Lumumba of Congo.

Those were the leaders they admired the most – more than anybody else.

The Pan-African Congress-USA was *not* a racist organisation. But its members frowned on racial integration. They believed that black people worldwide would be able to preserve, protect and promote their own interests and wellbeing *only if* they worked together as one people without integrating with members of other races in pursuit of their goals.

Racial integration was synonymous with racial suicide in a world where black people were the prime target by racists across the spectrum on a global scale.

We suffer as black people. And we are targeted as black people. Therefore we must work together as black people for our own survival. We are the only ones who are responsible for our wellbeing; nobody else is.

It was powerful logic and very appealing to the members of the organisation and even to some non-members.

Dr. Walter Rodney, who wrote *How Europe Underdeveloped Africa* and who had fierce pride in his racial identity and African heritage, also articulated the same position in his work, *The Groundings with My Brothers*, stating that as long as we are oppressed as black people, we must unite and work together as black people to end our oppression.

That is racial solidarity. The Pan-African Congress-USA advocated that relentlessly. Racial solidarity is not racism.

The Pan-African Congress-USA also sponsored a number of African students to study in the United States. The students came from Ghana, Tanzania, Nigeria and Sierra Leone. They all went to school in Detroit. I was one of them.

I have provided some information on the central figure in the Fihankra controversy, Kwadwo Akpan, who was one of the leaders of the organisation which sponsored me as a student in the early seventies. As I state in my book, *My Life as an African: Autobiographical Writings*:

"I was sponsored by the Pan-African Congress-USA, an organization founded in 1969 by a group of African Americans in Detroit, Michigan, to forge and strengthen ties between Africa and Black America, among other things. Sponsoring African students was one of the ways of achieving this goal.

The first student to be sponsored was Kojo Yankah. He attended Wayne State University during the same time I did and later the University of Michigan. He returned to Ghana....

We arrived in America as students at a time when the country was still going through dramatic changes as a result of the civil rights movement and the reaction to the racial injustices black Americans had been subjected to for centuries. Many of them, especially the young, had reacted by rioting in the sixties.

Detroit itself had been the scene of some of the worst riots in the nation's history which erupted in 1967 soon after Newark exploded only a few days earlier, and not long after Watts went up in flames in 1965. It was badly scarred and gutted buildings were a common sight in many parts of the city including the area where I lived, not far from 12th Street where the riots started.

In 1975, 12th Street was renamed Rosa Parks in honour of 'the mother of the civil rights movement' whom I had the chance to meet in the same year, together with US

243

Congressman Charles Diggs from Detroit, at an African event at Wayne State University where a member of the Pan-African Congress-USA, Nana Kwadwo Oluwale Akpan, showed a documentary he had filmed in Angola showing the brutalities perpetrated by the Portuguese colonial forces against innocent civilians in villages during the liberation struggle.

The film had many gruesome scenes, including gaping wounds, I will never forget. One old man had virtually been scalped. Others were burnt with napalm.

And there was much more that we saw in that documentary.

Rosa Parks, her husband Raymond, and her mother Leona McCauley moved from Montgomery, Alabama, to Detroit in 1957 at the urging of Rosa's younger brother Sylvester and amidst death threats – they also lost their jobs – because of her refusal to give up a seat to a white man on a city bus on 1 December 1955; an act that precipitated the modern civil rights movement but whose spirit had been harboured in the hearts and minds of most blacks across the nation for years, if not for centuries.

Her courageous act also catapulted a little-known Baptist minister, Dr. Martin Luther King, into the spotlight after she and others sought some help from him.

Dr. King was her pastor at Dexter Avenue Baptist Church and was new in Montgomery. Only 26 years old, he was chosen to lead the Montgomery Improvement Association, a new organization formed to direct the nascent civil rights struggle in that city....

Rosa Parks died years later at her home in Detroit on Monday, 24 October 2005, at the age of 92 and was buried in the same city. Her husband Raymond also died in Detroit before her in 1977. Her mother also died before her in Detroit. And both were buried in the same city.

Rosa Parks' long life and commitment to racial equality and dignity remained a source of inspiration to many people of all races who continued to carry on the struggle for justice across America and elsewhere. It is a struggle I have witnessed through the years." – (Godfrey Mwakikagile, *My Life as an African: Autobiographical Writings*, Dar es Salaam, Tanzania: New Africa Press, 2009, pp. 120 – 121, 122).

I go on to state in a chapter entitled "End of a Journey: Death of a Pan-African Congress Leader":

"In the last chapter, I mentioned some leaders of the Pan-African Congress-USA, an African American organisation which sponsored me as a student in Detroit, Michigan.

Some of them immigrated to Ghana in the early 1990s. And one of them died in 2008.

He was one of the people who played an important role in my life when I was a student in Detroit because he was an integral part of the collective leadership of an organisation which sponsored me and other African students in that city. His name was Kwadwo Akpan. We simply called him Kwadwo.

Kwadwo died in Togo and was buried in Ghana in the land of his ancestors: Africa. May his soul rest in peace.

I have included in this work some information about his life and death which is not in the third edition of my book, *Relations Between Africans and Africans*, because it was published before he died.

The articles about his death, reprinted below, were written by some of the people who knew him best.

One of them is Herb Boyd who taught at Wayne State University in Detroit when I was a student there in the early and mid-seventies.

He later became a prominent and nationally-renowned author.

One of his acclaimed works is on James Baldwin, an African American or black American author, who is acknowledged by many people – not just blacks – as one of the greatest writers in American history.

Boyd has also written about Malcolm X among many other subjects.

This is what he wrote about Kwadwo Akpan in his article published in *The Black World Today* (TBWT):

Noted Pan-Africanist, Kwadwo Oluwale Akpan, Makes His Transition

By Herb Boyd, Managing Editor, TBWT
Last updated Tuesday, 01 July 2008

The Black World Today
Randallstown, Maryland, USA

Wayne State University in the late sixties and the early seventies was a hotbed of political, cultural and economic activism. Such organizations as Uhuru, the Shrine of the Black Madonna, the Dodge Revolutionary Union Movement (later part of the League of Revolutionary Black Workers), the Republic of New Afrika, the Black Workers Congress, and Facing Reality owe their development to students and faculty at this urban-based college.

Kwadwo Oluwale Akpan, then Gerald Simmons, Jr., was part of this ferment, and lent his skills and consciousness to several political formations that emerged during this period, particularly the Pan-African Congress, where Ed Vaughn was such a pivotal figure.

Rarely was Kwadwo – and he adopted this name before he left Wayne State – without his camera and when a coterie of students, including Ozell Bonds, Bruce Williams, Lonnie Peek, Cathy Gamble, et al, formed the Association of Black Students, Kwadwo was among the group's leadership. Very few were as informed about the developments in Africa as he was, and it was only a matter of time before he began to venture to the continent, establishing ties in the business and political realm.

On May 30, Kwadwo, 63, made his transition in Lome, Togo, though for the past 13 years he lived in Ghana where he was the founder of FIHANKRA International and was enstooled as Chief Ye Fa Ogyamu in the historical township near Akosombo.

As an activist and community leader, he worked tirelessly for most of his life for the advancement of Africans throughout the Diaspora. Burial will be in Akosombo, Ghana. He leaves to mourn, his courageous wife, Majewa Akpan; loving parents, Gerald L. Simmons and Theresa S. Simmons; 8 children, 4 grandchildren, 2 brothers, and 2 sisters.

The photographic and political legacy of Nana Kwadwo O. Akpan

By Paul Lee
Special to *The Michigan Citizen*, Detroit, Michigan, USA

[In last week's issue of *The Michigan Citizen*, dated July 6th-July 12, 2008, we inadvertently published the first, uncorrected draft of the obituary of Nana Kwadwo O. Akpan by historical features writer Paul Lee. Because we believe that Nana Akpan's life and legacy are worthy of being remembered, we are presenting below the corrected, much fuller version of his obituary, along with a poem by Nana Akpan and an exclusive gallery of his photographs. — Ed.]

Nana Kwadwo Oluwale Akpan, formerly Gerald L. Simmons, Jr., 63, died of complications of a stroke on May 30, 2008, in Lomé, Togo, West Africa, where he was visiting for business and pleasure.

Although his name would be unfamiliar to young persons in Detroit and Michigan today, Nana Akpan, who was born in Memphis, Tenn., on Aug. 10, 1944, was a well-known and respected photographer, filmmaker and social activist during the civil-rights, Black Power and pan-African movements of the 1960s and '70s.

'There was a time in Detroit when we had a leader who was completely and totally dedicated to the liberation of black people, at home and abroad,' is how his friend Mwalimu Edward Vaughn, president of the Alabama NAACP conference, suggested Nana Akpan be remembered.

While few who knew Nana Akpan would question the depth of his pan-African commitment, some would beg to differ with this assessment – if only in private, out of respect for the departed, his family and friends.

Nana Akpan, they would contend, could be aloof, stubborn and seemingly self-interested.

This merely underlines the fact that his life, like all lives, was complex, but it was also one of great consequence — enough to provoke strong passions from divergent, though not necessarily contradictory, perspectives.

Photographer

During the period that has been called the U. S.'s second Reconstruction, and particularly in the wake of the July 21-27, 1967, Detroit Rebellion, Nana Akpan was a popular photographer, visually documenting the fast-evolving black rights movement.

'Black photographer -/Man, is that camera loaded with Tri-X and bullets?' Nana Akpan asked in a 1968 poem, 'TRI-X and BULLETS,' the former referring to Kodak's classic high-speed black and white photographic film.

His camera, the poem continued, was a 'weapon in my arsenal/to shoot/to expose … to kill./And in reality.' (See

248

sidebar for the complete poem.)

Among his many subjects was Jaramogi Abebe Agyeman, then known as the Rev. Albert B. Cleage, Jr., founder of the Shrines of the Black Madonna of the Pan African Orthodox Christian Church (PAOCC), who was Detroit's most prominent 'black militant' during the 1960s.

Nana Akpan had a long and varied relationship with the Shrine.

In April 1970, Jaramogi Agyeman hired him to photograph 'New Directions For the Black Church,' the historic First Annual Convention of the Black Christian Nationalist Movement, which codified the magnetic Detroit minister's revolutionary new Africa-centered creed, known as BCN.

(In 1978, the movement evolved into the PAOCC, a new black denomination.)

It appears that Nana Akpan's portrait of Jaramogi Agyeman, which appeared in last week's draft version of Nana Akpan's obituary, was taken at the 1970 BCN convention.

Photos by Nana Akpan also graced the cover of the BCN Second Biennial Convention booklet.

Nana Akpan also photographed the young Kwame Turé, then known as Stokely Carmichael, who in 1966 popularized the call for Black Power, a modern variant of black nationalism, which both reflected and helped accelerate the transformation of a wing of the modern civil-rights movement from one seeking racial integration to one that worked for black self-determination.

However, Nana Akpan also photographically chronicled Detroit's and the nation's booming musical scene. 'He took photos of every group that came to Detroit,' remembers Vaughn. He even went on the road with the popular Earth, Wind and Fire.

Nana Akpan's photographs appeared in *Black Consciousness*, a poetry journal; the popular Johnson Publications *Ebony* and *Jet*; *The Journal of Black Poetry*;

249

The Michigan Chronicle; and *Muhammad Speaks*, the organ of Elijah Muhammad's Nation of Islam.

He also published several collections of his photographs, including *Ex-posures In Black* (Detroit: ULOZI Photographics, 1968), which featured street scenes of everyday black life in Detroit, Harlem, Philadelphia and other cities.

It also included arresting images of several local and national literary, musical and political figures, including:

- Detroit poet Slick Campbell (later Abdul Jalil).

- Militant Pontiac attorney (and later Rev.) Milton R. Henry, also known as Abiodun Gaidi, who was called 'The Black Defender' (see gallery).

He was photographed at a 'Malcolm X Day' rally at Central United Church of Christ, the Shrine of the Black Madonna, on Feb. 21, 1968, the third anniversary of the Muslim and nationalist leader's assassination.

In the photo, the lower portion of the church's famous 18-foot Black Madonna and child chancel mural could be seen; at right, a painting of Malcolm X based on a photo by Henry's brother Laurence.

- Harlem reparations advocate Queen Mother (Audley) Moore (see gallery).

- Jazz pianist and composer Horace Silver.

- Jazz singer Nina Simone, the stage name of Eunice Kathleen Waymon, who was noted for her heartfelt, sometimes acid protest songs, including 'Mississippi Goddam' and 'To Be Young, Gifted and Black,' the latter written in memory of her late friend playwright Lorraine Hansberry.

- Venerable Detroit Garveyite Henry (Papa) Wells, also known as Anwar Pasha, who was a student of Master W. D. Fard, the mystical founder of the Nation of Islam (NOI) (see gallery).

Nana Akpan had a large three-feet by four-feet photograph on Detroit's famed 'Wall of Dignity,' a montage of black heroines and heroes on an exterior wall of Grace Episcopal Church on Rosa Parks Boulevard (formerly 12th Street) at Virginia Park.

Filmmaker

In 1969, Detroit activist, actor and black film archivist James E. Wheeler and a friend sold Nana Akpan a rare French Beaulieu 16mm motion picture camera.

'The most important thing for Black people is to develop means to communicate effectively with each other,' Nana Akpan wrote in *Ex-posures In Black*. 'It is essential that our efforts become as deliberate as possible, and I think that film is one of the most effective means we have to communicate.'

In 1972, it appears that Nana Akpan again memorialized Jaramogi Agyeman and the Shrines of the Black Madonna, this time on film.

He is credited, along with James Jewell, with filming an in-depth profile on 'Black Christian Nationalism' for *Black Journal*, the pioneering PBS black affairs series hosted by former Detroiter Tony Brown, which was broadcast on Nov. 28, 1972.

James Wheeler thinks that Nana Akpan might have used the movie camera that he sold him to film *Kwacha*, Nana Akpan's pioneering 1975 documentary on the guerilla struggle to liberate the south-central African nation of Angola from five centuries of colonial domination by Portugal.

The film graphically exposed Portuguese atrocities committed against black Angolans. In highlighting the liberation struggle, the documentary united Nana Akpan's belief in cameras and bullets.

'At that time,' says Wheeler, the founder-director of Concept East II and the Black Cinema Gallery, 'black filmmakers really weren't doing films like the ones that he did on Africa, which I think were very important,' particularly in terms of the 'revolutionary struggles.'

Recalls Vaughn: 'He was in the bush' with the guerilla fighters. 'It didn't even faze him that he was in danger.'

Angolan chameleon

However, Nana Akpan's support of the *União Nacional para a Independência Total de Angola* (National Union for the Total Independence of Angola, or UNITA), one of three ideologically and ethnically diverse Angolan guerilla movements, would create enduring suspicions.

UNITA, which was originally supported by the People's Republic of China, was led by the charismatic Jonas Savimbi.

Charles Simmons, who visited UNITA guerilla camps in 1973 as a reporter for *Muhammad Speaks*, observes, 'Savimbi was a chameleon of a character who would say different things to different audiences and was able to capture lots of support within the African American community [among those] who did not have access to international perspectives.'

For example, Simmons notes, 'Savimbi was sophisticated enough to understand what African Americans wanted to hear. He was friends with Ché, he was friends with Malcolm,' the Angolan leader claimed in exaggeration.

Savimbi was referring to Ernesto (Ché) Guevara, the legendary Argentine-Cuban guerilla leader, who Savimbi met during Guevara's 1964-65 African tour, and Malcolm X, who Savimbi might have met when both attended an Organization of African Unity (OAU) summit in Cairo, Egypt, in July 1964.

'That was heaven' to some U. S. pan-Africanists, Simmons noted. Many of them 'were intelligent and committed and thought that [Savimbi] was clean.'

Ed Vaughn, who also supported Savimbi, recalls: 'We were convinced that any Africa leader who espoused the concept of pan-Africanism was our friend.'

Cloud

However, some of Savimbi's Western admirers felt compelled to reevaluate their race-based enthusiasm for him after evidence emerged that he had begun to receive financial and military backing from the Central Intelligence Agency (CIA) and the then white-minority-ruled government of apartheid South Africa.

Tanzanian President Julius K. Nyerere and Zanzibari revolutionary leader Abdulrahman Mohamed Babu (who had actually been a close friend of Malcolm X) told Simmons that they were 'certain that Savimbi was getting support from South African apartheid and U. S. intelligence agencies.'

Despite this, Nana Akpan continued to support UNITA, perhaps, as Vaughn suggests, on the basis of British statesman Lord Palmerston's famous political dictum: 'Nations [and peoples] have no permanent friends and no permanent enemies. Only permanent interests.'

During the Reagan administration in the 1980s, Nana Akpan headed the Angola Peace Fund, which, according to Vaughn, was a UNITA front.

Nana Akpan's steadfast, mostly uncritical – if entirely sincere – association with UNITA would strain and, in some cases, completely rupture old political relationships and haunt his reputation for the balance of his life.

Nevertheless, he continued to be productive. He produced *Liberia – 1980 – After the Coup*, a 30-minute documentary on the bloody overthrow of the corrupt traditional Americo-Liberian government. It was based on films made by Nana Akpan during a visit to the West African nation that was founded by former U. S. slaves.

In assessing Nana Akpan's contributions as a pan-Africanist filmmaker, James Wheeler says that it is significant that he 'was working in the media to create positive images of black people' and made a 'conscious effort' to refashion the bonds of brother- and sisterhood between peoples of African descent.

Activist

As an activist and community leader, Nana Akpan worked tirelessly for the advancement of Africans throughout the Diaspora. And he did so in style. 'He was always neat to the bone,' recalls Vaughn.

Nana Akpan was an original member of Forum 65 and Forum 66, a black nationalist discussion group that began at the famous Vaughn's Book Store at 12135 Dexter Ave. at Monterey in 1965. The forums later sponsored the historic first and second annual black arts conferences in 1966 and 1967.

These conclaves, held at Jaramogi Agyeman's Central United Church of Christ, later renamed the Shrine of the Black Madonna, featured a wide variety of local and national black artists and leaders.

These included Turé, his quotable successor as chairman of the militant Student Nonviolent Coordinating Committee (SNCC), H. Rap Brown (later known as Imam Jamil Abdullah Al-Amin), and playwright LeRoi Jones (who would soon be known as Imamu Amiri Baraka).

Portraits of all three were later featured in *Ex-posures In Black* (see gallery for Brown and Jones photos).

Nana Akpan was also involved in local efforts to reform racist educational institutions. 'Kwadwo was with us at Wayne State University during the struggle to develop Black Studies there,' recalls friend Herb Boyd, managing editor of *The Black World Today* website.

Nana Akpan was the minister of communications for the Association of Black Students (ABS).

'Oh, my God!'

According to Vaughn, Nana Akpan's activism could be brave to the point of recklessness.

On Saturday, July 22, 1967, Nana Akpan, Vaughn, Kwame Atta (then known as Arthur Smith, or 'Smitty,' who worked at a Detroit post office branch with Vaughn) and Ken Hamlin (later a conservative radio talk show host who styles himself 'The Black Avenger') were detained by police in a suburb outside of Newark, N. J.

They were on their way home from picking up a load of books for Vaughn's bookstore at "Professer" Louis H. Michaux's famous National Memorial African Book Store at black Harlem's most celebrated intersection, Seventh Avenue and 125th Street.

'Jersey City went up that same night,' recalls Vaughn, referring to the uprising of that city's black community, 'and we could see the smoke and flames rising over the hills.'

This was only a week after the much larger rebellion in Newark, where African Americans finally rebelled against police brutality, political exclusion, urban renewal, inadequate housing and other injustices.

In fact, before stopping off in Harlem, Nana Akpan and the others had attended the First National Conference on Black Power, which was held in Newark from July 20-23.

(It was here that Nana Akpan met his first wife, Yoliswa, called "Yola." He featured her on the cover of *Ex-posures In Black* the following year.)

With Jersey City alight in the distance, the chief of a suburban police department, 'with about 15 burly cops with riot guns trained on us,' stopped the Detroit group, recalls Vaughn.

Searching the trunk, the chief pulled out the Yusuf Ali translation of the Qur'an, the Muslim holy book. 'Are you boys Muslims?' he asked.

'No, sir, I'm a Christian,' Vaughn replied, conscious of the fact that encounters with the police often proved fatal to African Americans.

The chief was next intrigued by *Color Me Brown* by Lucille H. Giles, one of the first black children's coloring books, put out by Johnson Publications.

The chief said that he would like it for his daughter. 'Naw, you're not either,' Vaughn vividly recalls Nana Akpan replying. 'You'll have to pay for it.'

'Oh, my God!' Vaughn thought, but the chief dutifully returned it to the trunk. 'Kwadwo was so stern when he told him,' Vaughn recalls with an amazed chuckle.

The next day, a Sunday, Detroit erupted in a rebellion that dwarfed all others, and wouldn't be surpassed until African Americans in Los Angeles exploded a quarter-century later, in 1992.

Pan-Africanist

In the 1970s, Nana Akpan was a member of the central committee of the Detroit-based Pan African Congress, U. S. A. (PAC), which sought the unification of Africans worldwide.

The PAC was organized in 1969 by Vaughn and Kwame Atta in the original Inner City Sub Center on Mack Avenue on Detroit's east side. '[Nana Akpan] didn't join at first,' recalls Vaughn. 'He was always inquisitive about stuff' and only joined the PAC "after investigating it."

Nana Akpan edited many of the PAC's publications, including *The Pan African Congress U. S. A.* pamphlet, which featured a Sankofa bird, an Akan symbol from Ghana, on its cover.

'He was always very technical and wanted to make sure that we didn't put out anything that wasn't first class,' remembers Vaughn. Because of this, 'we didn't put out anything that wasn't professional.'

Nana Akpan was also well-versed in the ideologies of pan-African thinkers such as Kwame Nkrumah, the visionary independence father and first president of the West African nation of Ghana; Ahmed Sékou Touré, the regal trades-union-leader-turned-president of Guinea, also in West Africa; and Julius Nyerere.

'[Nana Akpan] was the guiding force in terms of the ideology' of the PAC, says Vaughn.

Homeland

In 1995, the pan-Africanist Nana Akpan resettled in Ghana, where he was a co-founder of Fihankra International, a community of African Americans who were granted land by the Ghanaian government.

Fihankra, located in eastern Ghana near the banks of the Volta River between Accra, the capital, and Tema, the main seaport, describes itself as a 'Bridge to Land, Tradition and Opportunity.' As a sign of respect, Nana Akpan was enstooled as chief of Ye Fa Ogyamu, the historical township near Akosombo.

Vaughn credits him as the 'prime mover' behind the Ghanaian government's granting of dual citizenship to African Americans.

Although the law felt short of some African American's hopes, granting limited rights instead of full citizenship, Nana Akpan hailed its potential.

'....Each step forward moves us closer to our goal of re-integrating Africa with its Diaspora,' he said. 'Toward that objective, this law is a most significant step ahead while there will be continued dialogue to further improve relations between Diasporans and the government of Ghana.'

He traveled often to the U. S. to promote better pan-African relations. In June of last year (2007), he addressed the 1st Annual NAACP Alabama State Conference Economic Development Summit On Africa, arranged by

Vaughn and Dr. John Alford in Montgomery and Dothan, Alabama.

Burial will be in Akosombo. Nana Akpan leaves to mourn him his courageous wife, Majewa Akpan; eight children, Ewunike, Samwimbila, Adwoa, Osakwe, Aziza, Afriyie, Osonose and Isiko Akpan; two foster sons, Richard and Narciss Miller; four grandchildren, Maia, Nkosi, Nala Akpan, and Anthony Flowers; two brothers, Phillip and Stephen Simmons; his loving parents, Gerald L. Simmons, Sr., and Theresa S. Simmons; two sisters, Sharon Simmons-Lofton and Valerie (Simmons) Tyler; many nieces and nephews; and a host of friends and admirers throughout the pan-African world.

Memorial service to be held at a later date.

Herb Boyd and Paul Lee who wrote about Kwadwo Akpan and his death were just some of the many people from all walks of life who knew him.

One of the most prominent African scholars, Professor Ali Mazrui, also briefly wrote about Kwadwo Akpan in connection with a conference both attended in Washington D.C., in 1989. It had to do with Angola. As he stated in his *Mazrui Newsletter*, Eve of 1990:

"The Angola Peace Fund, based in Washington, D.C. invited me (in 1989) to a one-day symposium on 'Reconciliation in Angola: Perspectives on Africa's Future.'

Guess how may people were scheduled to speak? Yes, five in all.

Andre Franco de Sousa, one of the founders of MPLA (now the ruling party of Angola), made a moving case for genuine reconciliation.

Ambassador Herman Cohen, the United States Assistant Secretary of State for African affairs, tried to explain the Bush Administration's approach to the problems of Southern Africa.

Kwadwo O. Akpan spoke as the Executive Director of

the Angola Peace Fund, a private organization, led by African-Americans. The Fund is committed to the search for reconciliation in Angola.

Jonas Savimbi (leader of UNITA) was expected to turn up at the symposium, and was in the programme as one of the five speakers. Strict security precautions were taken towards the time of his scheduled arrival.

At the very last minute he sent his apologies. He was indeed in Washington, D.C. – but the pressure of official business kept him from our symposium. The participants and journalists at the symposium were of course most disappointed.

My own speech to the symposium included a sub-section on 'Heroic Villains in Recent African History.'

I compared the late Moise Tshombe of Zaire with Jonas Savimbi of Angola.

Perhaps it was just as well that Dr. Savimbi was not present to listen to what I had to say! There might have been an explosion!

On the other hand I did try to be fair and even-handed in my analysis." (Ibid., pp. 287 – 199).

Conclusion

IT IS impossible to cover all the ethnic groups in Ghana in a book of this size; it would have to be encyclopaedic, which is beyond the scope of my work.

I have focused on a broad category of groups in an attempt to present a comprehensive picture of the ethnic and cultural composition of the country and its landscape, fully aware of the limitations I have faced in pursuit of this goal.

The broad categories I have covered do not include or represent every ethnic group in Ghana; an omission that does not in any way imply the groups excluded are not important. It is my hope that the groups I have focused on are, in one way or another, enough to provide a profile that is representative of the country as a whole.

There are some researchers who have probably written about all the ethnic groups in Ghana in a comprehensive way. It is a task I have not attempted to handle besides providing a basic and simple introduction to one of the most fascinating countries in Africa.

Ghana already stands out for being the first country in sub-Saharan Africa to emerge from colonial rule under the leadership of Kwame Nkrumah. He was in a class by himself as the first leader to call for immediate continental unification under one government. He was also the last.

After he was overthrown in February 1966, Ghana lost her stature as a leading African nation and beacon of hope for those still suffering under white minority rule on the continent; a subject I have addressed in my forthcoming book, *Ghana after Nkrumah*.

There will never be another Nkrumah in terms of stature, commitment and accomplishment on a continental scale. As Nyerere said in his speech in Accra on Ghana's 40th independence anniversary in which he also paid tribute to Nkrumah as a great African leader:

"Prior to independence of Tanganyika, I had been advocating that East African countries should federate and then achieve independence as a single political unit. I had said publicly that I was willing to delay Tanganyika's independence in order to enable all three-mainland countries to achieve their independence together as a single federated state.

I made the suggestion because of my fear, proved correct by later events, that it would be very difficult to unite our countries if we let them achieve independence separately.

Once you multiply national anthems, national flags and national passports, seats at the United Nations, and individuals entitled to 21-gun salute, not to speak of a host of ministers, prime ministers, and envoys, you will have a whole army of powerful people with vested interests in keeping Africa balkanized. That was what Nkrumah encountered in 1965.

After the failure to establish the union government at the Accra summit of 1965, I heard one head of state express with relief that he was happy to be returning home to his country still head of state. To this day I cannot tell whether he was serious or joking. But he may well have been serious, because Kwame Nkrumah was very serious and the fear of a number of us to lose our precious status was quite palpable.

But I never believed that the 1965 Accra summit would have established a union government for Africa. When I say that we failed, that is not what I mean, for that clearly was an unrealistic objective for a single summit. What I mean is that we did not even discuss a mechanism for pursuing the objective of a politically united Africa. We had a Liberation Committee already. We should have at least had a Unity Committee or undertaken to establish one. We did not. And after Kwame Nkrumah was removed from the African political scene nobody took up the challenge again."

Nkrumah did not succeed in persuading other African leaders to unite their countries under one government. But he succeeded in uniting different ethnic groups in Ghana, built a strong nation and provided it with a solid national identity as a cohesive and stable political entity that still endures as a lasting testimony to his leadership.

The ethnic groups he united to form one nation still exist. They still have their own identities. But their separate identities have been submerged in a larger body to form a national identity that is one of the strongest in Africa.

Like the identities of other African countries, Ghana's national identity is a product of unity in diversity, different ethnic groups with different backgrounds, cultures and languages coming together to form one nation. And the diverse cultures are important. They are a source of strength for a country which, because of its very nature, survives and thrives on diversity. But they can not, and should not, be the end in themselves. As Nyerere said in his speech in Accra:

"Reject the return to the tribe. There is richness of culture out there which we must do everything we can to preserve and share.

But it is utter madness to think that if these artificial,

263

unviable states which we are trying to create are broken up into tribal components and we turn those into nation-states we might save ourselves. That kind of political and social atavism spells catastrophe for Africa. It would be the end of any kind of genuine development for Africa. It would fossilise Africa into a worse state than the one in which we are.

The future of Africa, the modernisation of Africa that has a place in the 21st century, is linked with its decolonisation and detribalisation. Tribal atavism would be giving up any hope for Africa. And of all the sins that Africa can commit, the sin of despair would be the most unforgivable.

Reject the nonsense of dividing the African peoples into Anglophones, Francophones, and Lusophones. This attempt to divide our peoples according to the language of their former colonial masters must be rejected with the firmness and utter contempt that it richly deserves....

This is my plea to the new generation of African leaders and African peoples: work for unity with the firm conviction that without unity, there is no future for Africa. That is, of course, assuming that we still want to have a place under the sun. I reject the glorification of the nation-state we inherited from colonialism, and the artificial nations we are trying to forge from that inheritance. We are all Africans trying very hard to be Ghanaians or Tanzanians. Fortunately for Africa, we have not been completely successful.

The outside world hardly recognises our Ghanaian-ness or Tanzanian-ness. What the outside world recognises about us is our Africanness."

Besides our common identity as Africans who live on the same continent and have a common history of being conquered and ruled by Europeans, our Africanness is also derived from our heritage, cultures and institutions which have existed since precolonial times, cemented by our

264

commitment to preserving our common identity which is a product of the diversity that characterises our continent; and so it is within our countries.

The diversity of the cultures and institutions in Ghana has not prevented the people from uniting to form one identity as Ghanaians. This identity, which is unity in diversity, is reflected by the different ethnic groups which collectively constitute the nation of Ghana.

In the midst of all those differences, it is impossible to legitimately claim that Ghana or any other country composed of many ethnic groups – as most countries are – has one culture. Yet there are many things the people of Ghana have in common which can be identified as Ghanaian and national in character.

One of the best attributes the country has is harmony among the different ethnic groups. And the most prominent symbol of their identity, besides the kente cloth, is the black star on their national flag to symbolise pride in African heritage and identity.

Incorporation of the black star into the national flag was inspired by the work of Marcus Garvey who formed a shipping company, the Black Star Line, for black people throughout the world.

Nkrumah himself, who suggested the national flag should have a black star on it, was inspired by Marcus Garvey during his student days in the United States and paid tribute to him in a speech when Ghana won independence on 6 March 1957.

Ghanaians are also proud of their place in the history of African liberation. Their country was the first in black Africa to win independence. It also produced a leader, Kwame Nkrumah, who was a symbol of Pan-Africanism and one of the strongest proponents of African unity. He wanted all the countries on the continent to unite under one government. He wanted them to unite right away or as soon as possible. He was also one of the strongest supporters of the African liberation movements.

He still stands out as a national symbol, although his opponents do not accord him such status. Renowned Kenya scholar, Professor Ali Mazrui, in a lecture at the University of Ghana in 2000 angered many Nkrumaists when he said Nkrumah "was a great African, but not a great Ghanaian."

Yet nothing has diminished Nkrumah's stature as a great Ghanaian as well, and not just a great African. Also, it was he who renamed the Gold Coast, "Ghana," a name of an empire in a bygone era but which Ghanaians have embraced with pride as a symbol of their identity as a nation.

Establishment of a unitary state by Nkrumah soon after independence, instead of a federation which would have given legitimacy to and strengthened regionalism and ethno-regional loyalties, has also solidified national identity among Ghanaians through the years. Instead of seeing themselves first as members of tribes and regions, many of them see themselves as Ghanaians first although there are still tribalists and regionalists among them.

There is a general feeling among many people across the country that they are united by a common identity which transcends ethnic and regional loyalties. Integrating students from different parts of the country, having them attend the same schools and colleges, has also helped to overcome ethnic and regional biases and strengthen national unity and identity.

There has also been a successful movement towards cultural integration among different ethnic groups, participating in cultural festivals of other groups, spreading customs and values from one group to another through social interaction including intermarriage, trade, and sometimes by sheer power of dominant groups spreading their cultures; for example, the Akan whose influence on other Ghanaians has been profound through the years and has even led to the virtual adoption of Twi, an Akan language, as a "national language."

266

However, the asymmetrical relationship between the north and the south, with the south tipping scales in its favour, remains a perennial problem despite attempts, now and then through the years, to end regional inequalities. Northerners are very conscious of this structural imbalance and will not rest until it is rectified.

There are inequalities in other parts of the country. But the disparity – across the spectrum – between the north and the south is the most pronounced. As Professor E. Gyimah-Boadi of the department of political science at the University of Ghana-Legon who was also the executive director of the Ghana Centre for Democratic Development, and Richard Asante, a Fellow at the Institute of African Affairs, also at the University of Ghana, stated in their work, *Ethnic Structure, Inequality and Governance of the Public Sector in Ghana*:

"Ethnic rivalries during the colonial era and the effect of colonialism on different groups and regions of the country, coupled with the uneven distribution of social and economic amenities in both the colonial and post-independence Ghana have all contributed to the inequalities and to some extent some of the present-day ethnic tensions within and among the various ethnic groups and the country in general.

Even though no part of Ghana is ethnically homogeneous, an overriding feature of the county's ethnic polarization is the north–south divide and the dominance of the southern half of Ghana in general, and in particular by the Akan group. This segment of Ghanaian society has enjoyed relative economic and political dominance in both the colonial and post-colonial times.

In addition, there has been a divide in Ghanaian politics between the populist and the elite strands in society and between the rural and urban populations.

The north–south flow of migration is emblematic of the ethno-regional inequalities that have developed in Ghana since colonial times when infrastructural development and productive projects had been concentrated in the south and left the north relatively underdeveloped." – (E. Gyimah-Boadi and Richard Asante, *Ethnic Structure, Inequality and Governance of the Public Sector in Ghana*, United Nations Research Institute for Social Development (UNRISD), 2004, pp. 1 – 2).

This demonstrates that despite the success Ghanaians have had in building a cohesive national entity in which they are all treated equal, they are all *not* treated equal. Inequalities between ethnic groups remain a problem. Regional inequalities are also real. Even tensions exist among some ethnic groups.

And there is also the perception among many Ghanaians, supported by evidence, that the Akan – mainly the Ashanti – as the main ethnic group are considered to be *the* Ghanaians, reinforced by some foreigners who wrongly equate "Ashanti" with "Ghana" as if there are no other Ghanaians. The question, "Are you Ashanti?," many Ghanaians are asked abroad is indicative of that; it is, in fact, damning evidence against the notion that all Ghanaians are considered equal although the country has remained peaceful through the years; an achievement partly attributed to authoritarian rule clamping down on the opposition and any elements which may cause unrest and chaos however legitimate the demands of those who demand change.

There is no question that little has changed in terms of dominance by the Akans in many areas of national life since independence; a harsh reality underscored by Professor Gyimah-Boadi and Richard Asante:

"Four decades into independence, inequalities are still pervasive in Ghanaian society. For example, the Akan dominance of the political system has largely persisted from Nkrumah's time to the present, notwithstanding the perception that the Rawlings-PNDC regime had ushered in a new period of Ewe predominance, especially in politics and in the public sector. And even if the claims of an emergent Ewe dominance were valid for the 1980s and 1990s, the pattern appears to have been reversed with the coming into power of the New Patriotic Party (NPP) government, which is largely perceived as a pro-Akan government.

Relative economic buoyancy and to some extent, authoritarian modes of political management may account for the relative success of post-colonial governments in managing conflicts in the first thirty years of independence.

But it is noteworthy that Ghana has not experienced any major eruption of ethno-regional conflicts, and the relationships between the social classes, religious groups have remained relatively stable even under neo-liberal structural adjustment reforms in the 1980s.

It is even more remarkable that the process of democratization in Ghana since the early 1990s has not been accompanied by or degenerated into violent conflict and instability, and widespread fears of an ethno-regionally-driven implosion in the aftermath of a return to multi-party constitutional rule after 11 years of authoritarian rule, under the Provisional National Defence Council (PNDC) have proved largely unfounded." – (Ibid., p. 4).

The country has also avoided domination – hence conflict – by a single ethnic group because of competing interests among the nation's largest groups; also because the largest group, the Akan, is not a monolithic whole. Ghana has also pursued policies through the decades aimed at achieving ethnic integration and fostering national unity:

"Despite the fact that the Akan group constitutes the

largest ethnic group in Ghana it is fragmented and cannot win competitive elections without appealing to the major ethnic groups....(And) even though the Akan ethnic group dominates the Ghanaian public sector, post colonial administrations have shown considerable sensitivity to the need for a measure of representation in politics and the public sector for the other four largest ethnic groups....

(Also) governance reforms and public policies in Ghana have tried to foster political inclusiveness and civic participation as a way to promote national unity....

Inequality and ethno-regional rivalry may cause tensions but they have not erupted in violent conflict largely because successive Ghanaian governments have adopted practices of symbolic distribution, representativeness and inclusion." – (Ibid., pp. 7 – 8).

Other ethnic groups besides the Akan are also divided within, a blessing in disguise that has helped to keep the country united without chaos and without the threat of fragmentation along ethno-regional lines or even secession by larger groups.

Even the underdeveloped north which is sometimes perceived to be a homogeneous whole – mainly united by poverty and underdevelopment contrasted with the south – ethnic divisions and differences characterise its true identity as much as they do the south:

"The broad ethnic groups, though useful catchalls, do not reveal the true extent of the complex nature of ethnicity in Ghana.

The various subdivisions in the main ethnic groups as well as the geographic distribution of these populations make understanding the intricacies of ethnicity in Ghana a complex affair. For example, the largest group, the Akans, consists of Asante, Fanti, Brono, Akyem, Akwapim, Kwahu, Denkyira, Wassa, Nzima, and Sefwi etc. and are spread over the Western, Central, Eastern, Ashanti and

Brong Ahafo regions, with an enclave in the Volta region.

Within these broader groups, jealousies and rivalries make distinctions between the subdivisions all the more important. For example, since the passage of the Emergency Powers Act by the Convention People's Party's government led by Dr. Kwame Nkrumah in 1958, which separated the Brong-Ahafo area in the Ashanti region and created it as a separate region with its own House of Chiefs, Brong-Akans and Ashanti–Akans have feuded persistently over whether or not Brong-Ahafo is vassal state of the Ashanti kingdom.

Furthermore, Akan settler farmers and their hosts in predominantly Akan cocoa growing areas in the Eastern Region, and Ashanti settler farmers and their hosts in the Western Region have clashed over settler rights versus landlord claims.

Ethnic rivalries of the colonial era and the effects of colonialism have also created tensions between Ashanti on the one hand, and Fantes on the other.

At the end of the 17th century there were a number of small states on the Gold Coast; by 1750 these had merged, by conquest or diplomacy, into two: the Asante Empire, and the Fantes.

By the 19th century, the Ashanti's were seeking mastery of the coast, especially access to the trading coast of Elmina. Thus, Ashanti's expansionist ambition of conquest and domination over the majority of their southern counterparts brought them into open confrontation with some of the states in the coast and the British colonial authorities.

Moreover, the Northern region like its counterparts in the South is also far from being homogeneous. There are no less than fifteen different ethnic groups in the region with varied histories, customs and traditions. Besides the Konkomba-Bimoba clash, most conflicts have been between 'majority' and 'minority' ethnic groups." – (Ibid., pp. 12 – 14).

The taproot of the problem in many of these conflicts is marginalisation of some groups and even exclusion from power and resource allocation and sharing at the local, regional and national levels. The chaos and insecurity caused by the conflicts has had a profound impact and longterm effects on the wellbeing of the people involved in those conflicts:

"These conflicts have left in their wake destruction of life and property. Even more alarming is the atmosphere of insecurity and distrust that these conflicts have engendered which has affected all socio-economic activities in the region.

Even though the immediate causes of these conflicts differ, the remote causes are similar if not the same.

They arise from several years of renegation of certain ethnic groups, so-called 'minority' groups to 'second rate citizens' in the traditional and political administration of the region, or attempts to by-pass some of the 'gates' in the system of rotation to the chiefship....

The term 'minority ethnic' groups as used in the Northern Region has nothing to do with population; rather it connotes those ethnic groups that did not form kingdoms or empires in the past. Collectively, the 'minority ethnic' groups far out-number the 'majority ethnic' groups in terms of numbers....

The majority ethnic groups have cunningly taken the lands of these areas to themselves through sometimes false information and manipulation of colonial authority. The impression created is that these four groups – Mamprusi, Dagomba, Gonja and Nanumba – own all the lands in the Northern region. They are therefore the 'landlords', the 'ruling class'. In fact the relation between the 'ruling class' and their 'landless subjects' is at best an acceptance of a situation of mutual mistrust and at worst, open confrontation." – (Ibid., pp. 13 – 15).

Ironically, ethnic loyalties have also contributed to harmony between groups, although there is always the potential – and the tendency – to exploit ethnic and regional differences, a phenomenon that is most pronounced in the political arena where politicians mobilise forces along ethno-regional lines demarcated by geography:

"Ghana's main ethnic groups are clumped regionally across the country.

The Ga-Adangbe is a small group in the South Eastern parts of Ghana, in particular the Eastern and the Greater Accra Regions.

The Ewes predominate in the east, near Ghana's border with the Republic of Togo, a country where Ewes also constitute one of the major-ethnic groups. Despite the fact that Ewes are found largely in the Volta region, there are many minority ethnic groups – such as the Likpe, the Avetime, Krachie and Nchumaru – that also live there.

Much further to the north, located in Ghana's Savannah zone, are two other major ethnic constellations, the Gurma in the North East and the Mole-Dagbani to the West.

This complex mix of ethnicity and regionalism has allowed political and cultural entrepreneurs to exploit divisions and sub-classifications to suit their purposes. For instance, an individual may subjectively cast as Akan, even though the person considers himself as non-Akan on the basis of paternity or maternity.

Moreover, in reality, Akyem or Brong affinity towards an Asante today may be less than towards a Ga, or Ewe, while an Asante's predilection towards a Dagomba may be stronger and more positive than towards say, a Fanti or a Denkyira.

Similarly, the expression 'Northerners' is often used as if the populace in Northern, Upper East and Upper West regions formed a single ethnic group even though most of the languages are not intelligible to one another.

Overall, the trajectory of census data in Ghana reveals that Ghana's ethnic groups are not confined to specific geographical areas. Internal migration and foreign immigration have rendered the various areas less and less homogeneous over time from the point of view of tribal distinction.

Surprisingly, despite this hodgepodge of ethnicities, Ghana's ethnic map is almost coterminous with its religious map.

Christians who constitute about 69% of the population and are predominantly Akan are found largely in the southern sections while Muslims who constitute about 16% live mainly in the Northern section.

Animists are evenly distributed among the various ethnic groups throughout the country (GSS, 2000).

The spatial distribution of the two major foreign religions, Islam and Christianity, almost coincides with the division of the country into the northern half which is poor and disadvantaged, and the southern half which is wealthy and more developed." – (Ibid., pp. 15 – 16).

The disparity between the north and the south was so serious when the country approached and later achieved independence that it threatened to split the country; so did regionalist elements especially among the Ewe in the eastern part where there was a strong irredentist movement seeking unification with their brethren across the border in Togo to establish an independent Ewe state:

"Inequality in Ghana, as in most societies, has been determined by factors such as geography, (especially when examining the differences between the poor north and the prosperous south, and the rural-urban divide), gender, disability and class.

More specifically, inequality of opportunities among the peoples of Ghana is often the result of the combined

274

effect of objective factors such as differential resource endowment, history and public policy, as well as subjective factors such as attitudes and prejudices.

Cumulatively, these effects have cut across regions. There are wide disparities with respect to the distribution of medical and health facilities, access to telephones, consumption of electricity, small-scale industries, schools and other key social services, particularly between the north and the south, rural-and urban areas. For example, at independence, having been largely neglected and left relatively underdeveloped under colonial rule, the northern region declared a social and economic distance from the rest of the country and its political leaders argued that their people were not ready to be governed as part of independent Ghana without special protections.

In the southeast, having been colonized by Germany, and governed later as part of the UN Trusteeship Territories together with Togoland, the Ewe exerted irredentist pressures towards their cousins in Togoland.

The Ashanti also demanded special protections for their cocoa and mineral wealth as well as their culture." – (Ibid., pp. 16 – 17).

There is a natural tendency among marginalised and disadvantaged groups to mobilise forces against dominant groups to protect and promote their interests. This happened during the struggle for independence when the people in the north formed political parties whose agenda sometimes militated against the interests of fellow northerners although the focus was mainly on resisting domination of the country by southerners even though Kwame Nkrumah, who emerged to be the most prominent leader during the struggle for independence and was a southerner and Akan himself, had a nationalist agenda embracing all ethnic groups:

"The assumption of office as General Secretary of the

UGCC by Nkrumah in 1947 was certainly an important turning point in the history of the UGCC and Ghana as a whole. His assumption of office not only boosted the party, but also provided a focal point for radical organization; this eventually led to his break with the UGCC and the formation of his own party, the CPP.

The outbreak of anti colonial riots in 1948 brought into sharp focus the ideological and political contradictions between Nkrumah and the rest of the conservative UGCC leadership. As a result, Nkrumah's supporters within the Committee of Youth Organizations (CYO), which he had established inside the UGCC, compelled him to break away to form the first mass political organization in the country, the Convention People's Party (CPP) (Austin 1976)....

The transition from nationalist political activity, almost entirely dominated by the intelligential or educated elites, to one in which the mass(es) dictated the pace and momentum of national politics is what produced an enduring polarization in the internal politics of the country.

The CPP won the general elections of 1952, 1954 and 1956.

The elections of 1954 witnessed the formation of political parties along regional and ethnic lines. For example, the Northern People's Party (NPP) was formed out of the fear of the people of the Northern and Upper Regions, especially of the educated people and chiefs, becoming dominated by the people of the south after independence. Its aim among others was to win respect for the culture of the people of the Northern Territories to ensure their just treatment, their protection against abuses, and their political and social development.

Closely connected with the NPP was the Muslim Association Party (MAP). This party was formed in 1954 out of the Gold Coast Muslim Association established in the early 1930s. As the name indicates it was formed primarily to cater for the interests of Muslims living in the

Zongo (Muslim quarters) of the main towns in the country.

The last two parties, the Togoland Congress (TC) and the Anlo Youth Association were formed in the present Volta Region. The TC was formed in 1951 out of a number of political associations which were already in existence in the region. These included the Togoland Union founded as early as 1943, the Togoland Youth Conference and the United Nations Association of Togoland." – (Ibid., pp. 22 – 24).

As the Gold Coast approached independence in the 1950s, ethnic differences led to further polarisation of the country to the detriment of national unity – considering the status of the Ashanti as *the* largest and dominant ethnic group – when the National liberation Movement was formed to protect their interests after the Convention People's Party emerged victorious at the polls:

"It was with anxiety that all the parties entered the elections in June 1954 but the results were decisive. The CPP won 72 out of the 104 seats, NPP 12, GCP 1, MAP 1, AYO and the TC won 1 and 3 seats respectively. The CPP won by a clear majority, and also won seats in all the regions of the country, 38 in the colony, 18 in Ashanti, 8 in trans-Volta and 8 in the North.

The first obvious reason behind the CPP's victory was its slogan 'self government now' and especially the way it fired the imagination of the public, the positive achievement of the CPP government in its first term of office (1951-54), better organization, and the popularity and charisma of Nkrumah.

However, three months after the 1954 elections, the National Liberation Movement (NLM) emerged which started, and essentially remained as, an Asante nationalist movement with its leadership concentrated in the hands of Ashanti people.

The NLM was largely an Ashanti–based movement

which, according to its founder, Baffour Osei Akoto (also a senior linguist of the Asante monarch), was an attempt by the Ashanti to safeguard its national identity and reverse the trend that threatened its traditional institutions with extinction.

In its effort to capture political power at the national level the NLM struck an alliance with Akyem Abuakwa and sought alliances with other ethnic and regionalist parties like the Anlo Youth Organization in the Volta Region and the Northern People's Party (NPP).

The aims of the NLM were, however, couched in general terms applicable to the whole of Ghana. The rise of the NLM affected the subsequent history of Ghana in two ways: it opened an era of violence, arson and anarchy which reigned in Kumasi and its immediate environs for about three years, and it also raised problems as to what kind of constitution independent Ghana should have and whether there should be any fresh elections before independence or not.

While the NLM insisted on a federal constitution, the CPP insisted that the constitution should be unitary.

On the question of fresh elections, the former argued that since it had just emerged after the 1954 elections, there should be new general elections to determine the popularity of the two parties.

It is against this background that the final round in the battle for independence began with the general elections of July 1956. The election was to determine the preference of Ghanaians in terms of the timing of political independence from British colonial rule. While the CPP campaigned on 'self government now' and a unitary state, the other parties wanted 'self government in the shortest possible time' and federation. The CPP was opposed on the electoral battlefield by the NLM and its allies.

The CPP won all the 44 seats in the colony; 8 out of the 13 in trans-Volta Region; 11 out of the 26 seats in the Northern Territories; 8 out of the 21 seats in Ashanti,

278

making a total of 71 seats, with a clear majority of thirty-eight.

In the case of the opposition groups, the NLM won 12 seats all in Ashanti; the NPP got 15 seats all in the North, TC 2, MAP 1 and the Federal Youth Organization (formerly the Anglo Youth Association), 1 seat.

The first reason for the CPP's success in the 1956 elections was the weakness of the opposition parties. Secondly the battle cries for federation and 'mate' (secession) of the NLM and its allies scared large number of voters elsewhere, though anti–CPP, were nevertheless opposed to federalism and secession.

The propaganda mounted by the CPP highlighting the threat of re-establishment of the Ashanti domination over the country in the event of an NLM victory also proved particularly effective in the southern Ghana.

In addition, the NLM concentrated too much on Ashanti, Akim, and sections of the Northern Region.

Though the CPP won the 1956 elections, the results show that the CPP was quite weak in Ashanti, the Volta and the Northern and Upper regions. On the basis of this, Busia and the opposition immediately after the release of the final results of the elections, announced that the election results justified NLM's call for a federal form of government, arguing that although the election had been fought over the issue, the CPP could not win the overall majority in both the Ashanti and Northern territories, consequently there was no alternative but federalism (Nkrumah 1972)." – (Ibid., 24 – 26).

The threat to national unity which was fuelled by secessionist sentiments and other centrifugal forces compelled Nkrumah's government to take radical measures to maintain Ghana's territorial integrity and concentrate power at the centre; a noble objective but which, ultimately, led to denial of freedom to the regions to manage their own affairs and allay fears among disadvantaged ethnic groups of being dominated by powerful ones:

"Antagonism was also developing in the various regions based on sectional interests. For example, in spite of the May 1956 plebiscite that was conducted by the UN to find out whether the then British Togoland (made up of the Trust Territories now Volta Region and parts of the Northern Region) wanted to join the Gold Coast, and the fact the CPP which campaigned for the area to join the Gold Coast won by 79 percent of the votes cast in favour of the union, the people of southern Togoland were still in open rebellion and even boycotted the independence celebrations.

Similarly, in Accra, tensions between the CPP and the Ga people grew worse and led to the formation of the nativist Ga Shifimokpee (the Ga Standfast Association) in 1957. This movement later joined forces with the opposition groups.

The antagonism was further worsened when after boycotting the Assembly, the opposition sent a delegation to London to press the case for a federal form of government.

The constitutional crises were later on diffused by the intervention of the British government who succeeded in persuading the parties to make a concession in their respective demands. Consequently, both parties agreed and regional safeguards were included in the Independence Constitution of 1957. Even though the Independence Constitution maintained the unitary state, it also conceded a greater measure of administrative power to the regions through the creation of the Regional Assemblies.

It is against this backdrop that the Nkrumah-led CPP government introduced a number of harsh and radical political measures, in an attempt to deal with the mounting ethnic tensions, which threatened to disintegrate the country.

The measures started innocuously with the passage of laws forbidding the formation of political parties along ethnic, religious and regional lines (Avoidance of Discrimination Act, December 1957), which served to suppress all existing parties that had raised the question of federalism such as the National Liberation Movement and the Togoland Congress Party. Indeed the dissolution in March 1959 of the quasi-federalist interim regional assemblies established under the 1957 Independence Constitution appears to have put a permanent lid on the issue of federalism and to some extent, decentralized local government.

Furthermore, the CPP suspended the NLM-dominated Kumasi City Council and ordered a probe into its activities, apparently to break the hold of the NLM in Kumasi.

Nkrumah also appointed CPP politicians as Chief Regional Commissioners in place of civil servants who were all British. This was done to strengthen the CPP in the regions.

Nkrumah also introduced the Emergency Powers Act in January 1958 and separated the Bono-Ahafo area in the Ashanti region and created it as a separate region with its own House of Chiefs, and also went on to recognize a host of chiefs who were pro-CPP in Ashanti as paramount chiefs. This explains some of the recurrent tensions between Ashantis and Bonos.

In short, Nkrumah and the CPP justified the use of totalitarian measures as necessary for containing the fissiparous tendencies that threatened national unity, integration and development.

The political measures were in large part meant to strengthen the CPP, concentrating power at the centre and weakening regional and ethnic sentiments and loyalties. It is also true that the measures contributed to a remarkable degree of peace, order and stability in the country." – (Ibid., pp. 28 – 20).

It is true that the country has enjoyed relative peace and stability since independence partly or largely because of centralisation of power, neutralising regional and ethnic threats to national unity.

Paradoxically, centralisation has fuelled the very same sentiments leaders have sought to suppress and eliminate because of curtailment of freedom enjoyed by the regions before consolidation of power at the centre under Nkrumah. This has led to demands for decentralisation, an issue that is now on the national agenda and whose legitimacy has been conceded by some of the leaders who came after Nkrumah.

Therefore, ethnic tensions and rivalries remain an issue even if it is dismissed as minor by some politicians who profess unity while they do exactly the opposite.

The best example of such tensions and rivalries are between the Ewe and the Ashanti in spite of the fact that social interactions between members of the two ethnic groups have taken place through the years even when they are feuding.

The rivalries between the two groups also assumed another dimension in the national context after the 1966 military coup against Nkrumah. As Professor Gyimah-Boadi and Richard Asante state concerning the Ewe-Ashanti rivalry in Ghanaian politics:

"The Avoidance of Discrimination Act introduced by the Nkrumah government in 1957 banned all organizations, parties and societies, which were confined to only 'particular tribal, racial and religious groups, which were used for political purposes'.

Under this law, almost all the existing opposition parties and associations became illegal.

In response to this bill all the opposition parties – NPP, MAP, NLM, WAY, AYA, and the Ga Shifimokpee – united to form the United Party (UP) in 1957 under the

282

leadership of Kofi Abrefa Busia.

However, the unity forged by two of the regional parties, the NLM in Ashanti and the AYO in Volta was short-lived.

In the 1966 coup which preceded the 1969 election, the 'comrades in crime' were an Ashanti (Major Afrifa) and an Ewe (Colonel Kotoka), perhaps in pursuit of the promotion of the ethnic interests manifested in the formation of the UP.

However, the death of Kotoka in 1967 during an attempted coup by Akan junior officers and the subsequent takeover of the military government and the National Liberation Council (NLC) leadership by Afrifa, marked the beginning of the parting of the ways between the Akans, in particular the Ashanti, and the Ewes (Hutchful 1979).

By the time the NLC handed over power in October 1969, the military regime had split into factions with the Ashanti and Ewes poles apart.

Furthermore, the ethnic backgrounds of the two leading parties and the voting pattern in the 1969 elections did not help matters.

Significantly, the absence of Ewes in Busia's cabinet and the disqualification of KA Gbedemah (an Ewe) and leader of the National Alliance of Liberals (NAL), the removal of the most senior Ewe officers in the Armed Forces and the dismissal of 568 public servants by the Busia administration ostensibly under the Transitional Provisions of the 1969 Constitution, and the perception that Ewes were over represented among the senior public servants affected by the retrenchment exercise, further deepened the Ashanti-Ewe rivalries.

Asante-Ewe rivalry in the NLC and Busia-Progress Party administrations appeared to have informed the politics of the next military administration – the Colonel Acheampong's National Redemption Council –NRC- (1972-75) and Supreme Military Council – SMC-

(1975-78).

Thus, in addition to trying to reflect ethnic and regional balance on the ruling Council, the Acheampong administrations attempted to foster de-politicization (Rothchild, 1978).

The NRC/SMC sought to institutionalize no-party politics in Ghana through the promulgation of the 'Redemption Charter,' and more stridently, through the military and civilian power sharing no-party Union Government (Unigov) concept.

The two projects that sought to position the NRC/SMC between Nkrumah and Busia were presented as alternatives to authoritarian rule under the military and multi-party civilian rule (Chazan, 1983).

In addition to the resurgence of Ewe irredentism in 1974 (Duodu, 1974), Acheampong's efforts to promote national unity and abate ethno-regional conflicts through no-party politics flopped miserably. Unigov and especially the referendum over it in 1977 proved exceptionally politically divisive, and paved the way for the palace coup of August 1979 and the ushering in of SMC 2 under the leadership of General F. W. K Akuffo (Chazan, 1983).

Asante-Ewe rivalry appeared to have surged in the multi-party contest that was staged in 1979, with Ewes voting decisively against the Popular Front Party (PFP) because of a perception that its leader, Victor Owusu, was an 'arch tribalist,' and the Peoples National Party (PNP) proved popular in the northern regions at least in part because the Party's presidential candidate, Dr. Hilla Limann, was 'native son.'

But Asante-Ewe rivalry had not featured much in the Third Republic and under Limann-PNP administration.

Ashanti-Ewe rivalry has persisted into Ghana's Fourth Republic, with Ashanti-Ewe exceptionalism in voting patterns. While other regions distribute their votes, Volta and Ashanti Regions concentrate their votes on their home-based parties in all the elections held in the 4th

Republic.

The NDC swept the votes in the Volta Region by 94.5 percent, 93.2 percent and 88.47 percent, respectively, in the 1992, 1996, and 2000 presidential elections, while the New Patriotic Party (NPP) won approximately 66 percent, 61 percent and 80 percent, respectively, in the Ashanti Region.

Indeed the two main parties, the NDC and NPP are largely perceived as Ewe- and Ashanti/Akan-based, respectively.

Therefore, even though the two leading candidates were Akan (NDC presidential candidate Mills is a Fante-Akan Akan and NPP candidate Kufuor is an Asante-Akan) in the 2000 presidential elections, the Volta Region voted overwhelmingly for Mills while Ashanti voted massively for Kufuor.

Indeed, even though the NDC presidential candidate in the 2000 election was not from the Volta Region, most of the leading members of that party, including Rawlings who was also designated as the 'Founder of the NDC' and Obed Asamoa (the party treasurer) hail from the Volta Region.

Similarly, both the NDC and NPP enjoyed considerable support from the traditional rulers of Volta and Ashanti regions, respectively." – (Ibid., pp. 30 – 33).

They go on to state:

"Nonetheless, deep-rooted Ashanti-Ewe cleavages have hardly presented a dire threat to the Ghanaian body-politic. A key reason is found in the fact that the Akan group is hardly a monolith. In fact the Akans are highly fragmented, and Ashanti's have not been able to mobilize the rest of the Akan sub-groups. In other words, the Akan group may be one linguistic and cultural group but it does not behave as cohesive political unit.

Partly for reasons of fear of Asante dominance and

285

lingering memories of Asante pre-colonial imperialism, elements of other Akan sub-groups such as Fantis, Akyems and Brongs do not always align themselves with Asante.

Moreover, the Asante and the Ewe together constitute only about 28 percent of the entire Ghanaian population. They are therefore compelled to seek alliances with other ethnic groups and political forces." – (Ibid., pp. 34 – 35).

Yet rivalries between the two groups persist and continue to be fuelled by ethnic loyalties and sentiments in spite of the higher ideal of Ghanaian identity they profess to share and cherish.

However, other factors have played a role in reducing or diluting the power of major ethnic groups in national politics:

"The regional impact on electoral outcomes in Ghana is very difficult to gauge mainly because some regions are largely coterminous with ethnic groups or sub-groups of ethnic groups while others are not. For example, different sections of the Akan sub-group tend to vote differently. Consequently, Akan voters often support and vote for individuals and candidates who are not Akans.

Similarly, non-Akan voters also support and vote for parties and individuals who are Akans.

Although, regional patterns of voting could therefore contain hidden ethnic dimensions, the trajectory of electoral politics in Ghana as depicted above shows that, even though ethnicity is important, it is nevertheless not the sole variable that determines the outcome of elections in Ghana.

The conscious efforts on the part of the political parties to present ethnically mixed presidential slates in elections (typical slates will combine an Ewe president with Akan vice president or Akan president with a northern vice) has contributed largely to the diffusion of ethnic imbalance in the voting pattern in presidential elections." – (Ibid., p.

35).

Although intermarriage has also taken place through the years among members of different ethnic groups across the country, transcending ethnic and regional boundaries, tensions and sometimes even animosity continue exist between some groups, yet not enough to tear the country apart. But challenges to the integrity of Ghana as a nation, and as a just collective entity taking into account the grievances of all groups, do exist and need to be addressed. As Professor Kenneth Agyemang Attafuah states in his paper, "Ethnic Diversity and Nation-Building in Ghana":

"Despite its significant strides in nation-building, Ghana, like many other African countries, remains severely fragmented, fractured and mired along ethnic lines, with other primeval ties and loyalties binding most people far more tightly than the State can currently dream of or claim.

The classic example is the traditional Asante-Ewe hostility which has been capitalized upon by nefarious politicians since Ghana's independence in 1957. This is in spite of great personal friendships and business partnerships across the two ethnic divides, as well as numerous flourishing marriages between women from matrilineal Asante and men from patrilineal Ewe ethnic groups that are considered hugely advantageous to the children of such marriages. A great number of Asante-Ewe concubinages also abound in Ghana.

Yet, it appears that the two ethnic groups are considered the most fearsome ethno-political enemies, with mutually strong suspicions and attributions of ill-will, and in their traditional settings, fantastic myths that justify out-group hostility and in-group solidarity, and, by extension, the maintenance of social distance and social exclusion of each other.

Mutually negative stereotypes and prejudicial attitudes also assail relationship between the large cluster of ethnic groups from the Northern parts of Ghana and those from the Southern parts.

Partly rooted in the nature of the colonial and post-colonial political economy, the systems of resource mobilization for economic production, and the unfair distribution of educational and development facilities, all of which have benefitted the resource-rich South to the disadvantage of the relatively resource-starved North, and which have largely been maintained to date, 'northerners' as individuals and groups often tend to be the object of vile discrimination in employment, housing and the provision of social services by 'southerners,' while the former also tend to find a scapegoat in the latter for virtually every personal or group failing.

At the root of the problem also lies the fact that the development of the resource-endowed South has been made possible by and with the critical supply of labour from the resource-deprived North.

The challenges that have attended the business of forging a sense of nationhood in Ghana have been daunting, longstanding and occasionally debilitating. Ethnic competition, rivalry, conflict, domination and marginalization often characterize inter-group relations in Ghana.

In parts of the country, particularly in the Bawku municipal area of the Upper East Region and parts of the Volta Region, contiguous ethnic groups are still caught up in pre-medieval rivalries and inter-ethnic warfare even in the face of long traditions of intermarriages and joking relationships. These internecine conflicts are often fuelled by incendiary politicians and acted out by idle armies of unemployed youths who are misled into the belief that their long-term economic prosperity is tied to the political fortunes of the politicians.

Occasionally, the inter-ethnic violence is spurred by

arguments and conflicts arising from the mundane activities of living. Indeed, in 1994, disputation deriving from haggling over the price of a guinea-fowl sparked off latent strife in one part of the Northern Region of Ghana, which quickly transformed into an explosive, full-blown war between two anciently contiguous ethnic groups – the Konkombas and the Nanumbas.

More than four thousand people died in that war and numerous others became internally displaced persons; thousands moved to the heart of Accra and established a 'temporary' slum settlement, known as Sodom and Gomorrah for its scale of unspeakable immorality, crime and violence." – (Kenneth Agyemang Attafuah, "Ethnic Diversity and Nation-Building in Ghana," *The Future of Africa*, in *Ethnic Diversity in Eastern Africa: Opportunities and Challenges*, Africa Health and Development International (AHADI) Nairobi, Kenya, 16 October 2009).

He goes on to state:

"The point is that Ghana has its fair share of inter-ethnic difficulties that frustrate and complicate the process of building a formidable nation out of the many distinct ethno-cultural groupings.

Yet, tensions in ethnic relations in Ghana have been sufficiently well-contained and well-managed; the country continues to pursue with zeal, even of lopsidedly at present, the agenda of nation-building. A veneer of inter-group hostilities is discernible in social and political life, especially as evidenced in voting patterns and free speech on the more than 320 private FM radio stations in the country.

Despite these major deficits in national integration, democratization and nation-building, the centrifugal forces of ethnic diversity have not been allowed to degenerate into full-scale armed conflicts and as witnessed in many

289

African countries such as Liberia, Ivory Cost, Nigeria, Kenya and Rwanda."– (Ibid.).

Therein lies Ghana's and Africa's future: The ability to contain ethnic conflicts and defuse ethnic tensions, as Ghana and a number of countries on the continent have done, which should be complemented with extensive devolution of power all the way down to the grassroots level to allay fears among members of "oppressed" ethnic groups – some of which are – and provide them with the opportunity and political power to make and implement decisions which affect their lives without being told what to do by regional and national rulers, in distant capitals, who ignore their needs and interests.

This will guarantee equality, enable members of *all* ethnic groups to participate in formulating local and national policies, and get a fair share of national resources, especially those which are found in their home areas but which are exploited and shipped away without the indigenous people getting anything in return.

Ethnic diversity by its very nature demands compromise, hence decentralisation, without which conflict is inevitable because of inequalities inherent in centralisation of power under highly regimented and centralised states dominated by a few people favouring some groups over others "in the name of the people" instead of letting the people themselves – of *all* ethnic groups – decide what is best for their own wellbeing and the wellbeing of the nation as a whole.

It is vital to peace and stability and even to national survival, instead of the reverse being the case as some opponents of decentralisation and devolution contend. You can *not* have genuine peace and stability in a country where some groups are dominated, oppressed and exploited by others. It is a recipe for catastrophe. Such domination, oppression and exploitation can be avoided and ended through decentralisation.

There is hardly any African country which has achieved true decentralisation or devolution or has even seriously attempted to do so.

Ghana under Rawlings is one of the few countries which tried to implement decentralisation. And it is one of the countries which may take the lead in that direction.

The imbalance between the north and the south can be a powerful motivating factor in pursuit of this goal; so should ethnic and regional inequalities in other African countries in pursuit of the same goal, complemented by affirmative action to help disadvantaged ethnic groups and regions catch up with the rest. As Professor Gyimah-Boadi and Richard Asante state with regard to decentralisation in the case of Ghana:

"A major problem facing post-colonial Ghana has been how to allow for a measure of local autonomy and self-government and promote effective local administration and efficient service delivery while keeping in check fissiparous tendencies at the local level and promoting national unity.

The 1957 Constitution prescribed a unitary system of government for Ghana. But it also established the quasi-federal Regional Assemblies to cater for the strong demand for federalism or some form of local autonomy. But a centralizing trend set in shortly after independence reflected in the scrapping of the Assemblies in less than two years and culminating in the 1960 Constitution and other amendments which centralized power in the hands of Kwame Nkrumah and the CPP.

This trend largely continued, notwithstanding episodic efforts to rekindle decentralization under post-Nkrumah governments. But the program launched by the Provisional National Defence Council (PNDC) in the late 1980s represents the most comprehensive effort at decentralization in post-colonial Ghana.

Proposals launched in 1987 culminated in the

291

introduction of the District Assemblies (DAs) Law (PNDC Law 207) in 1988. Its provisions for structure and functions around the District Assembles (DA) were incorporated in the 1992 Republican Constitution.

The main objective of decentralization in Ghana is the transfer of power, authority and responsibility from the central government to sub-national levels of government. The implicit objectives include popular participation, or 'power to the people' empowerment, equity, transparency, responsiveness, accountability, stability, efficiency, effectiveness, decongestion of the national capital and checking rural-urban drift and north–south divide in Ghana (Ayee 1999).

It sought to empower communities to be able to effectively participate in the making of decisions affecting the overall management and development of the rural areas. In furtherance of the objective, the 110 District Assemblies were created in 1988/89 as the main units of local government and given an unprecedented 86 functions that include planning, finance, budgeting, infrastructural development and security by their legislative instrument....

The District Assemblies are a hybrid form of decentralized authority, combining elected and appointed members....

In theory, the strength of the DA lies in the fact that the majority of the membership is elected by the local communities that they serve, and their membership can be terminated only by that electorate. In addition, it is only the electorate that can recall a member with whom they are displeased.

Another important feature of the present system of decentralized local government is the establishment of the District Assembly Common Fund (DACF) into which not less than 5 percent of total government revenues are paid and whose proceeds are shared according to a revenue sharing formula approved by parliament. This in addition to the 10 sources of revenue specified for the DAs represents a significant expansion of the financial base of the Assemblies.

Ghana's system of decentralized local government is aimed at promoting participatory democracy and development at the local level. The prohibition of partisan politics in the DAs and in DA elections is apparently aimed at ensuring consensus building and promoting national unity as well as development." – (Ibid., pp. 114, 115, 116).

Although this sounds very good, in practice, decentralisation in Ghana has been limited in scope because of government intervention. It is controlled by the central government. This defeats the purpose of true decentralisation. And its legitimacy as a genuine attempt to give power to the people is brought into question because it is only the central government which can remove from the district assemblies a significant of members it has appointed to act as a counterweight to elected representatives:

"The obvious aim was to create for the assemblies a local political structure that does not directly depend on central government. However, the translation of this apparatus into autonomous local decision-making, accountability, and popular local politics is constrained in a number of other ways by the design and actual operation of the assemblies....

The power of the members elected by the community is counterbalanced by the sizable proportion – 30 percent appointed, by the President, by whose consent alone they can be removed. Their primary allegiance is to the central government." – (Ibid., p. 117).

Although decentralisation has worked to a certain degree, it has not prevented conflict, one of the issues it can help resolve if power is truly in the hands of the people at the grassroots level through their elected representatives. There is always the potential for conflict between elected members and appointed members of the District Assemblies (DAs)s:

"The attempt to insulate the DAs from partisan politics has not worked effectively, especially following the resumption of partisan politics at the national level. Conflicts have pervaded the Assemblies, especially over roles and functions and over the establishment of districts and sitting of their capitals....

Additional conflicts in the DAs in the 4th Republic have arisen between MPs who are popularly elected and the government appointed DCE, especially where MP and the DCE belong to different political parties and their personalities are different.

Local conflicts also reflect keen competition over scarce resources, especially land and electricity. Since these resources are finite, conflict arises with respect to how personnel, money, land, power and amenities are shared. For example, land has been at the heart of the ethnic conflicts between the Konkombas on the one hand and the Nanumbas, Gonjas, Bimobas and Dagombas on the other, Nkonyas and Alavanyos, Pekis and Tsitos, the people of Akropong and Abiriw and the Kwahu Traditional Council and the Afram Plains.

They underscore a central fact (not normally openly acknowledged by government officials and pundits) of the post-colonial Ghanaian political economy – the unproven fear that ceding too much political, administrative and financial control to the local communities and districts would encourage centrifugal forces of separatism, successionism, and irridentism, and impede the project of national integration or at least undermine the ability of central government to protect the interests of minorities in the districts and local communities and or impart national values to the grassroots.

The strictures imposed on decentralization, especially central government control of the executive branch in the districts, local government funding (either through grants in aid or the current district assembly common fund) and the prohibitions against party politics are aimed at ensuring central government control over the districts and local communities. It may have been helpful to the protection of minorities and communal conflicts, but like all paternalistic controls, it also undermines local autonomy.

Thus, recurrent tensions between central government control and effective decentralization highlight the unresolved dilemmas in Ghana of how to combine local autonomy with the prevention of secession, irredentism, and other centrifugal pressures that impede national unity." – ((bid., pp. 118 – 120).

Adoption and implementation of affirmative action policies can play a major role in reducing inequalities across the spectrum, reduce ethnic and regional disparities and foster unity at the national level by enabling disadvantaged groups to catch up with the more developed ones and play an equal role in nation building.

They may antagonise many people who have educational and economic advantages over members of other groups because of colonial policies which favoured the south at the expense of the north. But in the long run, they will help to level the playing field and foster harmony and unity at the national level when those who lag behind other groups feel they are equal members of society. As Professor Gyimah-Boadi and Richard Asante state:

"While the term has not been officially used, affirmative action has featured in the social and economic policies of successive Ghanaian administrations in order to address the problem of inequality, especially among the regions. For example, special attention has been paid to the historically disadvantaged Northern regions, especially in the field of education.

Thus, in addition to the system of fee-free primary and middle school for all Ghanaians, special facilities were given to students from the North to avail themselves of secondary and university education under the 1961 Education Act introduced by the Nkrumah-CPP government. It was an important step in reducing the gap between the social classes, between the north and the south of the country and town and country, in terms of access to education (Ghana Human Development Report 1997).

Even in the choice of sites for state-owned enterprises, ethno-regional considerations were tolerated, sometimes in violation of economic rationality; a tomato factory was located in Tamale in the North even though it was far away from the main tomato producing and consuming markets in the southern parts of Ghana (Huq 1989).

The rural and agricultural development programs pursued by the Busia-PP government under its 'social Justice' program targeted the bridging of the rural-urban imbalance.

The program featuring an expanded program of feeder road construction and maintenance, enlarged program for rural water supplies operated by the Ghana Water and Sewerage Corporation with an increased subsidy from government, and extensive preventive medical care to the rural areas was intended to deal with the problems of employment and inequality.

These efforts helped to bring hope to Ghana's impoverished hinterlands.

Some impoverished rural masses saw new health centres, decent water, electricity and feeder roads springing up at places previously considered too remote for such projects. The communities in which these projects were located therefore developed a strong sense of identification with Busia and his party.

The Acheampong-NRC/SMC regime set up the National Council on Women and Development (NCWD) in 1975 following the international Women's Conference held in Mexico, to empower Ghanaian women.

In regards to education, the government pursued a two-fold policy of highlighting primary, middle and technical training at the expense of higher education, and of increasing per capita outlays in poorer areas.

The radical-populist military AFRC and PNDC governments of Flight Lieutenant JJ Rawlings focused initially on addressing non-elite workers/lower middle class grievances.

Under the banner of 'giving power to the people' economically and politically, the PNDC government established institutions which would allow public participation in decision-making, especially in respect of distribution.

The Workers' Defence Committee (WDC) was established to be involved in the day-to-day decision-making process of district councils, banks, company boards, various agencies and organizations.

In the townships of cities and in the villages of the rural areas, the People's Defence Committee (PDC), with their locally elected executive committee was to safeguard the day-to-day interests of the local people, protect tenants from unjust landlords and see that local government services were provided as required (Shillington 1992).

From the mid-1980s and especially under the neo-liberal economic reform program, the PNDC and later the NDC administrations also shifted to a rural development strategy, whose objectives were eventually captured in the Vision 2020 development plan document.

Under the Self-Help Electrification Projects (SHEP) and the District Capitals Electrification Project (DCEP) under this program, all the 110 district capitals in the country were connected to national electricity by the national grid.

The NDC government also improved the infrastructural facilities in the Northern Regions." – (Ibid., pp. 120 – 122).

They go on to state:

"The NDC also initiated 'free, compulsory and universal basic education' (FCUBE), in keeping with the state's obligation under the Constitution of 1992, and in Ghana's Vision 2020 agenda. FCUBE was directed towards making schooling from basic stage one to stage nine (i.e. from primary 1 to Junior Secondary School Form 3) free and compulsory for all school-age children by the year 2005.

The program provided a framework for focusing on equity, access to learning achievement and quality, gender issues and poverty reduction strategies within the education sector. At the same time, it created capacity-building opportunities through decentralization of education and the transfer of ownership and school management to the community and district assemblies. FCUBE covered targeted poverty-reduction activities and poverty focused activities. For instance though the FCUBE is nation-wide, the northern regions were particularly targeted with the view to increasing female participation in basic education.

Similar policies are being pursued under the NPP administration, albeit under the Ghana Poverty Reduction Strategy Paper (GPRSP) whose main goal is stated as ensuring sustainable equitable growth, accelerated poverty reduction and the protection of the vulnerable and excluded within a decentralized democratic government....

Successive civilian and military, or authoritarian and democratic regimes in Ghana have attempted to address the high levels of inequality by spreading the coverage of economic infrastructure (especially roads, bridges and post offices) and social services (clinics and health posts, schools, public measures, etc) in all regions.

Thus, post-colonial governments have recognized the need to initiate affirmative action programs as a means of addressing inequalities in the Ghanaian public sector in particular, and society in general. Such policies have been more general and have not directly targeted specific ethnic groups in Ghana but rather focused on disadvantaged and vulnerable communities and groups in the various regions." – (pp. 122 – 123, 124).

But in spite of good intentions, affirmative action policies have not been very successful. There are a number of reasons for that besides lack of adequate resources:

"Success in equalizing opportunities has been patchy and uneven. High levels of deprivation persist in many rural parts of Ghana and generally in the three northern regions.

Part of the blame must go to policy inconsistencies, gaps and continuities, poor design, inadequacy of resources, and the lack of commitment on the part of officials entrusted with policy. But at least in equal measure, outcomes have been highly uneven and poorly sustained on account of generally weak economic growth rate and frequent interruptions by military coups." – (pp. 124 – 125).

The context in which various ethnic groups have lived differently through the years in the region that became Ghana was partly set in the precolonial era and partly shaped by the colonial experience.

Inequalities among the groups can be attributed to differences in socio-economic conditions in different parts of the country, colonial policies which favoured some parts over others, and even how members of different ethnic groups responded to Western ways of life introduced by the missionaries and the colonial rulers;

some of them were more receptive than others.

It happened in other parts of Africa as well.

Northern Nigeria is a good example of how the people there reacted and responded to the introduction of education by the British colonial rulers, although this can not necessarily be equated to the way the people of northern Ghana – who lag behind their southern counterparts – responded to the introduction of Western ways of life, including education, in their region or regions. They were simply neglected by the colonial rulers. Even missionaries were discouraged by colonial administrators from going there.

But it does show there were consequences, in many parts of Africa, for groups which did not accept and adapt to new ways of life from Europe which turned out to be beneficial to members of groups which did, despite all the negative effects colonial rule had on the people across the continent – and there were many. As Margery Perham stated in the case of Northern of Nigeria contrasted with the southern part of the country:

"While most of the African colonies were taken over, even if by stages, as single entities, the three regions of Nigeria were annexed as separate dependencies at different dates and only brought together many years later. These different administrative beginnings might have mattered less if, in addition, the major tribal groups in each of the three main regions had not also been tribally as well as spatially separated from each other.

We must look more closely at this double divergence, that of colonial experience and of innate group character....

Each of these three dispersed administrations not only had its own character but was dealing with very different situations and different tribes.

In the West the Yoruba were a people of the robe, grouped within states, each centred upon a city. Some of these centres were very large – one, Ibadan, was indeed one of the largest indigenous towns of negro Africa – and each had its own complex and individual form of government and the sophistication which goes with civic life. Trade and industry were highly developed: there were numerous crafts, a highly complex religion and a history stretching back for many centuries.

These people on the whole accepted the white man's rule with great willingness but their own degree of civilisation prevented from being wholly submerged by it. Since their country was rather drier and more open than the forested region east of the Niger, they had never been so isolated from contacts with the north. The first explorers in the eighteen twenties give a picture of lively open cities into which some Hausa trade and people from the north could penetrate." – (Margery Perham, "Nigeria's Civil War," in Colin Legum and John Drsydale, eds., *Africa Contemporary Record: Annual Survey and Documents 1968 – 1969*, London: Africa Research Limited, 1969, pp. 1 – 2).

She goes on state:

"Very different was the situation east of the Niger as British influence and power spread. The tribes encountered along the coast numbered some which had become sophisticated as a result of their contacts with the outside world through the trade in slaves, palm-oil and other products. But, as the British presence was drawn irresistibly further inland, it met the more isolated groups, and above all the numerous Ibo people.

The physical conditions of Africa have made possible the virtual isolation from fully effective contacts with other peoples of large populations with resulting sharp contrasts in civilization.

The wet forests east of the Niger hindered the entry of other peoples, especially the warlike, slave-raiding, horse and cattle people of the north, but the dividing forests also prevented the Ibo developing any political organisation above the limited family or clan grouping.

To the British officials they seemed at once the most backward and the most intractable group of any size they had met in West Africa, and all attempts failed to find or create any form of chieftainship through which the administration could effectively administer these millions. The Niger Coast Protectorate was proclaimed in 1891. Yet, when I studied the Ibo administration forty years later, the British officials were still groping for some structure through which to advance a group regarded as the most difficult and backward in Nigeria.

Yet all who knew the Ibo recognized their immense vitality and their readiness to embrace all the new influences brought to them, including the Christian faith. As a result, without losing their native vigour, the Ibo forged ahead in the 'forties and 'fifties to become the most active and westernised group in Nigeria and they streamed out of their poor and overcrowded land to employ their energies and their newly-gained skills and education in other parts of the Protectorate.

They also showed a capacity, very obvious in today's crisis (the Nigerian civil war), to win the devotion of Europeans, official and unofficial, who worked with them. Add to this that their lack of chiefs and cities gave then an equalitarian unity." – (Ibid., pp. 2 – 3).

That was in sharp contrast with the north:

"We must now look northward at the third major group of Nigeria's population and again we are met with one of Africa's astonishing contrasts.

In the north a different climate with dry, open savannah country allowed the development of city-states, comparable with those of the Yoruba, but open to the penetration of Islam and to other influences carried, if somewhat tenuously, across the Sahara from the

Mediterranean region. Here the traveller could find himself in a world different scenically and culturally from that of the green south, with an apparently docile peasantry grouped around the large, well-built cities of red clay, with their mosques, their law-courts and their palaces housing the Emirs. These were served by numerous officials, attendants and mailed horsemen.

A religious revival early in the nineteenth century intensified the spirit of Islam and carried its influence further south over still pagan areas, always the hunting ground for slaves, and even led to the conquest of the most northern Yoruba state. But it left unsubdued between the Muslim Hausa emirates and the southern regions, a number of pagan groups forming what was later to be called the Middle Belt.

The Niger Company pushed up the great river but the occupation and government of the vast northern region was beyond its powers. So, in 1900 the British Government took over. It sent out Frederick, later Lord Lugard, to occupy and administer the north which he did within six crowded years....

In 1906 the two very contrasted southern regions were brought together and in 1914 Lugard came back to unite north and south. This was a union of three British administrations rather than three populations. For another thirty years or more there was no British policy from above or African pressure from below to stimulate a real unity....

Lugard's indirect rule, suffering the penalty of its initial success, was, in the view of later critics, maintained with such preservative effect in the Hausa states as to maintain the gap between them and the thrusting English-speaking pagan or Christian intelligentsia of the south. But it should be remembered that the administrators were dealing with a system of government congealed within a world faith which British rulers had everywhere learned from experience to treat with respect, and also that the resultant inertia of the north can be exaggerated.

There were educational and economic forces at work, but the government which directed them was not moved by any great sense of urgency until, after the end of the Second World War, the idea of independence began to be a serious prospect. It must also be remembered that the people of the Hausa States and the Kanuri of the ancient northern kingdom of Bornu had their own language, whereas in the south, English was increasingly the lingua franca of the people and opened them to the full impact of the new economic, political and religious influences.

A northern chief once reproached me about the failure of the British to spread the English language. I reminded him of the strong opposition to this and of an incident encountered in Bornu where there was great anger because the British would not give first place to Arabic in schools. 'Well,' he said, 'you should have forces us.' That would have been against the British tradition and would certainly have alienated the people." – (Ibid., pp. 3 – 4).

Perham goes on to explain:

"The result of these unabridged and, perhaps in the time, almost unbridgeable contrasts between the three main peoples was that they met the increasing impact of new political influence in their separate and different ways....The northern emirs, awakening to the danger of being by-passed politically and even isolated physically by the southerners, enclosed their loyal subjects in the designedly local and monolithic Northern Peoples Congress.

Independence was gained after some fourteen years of experiment, experience and consultation under British guidance, with the constitutional ideas moving increasingly in the direction of a loose federation of the original three regions.

The independence celebrations in October 1960 were

304

carried out with immense pomp and enthusiasm, but I must confess that when, as the guest of the new government, I watched the Union Jack hauled down and the new Nigerian flag run up, I had a sudden involuntary tremor of apprehension about the future. The new federal dawn was, indeed, soon clouded.

In spite of early attempts by the two southern parties (the Action Group of the Yoruba led by Chief Obafemi Awolowo and the predominantly Igbo National Council of Nigeria and the Cameroons – NCNC – led by Nnamdi Azikiwe) to break out of the situation in which each of the three regions had its own regional party, the political pattern with little exception tended towards that dangerous form.

The northern leaders had the strength of their great local authority and their unity, but were afraid for their communications with the ports (in the south) and resentful of the increasing influx of western-trained southerners, and especially Ibo, who flocked into their cities to monopolize much of the skilled and commercial employment." – (Ibid., pp. 4 – 5).

The parallels between Ghana and Nigeria are not exact. But there are strong similarities between the two, especially in terms of education and economic power, with the northern regions of both countries lagging behind their southern counterparts. This has posed a threat to national unity and stability in both countries.

Western influence in the southern regions has played a major role in tilting the "balance" in favour of southerners who are also predominantly Christian. Colonial policies created inequalities between northerners and southerners. The colonial rulers were mostly based in the southern part of both countries and deliberately ignored the north, especially in the Gold Coast.

In the case of Ghana, Professor Gyimah-Boadi and Richard Asante state the following with regard to

305

inequalities and tensions among different groups and disparities between the north and the south as well as in other parts of the country:

"Ghana is made up of diverse socio-cultural groups. Different socio-economic conditions and inter-group relations in the pre-colonial era combined with differential exposure to and incorporation into the colonial order set the stage for ethno-regional inequalities and rivalries after independence.

The north-south divide, rural-urban disparities, Ashanti–Ewe divide, overall dominance of the Akan group in economic and social life and in the public sector represent the main features of ethnic and regional polarization in Ghana.

This appears to reflect largely, the relatively strong factor endowment, greater exposure to western/colonial era commerce, education, and other social influences in the southern part of Ghana.

But there are also social class divisions, characterized by a vast rural and agrarian rural population and small urban elite.

Akans (who comprise about twenty sub-groups) constitute about half of the Ghanaian population. But like the other ethnic groups, they are very fragmented and have their own internal rivalries. Consequently, the Akan group hardly behaves as a coherent political unit. Different sections of the Akan group such as Fantes and Asantes tend to vote differently during elections.

This has contributed to the formation of cross-ethnic coalitions in which Akans vote for individuals and parties of non-Akan origin, and non-Akans support and vote for individual Akans candidates and Akan-dominated parties. Thus, even though the Akan group constitutes the largest ethnic group in the country, it is too fragmented to win competitive national elections without appealing to the other major ethnic groups in Ghana.

Fragmentation among the Akan group also implies that Akan-based parties can only be electorally competitive if they are able to broaden their support base by bringing on board non-Akans.

Similarly, the other major ethnic groups who cumulatively constitute about 50 percent of the population are equally fragmented and have their own inter- and intra-rivalries, which prevent them from behaving as coherent group to counter Akans.

Altogether, fragmentation among the various ethnic groups has encouraged cross-ethnic coalitions and thereby helped to foster crude but stable inter-ethnic relations in Ghana.

To be sure, the Ashanti-Ewe divide remains potent. The two groups have displayed the least flexibility in their voting behavior. The pattern of voting among Asante's and Ewes broadly suggests that the country is polarized along ethnic and political party lines. Indeed, just as in the 1969, 1992 and 1996 elections, the 2000 elections recorded partial bloc voting for the NPP in the Ashanti region and full bloc voting for the NDC in the Volta region.

However, at least for now, the Ashanti–Ewe divide does not pose a major threat to the Ghanaian body politic – largely because Ashantis constitute only about 15 percent of the Ghanaian population and have not been all that successful in mobilizing the other Akan sub-groups to vote along with them in elections.

Similarly, the Ewe ethnic group which constitutes only about 13 percent of the entire population is not large enough to win competitive national elections in Ghana, even with the full bloc voting in the Volta region.

Thus, the two groups have always been motivated to seek alliances with other major groups and regions of the country." – (pp. 125 – 126).

They go on to state:

"Institutional arrangements and public policies under successive governments are the main factors accounting for the relative success with which Ghana has been able to contain ethno-regional inequalities and rivalries. Ghana's governance institutions and public policies have been generally sensitive to the complex challenges presented by the heterogeneous nature of the society.

Electoral rules, decentralization programs, affirmative action and other social policies, and public service recruitment and political appointments under parliamentary and presidential constitutions and under military and civilian administrations have sought to address or at least have been sensitive to the problems of inequality and cleavage in Ghanaian society.

Thus, Ghana's electoral rules are based on the majoritarian winner-takes–all formula (which has serious drawbacks for effective representation). But it is also provides safeguards for groups who do not vote for the winning candidate or party.

Not getting many votes in the Volta Region has not discouraged President Kufuor from appointing Ewes to his cabinet. He seems to have done so partly to overcome negative perceptions of an NPP anti-Ewe bias and enhance his and the NPP's electability in the next elections.

Indeed, the electoral rules of the 4th Republic appear to promote pluralism within the party system because political parties are motivated to seek alliances across ethno-regional lines in order to be competitive, thereby fostering consensus building and political inclusiveness.

Outright prohibitions against the formation of ethno-regionally based parties, together with the cross ethnic coalition arithmetic of vote getting in Ghanaian elections, have helped to inhibit the formation of ethno-regional parties and encouraged previously ethnically/regionally-based parties to repackage their programs and transform themselves into national parties.

The pattern of appointments into the public service and

to political positions, fostered by constitutional provisions, notably those contained in the 1992 Constitution also help to promote political inclusiveness and national unity. While there is no formal requirement to factor ethno-regionalism into public sector recruitment, successive governments have been sensitive to ethno-regional imbalance and in practice adopted something of an ethnic mixing formulae, giving representation to all the major ethnic groups in cabinet and to some extent other key public sector institutions. This has helped to make governance institutions and public policies supportive of political inclusiveness, civic participation and national unity. It has also helped to mute Akan dominance of the Ghanaian public sector." pp. 127 – 129).

In spite of ethnic diversity and tensions as well as regional differences and rivalries, Ghana stands out as one of the most stable and united countries in Africa. And it can remain that way if Ghanaian identity takes precedence over other identities – ethnic and regional – for the sake of national unity. As Nkrumah would have said, "I am not Ghanaian because I was born in Ghana but because Ghana was born in me."

Appendix I

The Curse of Tribalism

Liz Sly, *Chicago Tribune*,

26 July 1995

BIMBILLA, Ghana --- Locals call it the "Guinea Fowl War" because it flared after a dispute between two tribesmen over one of the birds in the market of this small rural town. According to some accounts, the Nanumba tribesman who wanted the fowl bit off the thumb of the Konkomba tribesman who had bought it.

However, the small but vicious war that subsequently ravaged huge swaths of this remote farming region of northern Ghana in 1994 and earlier this year was far more complex than its farcical origins suggest.

It was not an important war by most standards, barely registering in the consciousness of Africa, let alone the world. But its multiple causes go a long way toward explaining why the continent seems so conflict-prone at this turbulent point in its history.

And the fact that it happened in Ghana, a country widely regarded as one of the most stable in Africa, suggests that few parts of the continent are immune to the lethal combination of poverty, ethnicity and weak government that made for conflict here.

At first sight, this was a classic tribal war, fought over the age-old issue of land and waged by bands of warrior youths, armed mainly with bows and arrows but also a smattering of AK-47s, who were summoned to battle by the beating of drums outside the homes of tribal leaders.

More than that, however, it was a traditional war fought for modern reasons that underline the dangers of trying to catapult Africa into the 20th century in a fraction of the time it took the rest of the world to arrive.

"This conflict is all about change, and how it affects people in different ways," said Sulemane Abudulai, a local land-tenure expert.

"If people had alternative sources of income, they wouldn't be fighting over land. If people felt they had a say in the modern hierarchy, they wouldn't be fighting over power. If they felt a sense of unity in that they're all Ghanaian and they're all poor, they wouldn't be fighting each other," he said.

"If they could relate to a bigger thing, a government, it would be different. But they can't. So they revert to tribalism, and it's poverty and ignorance that make you revert to your tribe."

And that, in essence, is what happened when modern reforms aimed at alleviating poverty intruded into this traditional backwater of African life.

This is a part of the world barely touched by the 20th century, where most people live in beehive huts nestled among palm trees, where a bicycle is a luxury and where local chiefs are carried on litters, shoulder-high among their subjects, flanked by warriors carrying bows and arrows and ancient rifles left behind a century ago by European slave traders.

There are some 60 languages spoken in northern Ghana alone, even though just 1.4 million people, or nearly 10 percent of the nation's population, live there. The story of the "Guinea Fowl War" concerns just three of those language groups, or tribes, living on relatively fertile land that is especially suitable for growing yams.

The conflict pitted two groups, the so-called chiefly tribes of Nanumbas and the Dagombas against the third, the Konkombas, who do not have chiefs. The Konkombas are thus the traditional equivalent of sharecroppers: They farm the land but do not have rights to it, and they pay for the privilege with gifts of yams to their Nanumba and Dagomba overlords.

Into this traditional arrangement stepped the 20th century. Under reforms demanded by the World Bank in return for continuing to give indebted Ghana financial support, farmers who previously had been obliged to sell their crops to the state at hugely depressed prices are now permitted to sell on the open market.

Such reforms have the potential to revolutionize the lives of rural people, as Nanumba farmer Tindana Dokurugu, 42, discovered when he experimented with the new system. Along with most subsistence farmers in Ghana, and elsewhere in Africa, he had never bothered to plant more than he could eat because there was no incentive.

Last year, however, he planted double the usual number of yams. "I ate half and I sold half," he said. "With the money I bought a motorcycle."

But the reformers had failed to take into account the fact that the sudden profitability of yam farming would lead to a surge in demand for land to grow yams. The result was conflict-between those who had rights to the newly profitable land and those who did not.

The scale of the conflict paled in comparison to the anarchy that has gripped Somalia and Liberia or the mass slaughter in Rwanda, but it was devastating for the residents and economy of this region.

In two rounds of fighting, last year and then again this year, "ethnic cleansing" saw Konkombas driven from areas in which Nanumbas or Dagombas were numerically

313

dominant, and Nanumbas and Dagombas were driven from Konkomba areas. Some 3,000 to 4,000 people are thought to have been killed, dozens of villages burned and tens of thousands of people forced to flee their land.

And Nanumba farmer Dokurugu, for whom free-market principles had brought temporary prosperity, is now worse off than before. "I lost my farm and my motorcycle was looted," he said. "Now I have nothing."

Sitting under the shade of a mango tree in the Nanumba stronghold of Bimbilla, not far from where the thumb-biting incident took place, a group of Nanumba farmers forced off their land by the fighting blamed the conflict on the new profitability of yams.

"We all realize the value of this yam business," said Salisu Wumbei, a prominent Nanumba tribesman. "But don't think it was us who started this to drive the Konkombas away. It is they who want to cripple us. They want us not to farm yams."

Konkombas also blame yams, but see things differently. "Before, the Nanumbas didn't want to farm because they had us to do everything," said Konkomba tribal leader Kenneth Wujangi. "Now it's profitable and they want to take it all. But we have lived on that land for generations and we want our rights. We don't respect their overlordship anymore."

But yams alone cannot explain why bloody conflict ensued from reforms that could have benefited everybody. Adam al Haji, an official with the Ministry of Agriculture, says economists overlook the realities of African life in their attempts to apply Western-style economic principles.

"The modern state is so preoccupied with reforming the economy it has forgotten the very way in which our people live," he said. "While all the brains of the country are being pushed to think in terms of economic reform, a very limited number of brains are looking at these grass-roots dynamics that cause conflict."

Those dynamics should have been addressed long ago,

when the modern African state took over from colonial rulers, said land-tenure expert Abudulai.

Few dispute the need for economic reforms that will help African farmers lift themselves out of subsistence-level poverty, he said. Rather, he argued, the fact that the reforms led to conflict reflects a broader failure on the part of the government to reconcile traditional tribal structures with modern principles of land ownership.

"Since independence, no government has managed to align the traditional way of doing things with the modern state, and there hasn't been much effort either," he said.

The result is the persistence of something regarded as one of the scourges of Africa: tribalism.

While the word "tribalism" has acquired negative connotations in the West, many Africans are proud to identify themselves as tribesmen and see nothing wrong with the concept, said Konkomba leader Wujangi.

"People who don't want to use the word tribe and describe us as ethnic or language groups, they're just being polite," he said. "Your tribe gives you a sense of belonging, a pride in who you are and what you are."

"It only becomes a problem when one tribe tries to dominate another, and that is what has happened here," Wujangi said.

Tribalism also becomes a problem when government fails to play a meaningful role in ordinary people's lives, something of which the farmers themselves are acutely aware.

Ultimately, Nanumba tribesman Wumbei said, it is not Konkombas who are at fault. "We blame the state," he said. "We invested our protection, our welfare, in central government. But the state has failed to protect us, so the traditional system kicked in."

"Traditional systems," as he put it, are kicking in across Africa as states confront the consequences of their failure to apply the European concept of nationhood to the reality of Africa's multiple ethnic groups.

In Africa, rights to land reside not with individuals but with tribes, whose chiefs allocate access to land on the tribes' behalf. When modern concepts of profitability and private ownership clash with traditional concerns for the well-being of all members of the tribe, conflict seems inevitable.

In Kenya, President Daniel arap Moi has been accused of fueling tribal conflict in the Rift Valley to suit his own political goals. But he would not have been able to do so had land not become increasingly scarce, and profitable, owing to steady privatization.

In South Africa, the conflict in KwaZulu-Natal province between Zulus loyal to the African National Congress and those who support the Inkatha Freedom Party is overwhelmingly political. But at its core lies the question of who will control local government and, thereby, rights to land, which currently reside with local, unelected chiefs.

Throw in poverty, common to all these situations, and it is easy to see why land becomes such a desperately emotive issue.

The picture postcard scenes of idyllic rural life in northern Ghana belie statistics that describe a desperately poor people for whom independence and modern government have brought few material benefits. "Ghana is a poor country, but the people here are far worse off than the national average," said Al Haji of the Agricultural Ministry.

"The main problem in this region is poverty," said Al Haji.

Only a quarter of all children attend school, and 3 of 4 people have no access to health services. Ten percent of Ghana's population live here, but the region has only 3 percent of the country's schools. The modern state is barely closer to these people's lives than were the British colonialists, who ruled northern Ghana indirectly through local tribal chiefs.

316

"To people here, the government in Accra (the capital) is another planet on a distant galaxy," said Abudulai. "Government brings you no benefit. Once in a while, a government official passes by waving the flag. That's the only government they know."

Appendix II

Kwame Nkrumah:
The one and only founding father

2014 Independence Day special

Kwame Botwe-Asamoah,
GhanaWeb, 13 March 2014

While Nkrumah was being treated as a criminal in prison, crowds gathered daily in front of the James Fort chanting the Party's songs/anthems, "There is Victory for US" etc. Nkrumah, on the other hand, was busy writing on sheets of toilet paper in darkness outlying the party's strategies on the next level of the struggle, as well as rewriting the Party's manifesto.

Notwithstanding its opposition to the Coussey Constitution, the CPP changed its mind and contested the first general elections in the history of the Gold Coast on February 8, 1951. Not only did Nkrumah win the Accra Central constituency by obtaining 22, 780 votes out of registered 23, 122 voters, but also the CPP won a sweeping victory by pulling 39 of the 43 popularly elected seats. Subsequently, Nkrumah was released from prison on

February 12, 1951 to become Leader of Government Business.

Shortly after the CPP victory in the 1951 election, the UGCC collapsed. So all along, "Kwame Nkrumah was the UGCC and the UGCC was Kwame Nkrumah."

Nonetheless, on October 14, 1951, Nkrumah, while a Leader of Government Business, invited all the political parties (including J. B. Danquah and Obetsebi Lamptey) to join the CPP in a conference to plan a nation-wide campaign of Positive Action, should the British Government "rejects a motion for self-government now," but none of them responded.

In the meantime, due to pressures from Nkrumah, the Governor, on March 5, 1952 addressed the Legislative Assembly and declared that the Leader of Government Business should disappear from the constitution and be replaced by the office of Prime Minister. Accordingly, Nkrumah was elected by a secret ballot in the Assembly on March 10 to the office of Prime Minister. Not surprisingly, Dr. Danquah characterized it as "window dressing."

The differences between Kwame Nkrumah's political ideology and economic philosophy and those J. B. Danquah manifested during the 1951 Cocoa Marketing Board Amendment debate in the Legislative Assembly.

While the CPP, led by Ohene Djan, argued for state control of the Gold Coast Marketing Board to generate revenue from the sale of cocoa to promote development in the country (like the Adomi Bridge, Volta River project, Tema Harbor and township, Okomfo Anokye Hospital, democratization of education and health services, construction of the University of Ghana campus at Legon, Kumasi College of Technology (now KNUST), Medical School, road construction etc.), the Opposition, led by Dr. Danquah, opposed it saying that the bill was in violation of the full enjoyment of private property; hence, the property-owning political party (UGCC, GCP, NLM, UP, PP, NPP).

320

The 1954 and 1956 General Elections

On June 10, 1953, Kwame Nkrumah tabled a motion in the Assembly on constitutional reform, popularly known as the "Motion of Destiny," in which he demanded self-government. This resulted in the 1954 general election on June 15, 1954, which the CPP won 72 out of the 104 parliamentary seats.

The Ghana Congress Party (GCP), formed by Prof. Busia in May 1952, only won one out of the 104 seats.

Dr. J.B. Danquah (also of the Ghana Congress Party) lost the parliamentary seat in the Central Akyem Abuakwa constituency. (Danquah's election to the Legislative Assembly in 1951 was through the municipal/and electoral college, and not by popular vote.) Like the UGCC, the Ghana Congress Party collapsed.

In 1954, the UN Trusteeship Visiting Team recommended that a plebiscite be held in the Trans-Volta under British rule for the people to decide whether they wanted a union with the imminent Gold Coast's independence. Due to the 1948 Nkrumah nation-wide tour, his United Gold Coast agenda, as well as the CPP campaign in the province, the majority of the people voted to cast their lot with the new country Ghana. S.G. Antor (conceivably, one of the Founding Fathers) of the Togoland Congress strongly campaigned against it.

That notwithstanding, the anticipated independence in 1956 as promised by the Van Lare Constitution was bludgeoned with the birth of the ethnocentric National Liberation Movement (NLM) in the Asante Region.

Launched (amidst slaughtering a sheep, the firing of muskets and chanting Asante war songs) by Bafour Osei Akoto with Prof. Kofi Abrefa Busia as its leader, the NLM accused the CPP government of using the cocoa farmers' money to develop the coastal region or Colony. Thus, the Asante "cocoa farmers would be better off if they would manage their own internal affairs."

But the real reason behind the launching of this anti-political party movement was to provide another opportunity for the opposition parties (NLM, NPP, Togoland Congress etc.) to punctuate the attainment of Ghana's independence under Kwame Nkrumah and his CPP government that year.

In doing so, they (including J. B. Danquah, Obetsebi and other members of the defunct UGCC and GCP) demanded federalism by boycotting all talks, forums, meetings etc. The British government yielded to the intrigues of the Opposition and decided to hold another general election in 1956 for the people to decide whether they wanted a "unitary government" or a "federal form of government."

In spite of the NLM terrorist acts, the CPP, again, won another decisive victory in the July 1956 election.

Prior to the election, Dr. Busia had written to inform the Governor that, "in accordance with the constitutional practice in the United Kingdom, the National Liberation Movement and its allies will expect Your Excellency to call upon Doctor K. A. Busia, their Parliamentary Leader, to form a Government should they win more than 52 seats at the election."

Yet after Nkrumah's CPP won the 1956 general election, Prof. Busia produced another theory saying that no constitution would be acceptable unless it was "favored by a majority of the people of every region into which the Gold Coast" was divided.

Dr. J. B. Danquah's Doctrine of Independence from the British Empire

In his March 6, 1944 speech marking the centenary of the infamous Bond of 1844, Danquah expressed his unflinching desire to place a self-governing Ghana under the British empire.

He said:

"I AM SOMETIMES MUCH SURPRISED WHEN I SEE MANY OF MY COUNTRYMEN TERRIFIED BY THE USE OF THAT WORD, 'SELF-GOVERNMENT.' THEY ARE TERRIFIED OF IT BECAUSE THEY THINK IT MEANS THE DESIRE TO BREAK AWAY FROM THE [BRITISH] EMPIRE AND BECOME INDEPENDENT OF THE BRITISH. IF IT COMES TO THAT, IF IT COMES TO A DECISION TO BREAK AWAY FROM THE BRITISH CONNECTION, I WOULD BE THE LAST [PERSON] TO EXPRESS SUCH A TERRIFIC WISH" (see the Historic Speeches of J. B. Danquah).

In his July 13, 1959 letter to Mr. Brockway in London, J. B. Danquah said, "I was against any election as premature and favoured Constituent Assembly," where the pre-ordained rulers would be selected to rule (see Historic Speeches of Danquah).

To understand Danquah's reason for disregarding the electoral process and disrespecting the CPP victories and Nkrumah's government, we must go to the root of Danquah's political ideology.

Aside from being a "tame student of Kant's moral philosophy" (Danquah, Vol. 1), Danquah (Busia included) echoed and practiced Edmund Burke's ideology of rule by the preordained elite.

Burke's political philosophy was developed at Oxford University into an ideology that the elite is born to rule the world. Thus, it does society great harm, Burke reasoned, if the masses (affirming Aristotle's views that the masses should have been slaves) are allowed to participate in governance by voting.

So, since Kwame Nkrumah was a goldsmith's son with some "NTAFO" (Northerners) in his 1951 government, Dr. Danquah remarked, and since the CPP was voted into power mostly by the "masses," the Danquah-Busia camp considered the CPP government illegitimate and dangerous to the society; hence, it must be destroyed by violence.

In fact, Danquah's elitism was manifested in his distaste and contempt for "this thing of masses," whom he viewed as "only individuals" and dismissed their aspirations as "emotions."

The Danquah-Busia Camp's Style of Democracy

On April 5, 1955, the Opposition led by Busia and Modesto Apaloo walked out of the Assembly, just after a Motion on a Select Committee to examine the whole question of the federal system of government had been seconded.

In their opinion, the Select Committee, comprising some CPP parliamentarians or the "homeless tramp and jackals" (*Liberator*, March 1956), was incompetent to deal with national matters.

Bafour Osei Akoto and the chiefs in the "National Liberation Movement" did not want their movement to be called "Party," since "party politics were contrary to the tenets of traditional rule."

Similarly, on March 14, 1956, Danquah and his brother Nana Ofori Atta II told a visiting parliamentarian delegation to Kyebi that "PARTY POLITICS is an alien political form which" had "created civil strife and violent dissension between father and son." Accordingly, if the British showed no understanding, Akyem Abuakwa would secede from the country "as a sovereign and independent state with the only rival of the Ashanti country."

During the Jackson Commission, Danquah categorically denounced the authority of the Kwame Nkrumah government saying that "the people of Akyem are not subjects to the laws of Ghana" (Jackson Commission's Report, 1958).

So, his recourse was to do what?

Dr. Busia's NLM referred to the CPP supporters in Asante as "those who belong to no family or clan, those who are strangers, not properly trained to appreciate the value of the true and noble Akan" *(Liberator,* December 20, 1955). A Party of "Founding Fathers?"

The Opposition led by Dr. Busia, refused to meet with Sir Frederick Bourne in Kumase, sent by the British government to resolve the impasse between the CPP government and Opposition. And when the government issued its constitutional proposal for the country's independence in the April White Paper of 1956, again, the Opposition boycotted its proceedings.

So, how would latter-day apologists lump the Opposition leaders together with Nkrumah as "Founding Fathers?"

On November 20, 1956, leaders of the NLM and NPP sent a resolution to the Secretary for Colonies in London, demanding a separate independence for Asante and Northern Territories.

Yesterday's Secessionists, today's Founding Fathers!

Terrorist Acts of the Danquah-Busia Camp

Dr. K. A. Busia and the NLM warned the British government in August of 1955 of grisly aftereffects, if the country attained independence under the CPP government. Hence, the Danquah-Busia camp resorted to the undemocratic methods and terrorist acts and bomb attacks to overthrow the democratically elected government of Kwame Nkrumah, before and after Ghana's independence.

Yesterday's Terrorists, Today's "Founding Fathers"!

On November 10, 1955, Nkrumah's house was bombed while he was resting and working in his house with his secretary and others because of a terrible cold. Danquah-Busia-Obetsebi Lamptey's style of democracy!!!

On the day that the CPP reopened its regional office in

Kumase after fourteen months of closure, Prof. Busia's NLM drove a jeep past the crowd and fired shots into it and wounded several people; it also killed a pregnant woman.

Earlier, Krobo Edusei's sister had been shot dead as she was preparing food in the backyard for her children; while Edusei's wife had survived a bomb blast.

Yesterday's Murderous, Today's "Founding Fathers"!

On the eve of Ghana's Independence on March 6, 1957, the Ewe Unificationists, led by S.G. Antor (Danquah's buddy), formed themselves into a ragged guerilla army in Alavanyo and prepared for armed insurrection with homemade guns against the CPP government. The Governor-General sent troops to the region to put down the revolt.

Yes, S. G. Antor (J. B. Danquah's loyal buddy, an ally of Prof. Busia, and one of President Kufour's heroes) by his (Antor's) terrorist acts also passes to be one of the "Founding Fathers."

Sabotaging Ghana's Independence:
Dr. Busia and the NLM

On August 3, 1956, the Opposition leaders boycotted the constitutional debate tabled by the CPP government regarding Ghana's independence.

"Founding Fathers" indeed!

Again, when the Parliament formally opened after the 1956 general election to deliberate on Nkrumah's Motion of Independence, Dr. Busia and the NLM, and NPP's parliamentarians were absent.

Reprehensible Saboteurs and not "Founding Fathers"!

When the British Governor, in his opening speech, introduced a Bill declaring that the Gold Coast would be a sovereign and independent State within the Commonwealth, Prof. Busia and the Opposition criticized the proposal saying that it was premature.

Saboteurs and not "Founding Fathers"!

Before independence, Dr. Busia traveled to London to make a plea to the British Government to deny granting independence to Ghana, "because the country is not ready for parliamentary democracy." He continued, "We still need you in the Gold Coast. Your experiment there [Gold Coast] is not complete. Sometimes I wonder why you seem such in a hurry to wash you hands off us."

What a Traitor!!!

Opposing and Attacking the Name Ghana and Flag for the New Nation

When the British Government conceded to Ghana's independence on March 6, 1957, and Nkrumah chose for Ghana's flag, Red for the blood of the martyrs, Gold for wealth, Green for the rich land and the Black Star in the center representing the freedom of Africans on the continent and in the Diaspora, Danquah-Busia camp opposed it.

The Danquah-Busia camp had previously associated themselves with the name Ghana, yet when Kwame Nkrumah proposed it (GHANA) as the name for the new nation-state, they not only opposed, but they also attacked it.

How can saboteurs become "Founding Fathers?"

Given all that have been discussed above, how on earth can any living sane person lump Kwame Nkrumah together with the fictitiously labeled "Big- Six" and/or ex-UGCC's Working Committee members etc., (who strongly opposed, condemned, sabotaged and distanced themselves from anything associated with Nkrumah, as well as bitterly decried him, bombed his house, terrorized members of his CPP, attempted secession from the country, and opposed the name, "Ghana" for the new nation-state and its flag, from 1948 to Ghana's independence on 6 March 1957) as "Founding Fathers?"

Where were they on the dais where Kwame Nkrumah stood and declared the Independence of Ghana, followed by the National Anthem as the rising FLAG of Ghana was replacing the downward British flag on the eve of Ghana's independence?

Also, where were they in the banquet hall where all those who mattered assembled to celebrate Ghana's independence?

The answer?

They were busy plotting to make the new nation-state ungovernable, and overthrow to the CPP Government by violence.

History, as a social science, is not a conjured tale, but an analysis of observable and verifiable invents.

The records of Ghana's political history are stored in print and electronic media of the time, primary materials and archives for all rational people to look into.

And until new data descends from MARS, KWAME NKRUMAH remains and will remain the ONE and ONLY FOUNDING FATHER of MODERN GHANA.

Appendix III

Ethnicity:
An African Predicament

Francis M. Deng, Brookings Institution
1 June 1997

History has stripped Africa's people of the dignity of building their nations on their own indigenous values, institutions, and heritage. The modern African state is the product of Europe, not Africa. To attempt at this late date to return to ancestral identities and resources as bases for building the modern African nation would risk the collapse of many countries. At the same time, to disregard ethnic realities would be to build on loose sand, also a high-risk exercise. Is it possible to consolidate the framework of the modern African state while giving recognition and maximum utility to the component elements of ethnicities, cultures, and aspirations for self-determination?

The Challenge of Ethnicity in Africa

Ethnicity is more than skin color or physical characteristics, more than language, song, and dance. It is the embodiment of values, institutions, and patterns of behavior, a composite whole representing a people's historical experience, aspirations, and world view. Deprive a people of their ethnicity, their culture, and you deprive them of their sense of direction or purpose.

Traditionally, African societies and even states functioned through an elaborate system based on the family, the lineage, the clan, the tribe, and ultimately a confederation of groups with ethnic, cultural, and linguistic characteristics in common. These were the units of social, economic, and political organizations and inter-communal relations.

In the process of colonial state-formation, groups were divided or brought together with little or no regard to their common characteristics or distinctive attributes. They were placed in new administrative frameworks, governed by new values, new institutions, and new operational principles and techniques. The autonomous local outlook of the old order was replaced by the control mechanisms of the state, in which the ultimate authority was an outsider, a foreigner. This mechanism functioned through the centralization of power, which ultimately rested on police and military force, the tools of authoritarian rule. This crude force was, however, softened by making use of traditional leaders as extended arms of state control over the tribes or the local communities, giving this externally imposed system a semblance of legitimacy for the masses. Adding to this appearance of legitimacy was the introduction of a welfare system by which the state provided meager social services and limited development opportunities to privileged sectors. National resources were otherwise extracted and exported as raw materials to feed the metropolitan industries of the colonial masters.

This new system undermined the people's indigenous system, which provided them with the means for pursuing their modest but sustainable life objectives, and replaced it with centrally controlled resources that were in short supply and subject to severely competitive demands. Development was conceived as a means of receiving basic

330

services from the state, rather than as a process of growth and collective accumulation of wealth that could in turn be invested in further growth. The localized, broad-based, low-risk, self-sustaining subsistence activities gave way to high-risk, stratifying competition for state power and scarce resources, a zero-sum conflict of identities based on tribalism or ethnicity. Independence removed the common enemy, the colonial oppressor, but actually sharpened the conflict over centralized power and control over national resources.

Today, virtually every African conflict has some ethno-regional dimension to it. Even those conflicts that may appear to be free of ethnic concerns involve factions and alliances built around ethnic loyalties. Analysts have tended to have one of two views of the role of ethnicity in these conflicts. Some see ethnicity as a source of conflict; others see it as a tool used by political entrepreneurs to promote their ambitions. In reality, it is both. Ethnicity, especially when combined with territorial identity, is a reality that exists independently of political maneuvers. To argue that ethnic groups are unwitting tools of political manipulation is to underestimate a fundamental social reality. On the other hand, ethnicity is clearly a resource for political manipulation and entrepreneurship.

Africa's Response to the Challenge

After independence Africans were eager to disavow tribalism as divisive. Unity was postulated in a way that assumed a mythical homogeneity amidst diversity. Kwame Nkrumah of Ghana outlawed parties organized on tribal or ethnic bases. Houphouet-Boigny of Côte d'Ivoire coopted ethnic groups through shrewd distribution of ministerial posts, civil service jobs, social services, and development projects. Julius Nyerere, a scion of tribal chieftaincy, stamped out tribalism by fostering nationalistic pride in

331

Tanganyika and later, Tanzania, born out of the union with Zanzibar. Jommo Kenyatta of Kenya forged a delicate alliance of ethnic groups behind the dominance of his Kenyan African National Union party. In South Africa, apartheid recognized and stratified races and ethnicities to an unsustainable degree. Post-apartheid South Africa, however, remains poised between a racially, ethnically, and tribally blind democratic system and a proud ethnic self-assertiveness, represented and exploited by Zulu nationalists, spearheaded by the emotive leadership of Chief Buthelezi.

Throughout Africa, the goal of safeguarding unity within the colonial state has preserved the stability of colonial borders while generating ethnic tensions and violence within those borders. Sudan offers an extreme example. The dominant North, a hybrid of Arab and African racial, cultural, and religious elements, is trying to resolve its identity crisis by being more Arab and Islamic than its prototypes. Worse, this distorted self-perception, heightened by the agendas of political elites, is projected as the framework for unifying and integrating the country, generating a devastating zero-sum conflict between the Arab-Muslim North and the indigenously African South, whose modern leadership is predominantly Christian.

The decision of the Founding Fathers of the Organization of African Unity to respect the colonial borders established a normative principle that has been followed with remarkable success. Secession movements have met with strong resistance from the OAU. Katanga tried to break away from the Congo (which became Zaire, now back to the Democratic Republic of the Congo) but failed. The secessionist Biafran war in Nigeria also failed. Somalia's attempt to take the Ogaden from Ethiopia was decisively thwarted. Southern Sudan struggled for 17 years to break away from the North and in the end settled for autonomy in 1972. When the fighting resumed in 1983, the stated goal was and remains the creation of a new

Sudan that would be free from any discrimination based on race, ethnicity, culture, or religion.

Eritrea's breakaway from Ethiopia is seen not as a case of violating colonial borders, but of upholding them, since Eritrea had been a colony under Italian rule. Likewise, the de facto breakaway of Northern Somalia is seen as a restoration of colonial borders, since the North had been governed separately by the British. Even in the Sudan, often said to be a good candidate for partition, should the country be divided, the division might be rationalized as an extension of the British colonial policy that governed the Sudan as two separate entities, one Arab-Islamic and the other indigenous African with rudiments of Christian Western influences.

In most African countries, the determination to preserve national unity following independence provided the motivation behind one-party rule, excessive centralization of power, oppressive authoritarian regimes, and systematic violation of human rights and fundamental liberties. These in turn have generated a reaction, manifested in heightened tension and the demand for a second liberation. Managing ethnic diversity within the unity of the colonial borders is a challenge that African states are reluctant to face, but cannot wish away.

Ethiopia, after Eritrea's breakaway, can claim credit for being the only African country trying to confront head-on the challenge of tribalism or ethnicity by recognizing territorially based ethnic groups, granting them not only a large measure of autonomy, but also the constitutional right of self-determination, even to the extent of secession. Ethiopia's leaders assert emphatically that they are committed to the right of self-determination, wherever it leads. Less idealistically, it can be argued that giving the people the right to determine their destiny leads them to believe that their interests will be provided for, if only to give them a reason to opt for unity.

The only sustainable unity is that based on mutual

understanding and agreement. Unfortunately, the normative framework for national unity in modern Africa is not the result of consensus. Except for post-apartheid South Africa, Africans won their independence without negotiating an internal social contract that would win and sustain national consensus. The constitutions for independence were laden with idealistic principles developed outside the continent. The regimes built on them lacked legitimacy and in most cases were soon overthrown with no remorse or regrets from the public. But these upheavals involved only a rotation of like-minded elites, or worse, military dictators, intent on occupying the seat of power vacated by the colonial masters. Such leaders soon became their colonial masters' images.

At the moment, for the overwhelming majority of African countries the quest for unity underscores the intensity of disunity. As long as the Africans avoid confronting the issue of ethnicity and fail to develop norms and means for managing diversity within the framework of unity, peace and stability will continue to elude the pluralistic state.

Models of Ethnic Configuration

African governments have responded to the challenge in varying ways, ranging from pragmatic management to blind neglect and catastrophic mismanagement. The particular form the ethnic policies of a country take may in large measure be dictated by the characteristics of its identity configuration.

A few states in Africa enjoy a high degree of homogeneity or, at least, a relatively inconsequential diversity. Botswana, for example, reflects exemplary cohesiveness, democracy, stability, and sustained growth.

Most African countries, particularly those in West

334

Africa (possibly excepting Nigeria), Kenya, and southern African countries (exclusive of South Africa), fall into a second category. These countries face significant ethnic pluralism that is nevertheless containable through an effective system of distribution that upholds the integrity and legitimacy of the state. The way the nations in this group perceive themselves is consonant with the self-perceptions of their component groups.

A third group of countries, including Zimbabwe, Namibia, and modern-day South Africa, suffers racial, ethnic, religious, or cultural divisions severe enough to require special arrangements to be mutually accommodating in an ambivalent form of unity in diversity. Burundi and Rwanda, as well as Sudan, are candidates for this category, though all also have aspects of the fourth, and final, category.

The fourth category, the zero-sum conflict situation, consists of states embroiled in acute crisis with no collective sense of identification, no shared values, and no common vision for the nation. The framework of the nation-state is perceived as an imposition by the colonial invaders, now perpetuated by the dominant group whose identity defines the national character. Such definition might be explicit, as in apartheid South Africa, where race and ethnicity were factors in allocating or denying the rights of citizenship, or in the Sudan, where the identification of the country as Arab and Islamic carries inherent stratification and discrimination on racial, ethnic, and religious grounds. These conflicts are the most difficult to manage within the unity framework; depending on the particular circumstance of the case, they may call for fundamental restructuring and perhaps partition.

Policy Implications for Nationbuilding

At present, most African countries are addressing the

racial and ethnic identity issues through a pacifying system of distribution and allocation—a form of ad hoc pragmatic management rather than a strategic approach. What makes the issue of identity particularly acute for the continent is that it touches not only on politics, but also on economics and the organizational capacity for a self-generating and sustainable development from within.

There are four policy options for managing pluralistic identities. One is to create a national framework with which all can identify without any distinction based on race, ethnicity, tribe, or religion. This option, of course, best suits those countries that are highly homogeneous. The second option is to create a pluralistic framework to accommodate nations that are racially, ethnically, culturally, or religiously diverse. Under this option, probably a federal arrangement, groups would accommodate each other on the basis of the principle of live and let live, but with a more uniting commitment to the common purpose of national identification. In the third case, for more seriously divided countries, some form of power sharing combined with decentralization, with identities being geographically defined, may be the answer. In the zero-sum conflict situations, federalism would expand into confederalism, paradoxically trying to reconcile unity with separation. Where even this degree of accommodation is not workable, and where territorial configurations permit, partition ought to be accepted.

The Role of the International Community

How are these options to be brought about? Deciding which option to adopt is, of course, in the first place part of the sovereign right of the people of the country. But regional and international actors also have a responsibility that cannot be abdicated in the name of national sovereignty. By its very nature, sovereignty implies a tension between the demand for internal solutions and the need for corrective remedies from the outside. In other words, the responsibilities of sovereignty require both internal and external accountability, which are inherently at odds, especially since the need for external involvement is commensurate with the failure of internal systems. Given the ambivalence of the international system about intervention, this responsibility should belong first to the subregional and regional actors, with the international community, through the United Nations, as the ultimate resort.

The interconnectedness of the conflicts of neighboring countries means that preventing, managing, or resolving conflicts is becoming recognized as a matter of interest and concern not only to the countries directly involved, but also to the region as a whole. Regional awakening to the common threat of internal conflict is still nascent, but the importance of the shared threat is being increasingly realized, especially in view of the tendency toward isolationism in Europe and the United States, the only powers still capable of effectively intervening for humanitarian reasons or for the cause of peace, security, and stability in other parts of the world.

Reconciling Two Conflicting Paths

Final accountability for the responsibilities of sovereignty must ultimately fall on the international community, more specifically the United Nations. The intervention of international financial institutions in the affairs of sovereign countries to ensure more efficient management of their economies has now become a truism. International concern with issues of governance, such as democracy and respect for fundamental human rights, has also become widely accepted, despite the lingering resistance of vulnerable regimes. Beyond the issue of protection of minorities, long recognized as a legitimate concern for the international community, the politics and conflicts of identity and their impact on the prospects for peace, stability, development, and nation building must also be recognized as critical items on the agenda of a responsible and accountable sovereignty.

Insofar as the modern African state is the creation of European conquest, restructuring the continent, linking it to the international system, and reconceptualizing and reconstituting the state will require the cooperation of Africa's global partners. Outside actors can offer an objective and impartial perspective that can be pivotal to balancing the concerns of the internal actors. In addition, the international legitimacy of any new arrangements, which is necessary for building support from outside sources, can best be ensured by enlisting international partners in the search for effective solutions to these internal crises.

Post-colonial Africa stands poised between rediscovering its roots—its indigenous values, institutions, and experiences—and pursuing the logic of the colonial state in the context of universalizing modernity, primarily based on Western experience. The resulting tensions cannot be easily resolved. But an eclectic process that fashions a system in which ethnic groups can play a constructive role in the modern African state could significantly reduce the tension, foster cooperation, and facilitate the process of nation building.

www.ingramcontent.com/pod-product-compliance
Lightning Source LLC
Chambersburg PA
CBHW050454270326
41927CB00009B/1746